Daily Life in Late Antiquity

Daily Life in Late Antiquity is the first comprehensive study of lived experience in the Late Roman Empire, from ca. 250 to 600 CE. Each of the six topical chapters highlights historical "everyday" people, along with spaces and objects, whose lives operate as windows into the late ancient economy, social relations, military service, religious systems, cultural habits, and the material environment. However, it is nevertheless grounded in late ancient primary sources – many of which are available in accessible English translations – and the most recent cutting-edge scholarship by specialists in fields such as archaeology, social history, religious studies, and environmental history. From Manichean rituals to military service, gladiatorial combat to garbage collection, patrician households to peasant families, *Daily Life in Late Antiquity* introduces readers to the world of Late Antiquity from the bottom up.

Kristina Sessa is Associate Professor at The Ohio State University and is the author of *The Formation of Papal Authority in Late Antique Italy* (Cambridge University Press, 2012). She is presently writing a book about war, environmental crisis, and the formation of Christian institutions in the late Roman West. Her scholarship has been supported by awards from the American Council of Learned Societies, the American Academy in Rome, and the Italian Academy for Advanced Studies at Columbia University.

Daily Life in Late Antiquity

KRISTINA SESSA

The Ohio State University

CAMBRIDGE
UNIVERSITY PRESS

CAMBRIDGE
UNIVERSITY PRESS

University Printing House, Cambridge CB2 8BS, United Kingdom

One Liberty Plaza, 20th Floor, New York, NY 10006, USA

477 Williamstown Road, Port Melbourne, VIC 3207, Australia

314–321, 3rd Floor, Plot 3, Splendor Forum, Jasola District Centre,
New Delhi – 110025, India

79 Anson Road, #06–04/06, Singapore 079906

Cambridge University Press is part of the University of Cambridge.

It furthers the University's mission by disseminating knowledge in the pursuit of
education, learning, and research at the highest international levels of excellence.

www.cambridge.org
Information on this title: www.cambridge.org/9780521148405
DOI: 10.1017/9780511819360

First published 2018
Reprinted 2019

Printed in the United Kingdom by TJ International Ltd. Padstow Cornwall

A catalogue record for this publication is available from the British Library.

Library of Congress Cataloging-in-Publication Data
NAMES: Sessa, Kristina, author.
TITLE: Daily life in late antiquity / Kristina Sessa, The Ohio State University.
DESCRIPTION: New York : Cambridge University Press, 2018. | Includes
    bibliographical references.
IDENTIFIERS: LCCN 2018001757 | ISBN 9780521766104 (hardback) |
    ISBN 9780521148405 (pbk.)
SUBJECTS: LCSH: Rome–History–Empire, 284-476. | Rome–Social life and customs. |
    Rome–Civilization.
CLASSIFICATION: LCC DG311 .S55 2018 | DDC 937/.06–dc23
    LC record available at https://lccn.loc.gov/2018001757

ISBN 978-0-521-76610-4 Hardback
ISBN 978-0-521-14840-5 Paperback

Contents

Illustrations

Acknowledgments

A book that attempts to cover so many different areas of late Roman history necessarily involves the help and critical insight of many people. Shane Bjornlie, Kim Bowes, David Brakke, Cam Grey, Lucy Grig, Julia Hillner, Anthony Kaldellis, and Carolina Lopez-Ruiz read individual chapters of this book. All gave me sage, detailed advice on how to improve sections and let me know where I had run afoul of the facts. Needless to say, any remaining errors are my own, and I could not have completed this project without them. I also want to thank my OSU writing group co-members, Theodora Dragostinova, Lilia Fernández (now at Rutgers University), Robin Judd, and Mytheli Sreenivas. They cheerfully read and commented on several chapters, and helped me shape the narrative so that it was more interesting and accessible to non-specialists. Collecting images for this book proved more challenging than I had imagined, and I want to thank Kim Bowes, Dallas Deforest, Richard Hodges, and Caroline T. Schroeder for allowing me to use material from their personal archives and for assisting with the captions. Additionally, I am especially grateful to Giuliano Volpe, who graciously sent me high-quality images of the archaeological remains of the *stibadium* at the Villa di Faragola in Foggia, along with his computer reconstruction of it. As always, Chris Otter offered advice, support, editing, inspiration, and even a drawing of a spoon.

Writing a book for a general audience requires a different voice from the one I normally use in my scholarship. As I was crafting the manuscript, my imagined reader was my late mother, Alice B. Sessa (1944–2003). While not an historian by training (though she did have a master's degree in Spanish literature), my mother was deeply fascinated by the past and by many of the questions at the heart of this book. In my case, "write so your mother can understand it" was more than just a clichéd imperative; for me, it was the continuation of a conversation started long ago at the kitchen table, when my mother helped me write an overly ambitious fourth-grade report on the entire history of Japan. I miss you, Mom. This book is for you.

Introduction

Studying Daily Life in the Late Roman Empire

WHAT IS LATE ANTIQUITY?

Scholars today study the period between "the end of Rome" and "the beginning of the Middle Ages" as a distinct historical epoch. We call the period "Late Antiquity" or "the late Roman Empire," and this book uses both phrases interchangeably. Historians debate when Late Antiquity began and ended, but all agree that any periodization is strictly a modern convention. For a number of reasons, this book will focus on the period 250–600 CE. Most would concur that the second half of the third century marked the start of Late Antiquity, mainly because this was a time of unrest as well as major political, economic, and military reforms that came to characterize the period (see next section). Ending Late Antiquity in the year 600 CE is arguably more arbitrary, but it makes some sense. By 600, the western regions of the Roman Empire (Britain, Spain, Gaul, Italy, and North Africa) were largely under the control of post-Roman barbarian governments. While many cultural aspects of the Roman Empire endured within these new post-Roman kingdoms, their political and administrative fragmentation makes it hard to talk about them as a coherent entity. In the Empire's eastern regions (Egypt, Greece, Asia Minor, and the Near East, e.g., Syria and Palestine), the Roman emperor continued to rule over a single polity into the middle of the seventh century, when invasions by Slavs, Avars, and Arabs led to significant territorial loss. After that, the eastern Roman Empire was reduced to the provinces of Greece and Asia Minor and the capital

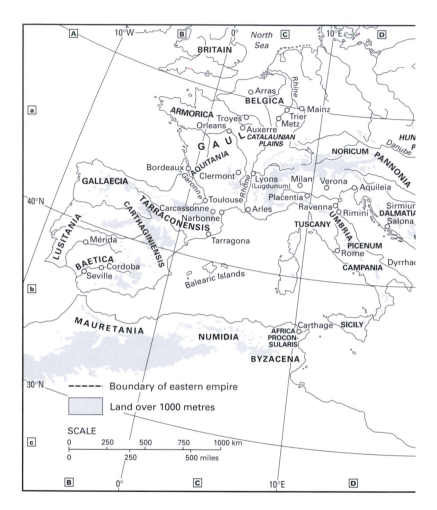

FIGURE 0.1 Map of the late Roman Empire, ca. 400 CE, from *Cambridge Ancient Histories*, vol. 14, p. 16.

city of Constantinople. Moreover, by concluding our study in the year 600 CE, we avoid the challenge of examining daily life during the rise of Islam and the emergence of the Arab caliphate in the seventh century. Islam is a genuine late antique phenomenon that should be studied in relation both to other monotheistic religions of the day (e.g., Christianity and Judaism) and to specific developments in regional politics and social relations in the Arabian peninsula. However, the study of early Islam requires expert knowledge of a very different source base from the one that we use to examine the late

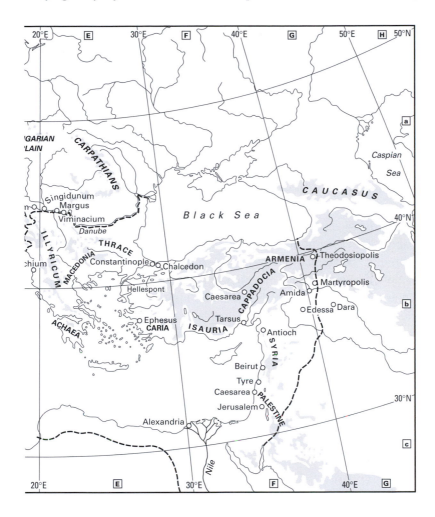

Roman Empire. Imperfect as the year 600 CE may be, one has to end a textbook – and a class – somewhere (Figure 0.1).

STUDYING DAILY LIFE IN THE DEEP PAST:
PROBLEMS AND POSSIBILITIES

There are hundreds of books on "daily life" in the past. Since the 1960s, it has been among the most popular genres of historical writing, especially for students and general audiences who want to know how ordinary people once lived. In fact, German historians in the 1970s coined a term for this particular approach to history, *Alltagsgeschichte*, or "everyday history." They were especially interested in how regular people lived under the Nazis in the 1930s and 1940s, and believed that an understanding of everyday experiences under Nazism would explain the rise of the Third Reich better than conventional political approaches. In fact, this "bottom up" approach to the past was already well under way in the study of Roman history. The French scholar Jérôme Carcopino's *Daily Life in Ancient Rome*, first published in 1941, broke new ground with its distinct focus on housing, social etiquette, leisure activities, and work in the city of Rome during the second century. As Carcopino's lively study of the everyday makes clear, the quotidian habits of men, women, and children were central to the history of a great imperial state.

Not all historians, however, have always accepted the study of daily life as a legitimate type of history. The approach has been criticized for being essentially descriptive and lacking in analysis (i.e., for only describing how people did something, rather than explaining why they did it); for making too much of seemingly trivial practices or banal objects, such as breastfeeding or children's toys; and for treating aspects of daily life in a certain time period as if they are unchanging phenomena. Since the 1980s and 1990s, historians have redressed the more relevant criticisms. As a result, the study of daily life has become more analytic in approach, as scholars now typically explain why people behaved and thought the way they did. They also attend to how the everyday changes over time and have come to appreciate the importance of daily life for understanding the impact, scope, and meaning of broad political, social, and cultural developments. Consequently, the study of ordinary people doing ordinary things has become central to how we understand the past.

Studying daily life in the deep past, in a period such as Late Antiquity, brings special challenges, however. First, we have to appreciate the extraordinary fundamental differences that separate modern Western society (among others) from late Roman society. One cannot exaggerate the extent to which electric lighting, fossil fuel–powered engines, modern medical procedures and medicines (especially vaccines), synthetic fertilizer (among other technologies and resources), and social safety nets shape our lives today. Imagine a world where none of these exist, and you will find yourself in the late Roman Empire, where communication between cities could take weeks or even months; where the average life expectancy at birth was twenty-five years; where everything you ate, wore, or used had to be produced by hand from natural materials; where your primary source of indoor lighting was oil lamps; and where those who had no means were left to die.

Second, there are the problems associated with the ancient sources themselves. Unlike historians who examine daily life in Victorian London, who have access to a vast array of archival sources, scholars of Late Antiquity have few large-scale datasets or more personal accounts by individuals, such as memoirs. For instance, in addition to the absence of standardized death, birth, and baptismal records (beyond what is written on tombstones), there are few late ancient autobiographical writings and no wide-scale publications such as newspapers authored by and/or aimed at a broader section of society. In short, we have few sources that offer direct insight into the emotional and intellectual worlds of ordinary people. In fact, our only significant source of documentary records is Egypt, where the dry climate has preserved hundreds of thousands of papyrus sheets, which were used by individuals to record information about quotidian matters such as taxes, lawsuits, labor arrangements, property matters, and personal communication.

Additionally, many of our best sources for daily life in Late Antiquity are prescriptive, meaning that they denote what behavior *should* look like in an ideal sense, rather than describe how it was really conducted. The sermons of Christian bishops, Talmudic interpretations, imperial law codes, and elite correspondence were not created to help historians in the twenty-first century decipher how regular people lived in Late Antiquity. Also, elite adult men authored most of our extant written documents, and as a result, we do not have easy access to the experiences of non-elites, women, and children.

Despite these challenges, we can use ancient sources with care to derive knowledge about the daily experiences of people from a large cross-section of society. First, historians can "read against the grain," meaning that we can take into account ideological frameworks that might structure how a particular author presents a topic and look for details that do not directly support that framework. For example, an aristocrat's account of his rural villa in Gaul and the crudeness of those who labored on it will be oriented around his own presuppositions about "rustics" and their inherent inferiority to elites. Yet, were this same author to note that a particular rustic could read and write, or that she had connections to families on a neighboring estate – details that seemingly go against the notion that peasants are illiterate, one-dimensional nonentities – then we might seize upon these comments as indicative of how some peasants actually lived, precisely because they are not stereotypical. Second, the fact that women are not well represented in the evidence does not mean that they are not represented at all. We have a relatively large number of papyrus texts from Egypt that were written by, for, or about real women, and these texts help us to correct the inherent patriarchal biases of the majority of our sources.[1] Of course, gender was experienced very differently in Late Antiquity than it is today, and we should not expect that late Roman women had the same desires, choices, and expectations that modern American women do.

Third, scholars of daily life must practice the art of inferential thinking and speculative history. There are many holes in our evidence and a total absence of sources for certain aspects of everyday life. For instance, scholars still do not really know what women did during their menstrual cycles to collect their blood and stay clean. Unsurprisingly, none of our normative, prescriptive sources – including a large number of medical texts – address the practicalities of getting your period in an age before adhesive-strip pads or tampons, or, more to the point perhaps, when most people did not regularly wear underwear. To make up for these missing data, historians of daily life have a few tools in their kit: they can draw inferences (we know that women in Alexandria collected what our texts call *phulakia*, or "protection," which were probably used menstrual rags, and hence we can infer that women used pads to absorb their menstrual blood and that there was some kind of recycling system); they can use comparative evidence from other premodern societies (in the European Middle Ages, women wore belts with linen or woolen pads during menstruation); and they simply make educated guesses (we know that women sometimes wore underwear for athletic contests, so perhaps they also did when they had their periods, and used it to hold menstrual pads in place). At times in this book, we will also "fill in the blanks" in order to create a cohesive narrative about everyday life, and all readers should understand that such is the nature of the evidence and the interpretive challenge of our subject matter.

HISTORICAL CONTEXTS AT A GLANCE

A history of daily life cannot be studied entirely apart from its broader geographical, political, social, and cultural contexts. The goal of this section is to provide readers with a brief introduction to the major changes that took place within the Roman imperial government, society, and religious systems between 250 and 600 CE.

Geography, Government, and Administration

In 250 CE, the Roman Empire was governed in much the same way that it had been since the first century CE: as a militarized autocratic polity, ruled by an emperor and his court. The emperor's capital was in Rome, which was the largest, grandest, and most heavily populated city in the Empire. The Senate, a collegial body of largely appointed male officials, still met regularly in Rome and issued decrees of its own. Nevertheless, the rule of law, control of the army, and economic decisions lay in the hands of the imperial court. To govern an empire that stretched from Britain to the Tigris and Euphrates Rivers, the emperor relied on governors and a string of lesser officials, who collected taxes, operated the extensive legal system, commanded the armies, and oversaw the general maintenance of law and order in the Empire's many provinces. The province was the basic administrative-geographic unit of the Roman Empire, and there were around fifty provinces in 250 CE. Each province was governed by an appointed official, who was responsible for tax collection and the law courts, which were just as important in maintaining law and order as the army. The Roman army was divided into legions (each approximately 5,200 troops) that were stationed around the Empire, but were especially concentrated along its major frontiers: the southern banks of the Danube River and the western shores of the Rhine; in the far east, where Rome bordered on the Parthian (and later Persian) Empire, the only other superpower; and in Egypt, the primary source of the Empire's grain supply.

The structure of the Roman government, the provincial administration, and the army remained largely unchanged between 250 and 285 CE. All these institutions, however, were placed under considerable pressure, because there was extreme political instability within the imperial court and an increase in predatory attacks by non-Roman armies and war bands within the Empire. Between 235 and 284 CE, there were at least twenty-six different emperors, most of whom rose to power – and were subsequently removed from it – via assassination and/or military coup. The Roman frontier, which had long been a stable feature of the Empire, began to break down from ca. 240 CE. From 240 to 275 CE, the Roman armies engaged repeatedly with enemy militias originating from just beyond the frontiers. These forces were more interested in raiding and collecting plunder than seizing territory, but their incursions were at times deep within the Empire. One emperor, Decius (r. 249–251 CE), was killed in battle against the Goths, a Germanic-speaking people from north of the Danube. Imperial usurpers in Gaul and Syria also established independent states within the Empire. The emperor Aurelian (r. 270–275 CE) eventually recaptured Gaul and Britain from Tetricus (r. 271–274 CE) and the Palmyrene region in Syria from Zenobia (r. 267–275 CE), whose husband had governed the region since 260 CE. There was also a major pandemic between 250 and 270 CE (the "plague of Cyprian," which was probably a form of hemorrhagic fever) that fatally impacted communities throughout the Empire.

Rome did not collapse under these conditions. In 284 CE, a new emperor came to power, Diocletian (r. 284–305 CE), who drove some of the most important political and administrative changes in the Empire's history. His most lasting contribution was to reorganize the way that the Empire was ruled, insisting that a single emperor in Rome was insufficient to deal with the many problems occurring along Rome's frontiers. He divided the Empire into four administrative quadrants, two overseen by emperors (*augusti*) and two overseen by junior emperors called "Caesars" (*caesares*). Scholars call this new government the tetrarchy, meaning "rule of four." Diocletian, in other words, decided that Rome was best ruled not by a single man, but by a coalition of rulers, each of whom had responsibility for a particular region, working together as a unit. Diocletian also reckoned that it made better sense for the imperial headquarters to be closer to the frontiers, where unrest was most intense. Consequently, he periodically established new capitals, such as Trier, Milan, Sirmium, and Nicomedia. With the intention of creating a more efficient government, Diocletian redrew provincial boundaries, creating more smaller provinces that were grouped into larger units called dioceses. After his reforms, there were a hundred provinces and twelve dioceses. Henceforth, the size of the Roman imperial administration grew rapidly.

Additionally, Diocletian oversaw a reform of the army, since each quadrant needed a separate force, and attempted to both stem inflation through price fixing and reform the religious environment by requiring individual acts of sacrifice to the imperial gods – an act that was largely targeted at Christians and led to large-scale persecutions. And in order to pay for all these costly reforms, the emperor raised taxes and reorganized the system by which the Empire assessed taxes and collected revenues.

Diocletian's reforms were durable, but they did not continue unchanged. Following his final abdication in 305 CE, the tetrarchy dissolved, and henceforth one or two leaders ruled Rome, not four.[2] For most of its future history, the Empire remained administratively split into two halves, one encompassing the western provinces with a capital first in Milan and then Ravenna, and the other constituting the eastern provinces with a capital in Constantinople, named for the emperor Constantine (r. 312–337 CE), who founded it. Additionally, the Roman army was divided into separate eastern and western organizations, each commanded by a different set and number of high generals.

In this book, we shall use the terms "the West" and "the East" to refer to these two parts of the Empire. Generally speaking, by the West we mean provinces in Britain, Spain, Gaul, Italy, Illyricum (the former Yugoslavia), and North Africa. By the East, we mean Egypt, as well as provinces in Greece, Thrace, Asia Minor (modern Turkey), Syria, and Palestine (including what is now Jordan and Israel). Culturally speaking, more connected East and West than separated them, but the main difference was linguistic: while Latin was the common tongue in the West, Greek along with Egyptian (i.e., Coptic) and several Semitic languages (e.g., Aramaic and later Syriac) were the primary spoken and written languages in the East. Northern non-Roman peoples, discussed more in the next section, spoke a variety of languages, such as Gothic. Although some of these groups became major political powers in the late Roman Empire, their languages only rarely entered the written record.[3] However, we should assume that spoken tongues differed enormously across the Empire.

Changing Geopolitics: West versus East

For much of the fourth century, the Empire was prosperous and stable. Beginning in the late fourth century, however, shifting political and military conditions in the West set off a process of fragmentation, whereby the Roman state ceased to rule large swaths of territory that had previously been within its frontiers. By 410 CE, the army and administration had effectively abandoned Britain, which had been experiencing heavy raiding from Saxon troops. After 406 CE, when bands of Alans, Sueves, and Vandals crossed the Rhine into northern Gaul, attacking cities and towns, the Roman army did little to halt their progress, forcing the region's inhabitants to fend for themselves. While the history of every region is different, virtually all western imperial territories came to be ruled by non-Roman polities over the course of the fifth century: the Franks, Burgundians, and Visigoths in Gaul; the Vandals, first in Spain and then in North Africa; and the Ostrogoths in Italy and southern Gaul. The last reigning western Roman emperor, Romulus Augustulus, was deposed in 476 CE, and from that date forward there was a single Roman emperor and imperial court in Constantinople.[4]

These arrangements in the West remained the status quo until the middle of the sixth century, when the emperor Justinian (r. 527–565 CE) launched a campaign to restore some of the lost western provinces to imperial rule. Although these wars of reconquest (often referred to as the Justinianic Wars) were successful in the short run – by 554 CE, Italy, North Africa, and southern Spain were administratively reintegrated into the Roman Empire – they ultimately could not stem the tide of political fragmentation in the West. By the end of the sixth century, Gaul and Spain were entirely ruled by post-Roman kingdoms (the Franks and Visigoths, respectively), while Italy was further divided into Lombard duchies and imperial-controlled regions. North Africa remained under nominal imperial control until the seventh century, when it fell to Arab armies.

In contrast, the East was ruled by Roman emperors in Constantinople as a coherent whole throughout Late Antiquity. To be sure, there were numerous internal political crises, such as when Phocas led a rebellion that unseated the emperor Maurice in 602 CE. There were also extensive hostilities with Persia (also known as the Sasanian Empire), the other dominant imperial state, which stretched from the eastern shores of the Arabian peninsula to modern Afghanistan and was centered in what are today Iran and Iraq. In fact, throughout the sixth century, Rome was intermittently at war with the Sasanians, who constantly pushed against the frontiers separating the two great empires. As already mentioned, the East underwent a geopolitical fragmentation similar to the West in the later seventh and eighth centuries, when Slavic, Avar, Persian, and Arab armies gradually took control over large swaths of the Empire.

What caused the Roman Empire to break apart? Whereas historians at one time pointed their fingers at predatory barbarian nations migrating en masse over the frontiers and wreaking havoc on the Roman state, scholars now emphasize internal structural problems as well as the unintended consequences of new practices. For instance, the abandonment of Britain took place over several decades, beginning in the late fourth century, when a Roman usurper in Gaul pulled imperial troops out of Britain to assist in an attempt to establish an independent state. In the early fifth century, when Britain faced intense Saxon raiding, the western emperor Honorius (r. 393–423 CE) could offer no military support, because he was fighting in Italy against two separate barbarian armies, one led by the Goth Alaric (ca. 370–410 CE). Alaric had spent his adult life within the Empire fighting for Rome as a leading commander in the Roman army, as did many barbarians. His internal revolt against Rome was a pure power grab made possible by the Empire's practice of recruiting non-Roman armies (that is, soldiers from outside the Empire) to fight their wars both foreign and civil, and settling many of these veterans on Roman land. In short, when Honorius told the Roman cities in Britain to fend for themselves in 410 CE (the same year Alaric sacked the city of Rome), he responded to a crisis that was the sum product of a perfect storm of conditions, many of which were of Rome's own making.

Moreover, historians now question whether these post-Roman polities were truly ethnic states wholly different from, or hostile to, the Roman world. Discussion of barbarian identity has become central to how historians view this period. To be clear, scholars today use the term "barbarian" in a neutral sense (as we shall use it here), to refer to people of non-Roman backgrounds, whose language, customs, and perceived origins place them outside the traditional classical Greco-Roman world. But precisely what it meant to be a barbarian in cultural terms remains elusive to us, in large part because we have very little writing by people who actually self-identified as barbarians and presented themselves as culturally distinct from Romans and Greeks. What is more, assimilation was clearly a significant force in Late Antiquity, as many barbarians came to adopt Roman customs, languages, and even political frameworks, and as many Romans took on barbarian traditions, such as wearing trousers.

What we can say is that the barbarian kingdoms in the West were independent regimes, with their own administrations, armies, and legal systems. Barbarian rulers often communicated directly with the Roman emperor and, in some cases, were officially recognized by him. In fact, most barbarian courts worked with, rather than against, the Roman government now centered in the East at Constantinople. These were not, in other words, anti-Roman regimes; on the contrary, most barbarian administrations comprised Romans and non-Romans, and most barbarian leaders adopted Roman imperial governing practices, especially in the areas of law, diplomacy, and tax collection. All, for instance, conducted their administrative affairs in Latin and exchanged letters that were rhetorically indistinguishable from official imperial correspondence. Most were Christian states as well, although some ruling families embraced Arianism, a non-Nicene form of Christianity. Consequently, rather than interpret the rise of new barbarian kingdoms as a sign of the "end" or "decline" of the Roman Empire, we now study them as integral parts of a changing late Roman world.

Late Roman Social Relations: A Primer

Late ancient society was, by modern American standards, highly and precisely stratified. Although there was considerable fluidity in this society (it was not a caste system), late ancient people were acutely aware of their relative legal and social position in the community. Perhaps the most fundamental distinction between persons was legal: were you a slave, and hence owned by someone else, or free? Free persons, whether freeborn or freed through a legal process called manumission (whom the Romans called "freedmen"), had access to legal rights and social inclusion. Slaves, alternatively, had no legal rights and no claims to social inclusion. Men, women, and children could all be enslaved, but manumission was common enough that freedom was always a hope for slaves. Although citizenship had once been a limited legal privilege in the Roman Empire, by Late Antiquity most free or freed inhabitants were technically Roman citizens, and hence citizenship ceased having much meaning as a legal status.

Among the legally free, there was considerable variation in social rank. Social status was determined by a cluster of factors: birth, marriage, wealth, and, increasingly in the late Roman Empire, public office,

the last of which was open only to male citizens. Late Romans recognized social prestige through both bloodlines and marriage ties, meaning that women could bring status to their households. Aristocratic
status was itself highly stratified, as elites from the Empire's major urban
cities, namely Rome, Alexandria, and Constantinople, would have been
seen as considerably more prestigious than those who hailed from
provincial towns. Especially elite were those aristocrats whose families
had served in the Senate, a group whom scholars call the senatorial
aristocracy, or simply "senators." Wealth also mattered, but what concerned the late Romans most was not how rich you were, but the source
of your riches. Only the ownership of real estate (e.g., farms, villas,
houses, and other urban buildings) mattered in terms of status. Those
who made their fortunes through trade, artisanal craftwork, or banking
were able to purchase the finest comforts, but they could not buy an
aristocratic reputation through entrepreneurial enterprises. Only
investment in property and office holding, or perhaps an exceptionally
good marriage, could bring them that.

The importance of holding office for aristocratic status was hardly
new (entrance to the Senate had always conferred social prestige in
Rome), but it took on much greater significance in Late Antiquity.
When Constantine established a second Senate in Constantinople, he
doubled the number of positions that elevated men to the highest
level of elite society, the senatorial aristocracy. In response to this
influx of new senators (hence men eligible for senatorial aristocratic
status), the emperor Valentinian (r. 364–375 CE) created three new
grades of senatorial status so that social hierarchies would remain
clear. The lowest (*clarissimus*) was accessible by birth and thus open
to any man born into a senatorial aristocratic family. However,
in order to achieve the two higher ranks, *spectabilis* and *illustris* (the
highest), men had to obtain public office within the imperial administration or military.[5] In short, the senatorial aristocracy became both
more and less accessible: more men of undistinguished birth could
achieve elite status through imperial appointment to an office,
but fewer could claim a place within its highest levels. To be clear,
not all late ancient elites were senatorial aristocrats with honors
such as *illustris*. The late Roman Empire was home to a large number
of provincial elites, landowning men and women who were important
figures in their cities and towns and, in the case of men, served

as local officials in the municipal government, but had no claim to membership within the senatorial aristocracy. Scholars often refer to these office-holding provincial elites as members of the "curial" class.[6] What is more, not all provincial elites were wealthy. We know the personal story of at least one provincial notable, Augustine of Hippo (d. 430), whose father was too poor to pay for his education abroad.

Of course, the elite status system in Late Antiquity was hardly a meritocracy. Patronage was the key to obtaining the office that brought you status. Patronage is a system of social reciprocity. It involves persons (men and women) of higher status, wealth, or office called "patrons," who take on "clients," that is, people of lower position. On the one hand, the patron offers the client connections to help acquire an office (men only), perhaps money in a time of need, assistance in the legal system, and in some cases even physical protection. On the other hand, clients are expected to support their patrons politically, to provide them with favors on demand in areas of official work and private enterprise, and to attend gatherings and parties where they can be "seen" among the patron's entourage.

Non-elites, who comprised the majority of late Roman society, occupied various places within the social hierarchy, some of which are admittedly harder to reconstruct with precision than others. Certain professions, such as acting and prostitution, carried precise legal penalties and social stigma, and were thus seen as disreputable. However, for most other non-elites, social position was determined more by local conditions and relative wealth than by profession. Artisans and merchants perhaps constituted something like a "middle class," along with physicians and bankers. Again, only landed property really counted in terms of social status, and those who worked with their hands or with money were not considered among the truly elite. Similarly, freeborn rural peasants might have had status within their village, especially if they owned a bit of property, but were viewed outside it as no more prestigious than slaves. Slaves, too, had social hierarchies. Those slaves who worked inside homes in close connection with their owners (often taking on oversight of other slaves and freedmen) wielded considerably more social power than those who labored in a workshop or cleaned the city sewers.

An Epoch of Religious Diversity and Change

Late Antiquity is characterized by an astounding diversity of religious practice and thought. There were four major religious systems at that time, each of which must be understood not as a monolithic entity, but as a related group of sects and movements: Judaism, classical paganism, Christianity, and Manichaeism. For much of the time, late Roman Jews, pagans, Christians, and Manicheans quietly and peacefully coexisted, living and worshipping side-by-side, especially in cities, where there was considerable cultural diversity. Late Romans were also open to the notion of religious "exchange" across systems. As we shall see, people commonly borrowed ideas, symbols, and rites from multiple systems, combining them into a practice that defies easy categorization (often to modern scholars' frustration). And like everything else in Late Antiquity, these religious systems were themselves in flux.

For Christians, the fourth century witnessed the emergence of Christianity not only as a licit religion, but also as an imperially sanctioned, supported, and protected institution. Beginning with the emperor Constantine's initial embrace of Christianity in 312 CE, virtually every subsequent emperor was Christian and used his private fortune and public authority to support the religion. Proclaimed as Rome's official religion by the emperor Theodosius I (r. 379–395 CE) in 380 CE, Christianity rapidly became the dominant Mediterranean cult favored by its most elite citizens. As money poured in and more elites joined the ranks, the church and its leaders gradually took shape as a spiritual, political, social, and economic force in communities across the Empire.

For Jews, Late Antiquity brought profound changes in leadership and legal traditions. With the demise of the Jewish priesthood following the Roman destruction of the great temple in Jerusalem in 70 CE, Jews began to turn to local leaders, the rabbis. Rabbis ("rabbi" or "rebbi" is Hebrew for "teacher" or "master") had been around for millennia, but they began to form a more institutionalized core of Judaism during Late Antiquity. The rabbis were not priests, but rather teachers and interpreters of Jewish Scripture and law. In Palestine and Mesopotamia (or what Jewish sources call Babylonia), rabbinic schools developed where men studied Scripture and the various Jewish legal traditions, which were codified and systematized during

Late Antiquity in what is known as the Talmud. Although the rabbis were very powerful in Palestine and Mesopotamia, it would take many more centuries for the rabbinic movement to become the norm for Jews all over the world.

Paganism arguably underwent the most drastic changes of all late ancient religions. As Christianity increased in popularity and power, traditional forms of paganism – that is, the worship in temples of multiple gods through ritual sacrifice and the interventions of priests – began to wane. The state delivered the biggest blows, which sequentially outlawed most forms of sacrifice, ended subsidies to support temples and priesthoods, and eventually commanded by fiat (the law of 380 CE mentioned earlier) that all citizens practice Christianity.[7] However, the drift away from classical paganism was slow and uneven, and because of the fluid nature of lived religion, it endured in hybrid forms. Most importantly, many late Romans came to perceive pagan mythology as a form of classical culture, and therefore were comfortable integrating its symbols and stories into their surroundings, as we shall see in this book.

Paganism, moreover, was in a sense reborn during Late Antiquity through the emergence of Neoplatonism. As the name suggest, Neoplatonists saw themselves as followers of the ancient Greek philosopher Plato (d. 347 BCE) and his metaphysical ideas about the division of the cosmos into a higher, ineffable realm of knowledge that was immaterial and a lower, material world, in which humans live. Neoplatonists associated the higher realm with a divine hierarchy presided over by the "Father" or the "Mind." The goal of practice was to transcend the material world so as to become part of the divine world. Neoplatonists believed that they could achieve this goal regularly through intensive philosophical study and the performance of esoteric rites called theurgy ("the divine work"), which in some cases involved divination and/or the mediation of natural objects, such as stones or plants. Most Neoplatonists were highly educated, elite city-dwellers. Until ca. 529 CE, when the emperor Justinian shut down their schools, Neoplatonists practiced openly in cities such as Alexandria, Constantinople, and Athens.

Late Antiquity also produced one of the most successful missionary religions in history, Manichaeism. Manichaeism is another Mediterranean monotheism, with close ties to Christianity. Its founder, Mani

(216–274 CE), came from a Persian family, and asserted that he was a prophet continuing the work of Jesus Christ. Mani taught that the cosmos was divided between a divine good or "light," and evil dark matter.[8] "Light" and "dark" were once locked in battle, which led to the creation of humanity and the earth. Consequently, the world is made up of dark evil matter, but contains particles of light that are found in all living things. Jesus, Mani claimed, was the son of light, who came to teach humans the truth about the cosmos and methods for cleansing their souls of dark matter and releasing the light. Release could be achieved through living a virtuous life that was, for instance, devoid of killing, lying, or consuming animal meat. Mani wrote numerous texts that outlined a new religious institution with two levels of membership: the "Elect" (the elites who spent their days in study and prayer) and the "Hearers" (non-elites who attended the Elect's daily needs). Manichaeism was extremely popular in the Late Empire. In the West, it attracted many followers, such as Augustine (354–430 CE), who had been a Manichaean Hearer before becoming a Christian bishop. In the East, Manichaeism spread to the Indus Valley and into China, where it flourished until the Middle Ages.

The last, but perhaps most important, religious transformation in Late Antiquity is the gradual decline of tolerance for diversity and difference. When Emperor Theodosius I declared Christianity to be the official religion of the Empire in 380 CE, he did not mean all forms of Christianity, only the form associated with a particular theology, what scholars call Nicene Christianity.[9] Other forms of Christianity, not to mention other religions, such as paganism, Manichaeism, and Judaism, were increasingly attacked both formally by the state and informally by local communities. Manicheans, for example, were regularly targeted by imperial legislation. These laws expressly prohibited them from congregating in public and private spaces, exiled members, called for the burning of their books, expropriated their property, and placed heavy fines on Christians who did not report them. Jewish communities, too, suffered in an environment of increasing intolerance. Our sources show that mobs occasionally burned down synagogues and attacked individual Jews, and that the state barred all Jews from holding public office in the early fifth century. By the sixth century, the emperor Justinian had excluded anyone who was not an orthodox Christian from serving in the government, including the army. Those who were not considered orthodox, whom the church and state branded "heretics," were punished with fines and imprisonment. In short, for some men and women in Late Antiquity, daily devotion to their chosen rites and beliefs brought challenges and even danger.

HOW TO USE THIS BOOK

Daily Life in Late Antiquity is written for students and general readers. It does not assume any background in ancient history. Consequently, it contains few formal bibliographic references or expansions in the form of footnotes or endnotes. Readers interested in pursuing a topic further should consult the recommended titles in the "Further Reading" section at the end of each chapter, which offers a select list of primary and secondary sources available in English. This book aims to introduce readers to the whole of the late Roman world, which means that it cannot offer the specificity of Bertrand Lançon's *Rome in Late Antiquity: Everyday Life and Urban Change, AD 312–609* (trans. A. Nevill, New York, 2000), the only other available study of late ancient daily life, albeit one that examines the city of Rome exclusively. At the end of this introduction, readers will find a list of more general studies of Late Antiquity that they can consult alongside this study of daily life.

The book has six chapters, each of which describes and analyzes everyday life through topics that would have been recognizable to men and women living in Late Antiquity. Chapter 1, "Rural Life," examines the quotidian experiences of the vast majority of the late Empire's population, who lived and worked in the countryside. It also explores the production and consumption (from farm to table) of four major late Roman commodities: wheat, olive oil, wine, and pork. Chapter 2, "Urban Life," looks at daily life in late Roman cities, paying close attention to both the changing physical environment and the types of activities that typically went on in late ancient urban centers, from industry and trade to prostitution and chariot racing. Chapter 3, "The Household," focuses on the late Roman world's most important social institution, with extensive discussion of marriage, divorce, childhood, slavery, and domestic space. Chapter 4, "The State in Everyday Life," presents an angle that is typically ignored in books about daily life: the manifold ways in which the Roman imperial state was part of ordinary people's everyday experiences. Here we explore the late Roman army, tax collection and payment, and the court system, which was used by peasants and senators alike. Chapter 5, "Body and Mind," examines how late Romans cared for their health and well-being through discussion of not only medicine, disease, and health care, but also sexuality, elite education (care of the mind), and dress. Chapter 6, "Religion in Daily Life," looks at how different religious communities (Jewish, pagan, Christian, and Manichaean) practiced their faith in Late Antiquity, as well as how they dealt with death and burial.

Each chapter opens with a profile of a real person or persons who lived in Late Antiquity. They have been chosen because aspects of their life resonate strongly with the chapter's main theme. The two exceptions are Chapters 2 and 6. Chapter 2 profiles not two people, but two cities (Ephesus and Brixia, the Roman name for modern Brescia in Italy). Chapter 6, on religion, opens with a discussion of a magical amulet from what is today the Balkans, whose inscription reveals a great deal about lived religion. Throughout this book, I have included as much primary evidence as possible to illustrate the many different experiences of daily life. Virtually all the original sources presented here are available in English translation for interested readers, and I have listed the references in the "Further Reading" sections. Teachers using this book thus might consider assigning some of these primary sources to use alongside the textbook. At the time of writing, there are two excellent collections of primary source material in English translation. R. Mathisen, *People, Personal Expression, and Social Relations in Late Antiquity* (Ann Arbor, MI, 2003, 2 vols.) provides extensive citations from late Roman sources emanating from Gaul and the West that are focused largely on the theme of daily life. M. Maas, *Readings in Late Antiquity: A Sourcebook* (London, 2009, 2nd ed.) covers more ground thematically and geographically (with extensive translated passages from east Roman sources), and includes sources on everyday life that supplement the material in this book.

It goes without saying that a book about lived experience within a vast and diverse empire over a 350-year period cannot be exhaustive or comprehensive. Not all readers, for instance, will agree with the decision to downplay aspects of high culture (art, literature, and philosophy) and to emphasize instead more mundane state-driven activities, such as tax assessment or the importance of practice (instead of theology) in the experience of religion. Hopefully, all will concur that beginning with the countryside, where at least 80 percent of the late Empire's inhabitants resided, is the right way to start a book on daily life. I have also endeavored to capture the dynamism that characterizes this period in history, to draw attention to ways in which thoughts and practices changed over time, as well as how they differed across the many distinct regions of the late Empire. The East and West had a great deal in common, to be sure, but their differing geopolitical trajectories led to some distinction in terms of how life was lived on the ground.

Further Reading

P. Brown, *The World of Late Antiquity, AD 150–750* (New York, 1972) and *The Rise of Western Christendom: Triumph and Diversity, AD 200–1000* (Chichester, UK, 2013, 3rd ed.) focus heavily on the cultural and religious history of the late Roman Empire. Brown's pathbreaking work has helped define Late Antiquity as a field. Students are encouraged to read these two studies along with Brown's more thematic monographs.

A. H. M. Jones, *The Later Roman Empire AD 284–602 CE: A Social, Economic, and Political Survey*, 2 vols. (Baltimore, 1964) remains the most comprehensive study of the political, social, and administrative institutions of the late Roman Empire. Readers looking for a more succinct book on these topics can consult S. Mitchell, *A History of the Later Roman Empire, 284–641 AD* (Malden, MA, 2015, 2nd ed.), which covers some religious developments as well. Both books include broad narratives of late ancient history, but readers can also use the still valuable study by J. Bury, *History of the Later Roman Empire*, 2 vols. (New York, 1958, reprint of the original published in 1911).

A. Cameron's two volumes, *The Later Roman Empire* (Cambridge, MA, 1993) and *The Mediterranean World in Late Antiquity, AD 395–700* (London, 1993), offer more streamlined discussion that synthesizes political, social, cultural, and religious developments. Readers interested in an even more condensed account of the period can consult G. Clark, *Late Antiquity: A Very Short Introduction* (Oxford, 2011).

Finally, there are several handbooks and encyclopedias dedicated to Late Antiquity, which contain entries and essays on particular topics.

Cambridge Ancient Histories, vols. 12–14 (Cambridge, 2000).

Interpreting Late Antiquity: Essays on the Postclassical World, eds. G. Bowersock, P. Brown, and O. Grabar (Cambridge, MA, 2001).

A Companion to Late Antiquity, ed. P. Rousseau (Chichester, UK, 2009).

The Oxford Handbook of Late Antiquity, ed. S. Johnson (Oxford, 2012).

1

Rural Life

Aurelius Sakaon (d. ca. 340 CE) was an important man with a scar on his left shin who lived in an Egyptian village called Theadelphia (now Batn-Ihrit). Theadelphia sat in the Fayoum Oasis, a fertile stretch of land west of the Nile River in northern Egypt. Sakaon, who died in his seventies, carved out a relatively comfortable existence for an illiterate peasant farmer. He owned his own house in the village and could afford to keep it going without taking in tenants. He also probably had enough income to rent additional land for farming and pasturing his animals. He married twice and, according to a census record dated 310 CE, was part of a household that included his sixteen-year-old son, two brothers, a nineteen-year-old nephew, and at least four other male relatives. We should assume that Sakaon's household included female members as well, despite their absence from the census record. In some cases, these records only list male members who were or had been eligible for military service.

Like the lives of all late ancient peasants, Sakaon's life revolved around the seasons and the land, and some aspect of agriculture occupied him every day of the year. One property that he cultivated was good for cereal farming, and so Sakaon spent the spring driving a team of oxen with a plow to prepare the fields for seeding, a job he and his family accomplished manually with seed either reserved from the previous year's harvest or purchased from the market. Water was a problem for Theadelphians, because the village sat at the top of a hill far from the Nile and was fed by an aging irrigation system. Consequently, Sakaon and his family labored to keep the fields watered – a task made all the more difficult when villages closer to the source periodically siphoned off water. After harvesting the wheat, Sakaon would separate a prearranged portion for taxes, allotting the rest to his family and perhaps rent. In especially good years, he might have a surplus, which he could sell at the market for cash and use the money to purchase some fancy tableware or dyed clothes. He also kept small herds of sheep and goats, whose wool or hair could be spun into thread and milk turned to cheese. And although Sakaon could neither read nor write the local dialect of Coptic, let alone Latin or Greek, he had the money and sense to pay professional clerks to draw up petitions so that he could challenge neighbors and relatives in court over stolen sheep, reneged contracts, water rights, and disputed marriage arrangements.

Two hundred and fifty years later, another landowner from Egypt, Flavius Strategius Apion II (d. 579 CE), took stock of his vast agricultural empire. He and his family owned tens of thousands of acres of fertile arable land in Oxyrhynchus, a lowland region that sat closer to the Nile than Theadelphia and so benefited from easier and more certain irrigation. His heirs – a daughter or daughter-in-law called Proiecta and two male relatives named Apion III and Georgios – inherited what was, by the sixth century, the single largest landholding in all of Egypt. According to one estimate, the Apiones owned forty-seven thousand acres in Oxyrhynchus, a figure that, if accurate, meant that this single family contributed one-third of the region's total taxes. A man of Strategius Apion II's stature, whose father and grandfather hailed from the highest stratum of the senatorial aristocracy, did not dirty his hands in the daily grind of cereal farming and animal husbandry. He instead employed an elaborate, hierarchically organized household administration, replete with salaried managers, revenue collectors, bankers, clerks, legal experts, and field bosses. From an urban residence in Constantinople or Alexandria, Strategius Apion II administered his vast rural landholdings and workforce, which included both peasant tenants and slaves. And although he was rarely physically present on the fields, he closely monitored his estates' productivity, eager for news that his yields were large, his taxes paid, and his net income could sufficiently cover his household's elaborate lifestyle. It is also likely that some of the estates Strategius Apion II oversaw actually belonged to the emperor, and that managing them was both a burden and a privilege. This was a common arrangement in Late Antiquity, and it added another level of complexity to the challenge of large-scale agriculture.

Aurelius Sakaon and Flavius Strategius Apion II were property owners from late ancient Egypt whose lives were tethered to the land. Between 80 and 90 percent of the late Roman population resided in the countryside. By any measure, agriculture was the basis of the late ancient economy for rich and poor alike. Whether you were a wealthy landholder like Strategius Apion II or a peasant like Sakaon, the countryside was the source of your livelihood. Agriculturalists not only grew the wheat, picked the olives, and raised the animals, but also produced the olive oil, fermented the wine, spun the wool, and made the ceramic vessels that were used at home, sold at local markets, and transported to cities across the Empire. As we shall see in the next section and in greater detail in Chapter 4, the late Roman tax system was tightly intertwined with rural life and agricultural production, as the state regularly exploited private land and rural labor to sustain its massive armies and feed its largest cities. For the vast majority of late ancient rustics, who were illiterate and lowborn, farm work was the primary means of survival. A bad harvest, a flooded storage facility, or crushing taxes could send a man like Sakaon into destitution at any moment. Alternatively, for the wealthiest late Roman citizens, such as Strategius Apion II and his heirs, landownership and agricultural production enabled a privileged life of leisure and luxury. Each man, in other words, represents one side of the late Empire's most important coin.

We begin with Aurelius Sakaon and Flavius Strategius Apion II not because either man is necessarily typical, but because we happen to know a great deal about their daily lives. Significantly, both men hailed from Egypt. In Late Antiquity, Egypt was part of the East, that is, the eastern regions of the Empire that were governed by the emperor from his capital in Constantinople. While we tend to think of Egypt as a desert, parts were (and still are) extraordinarily fertile because of the Nile's annual flooding cycle. Consequently, Egypt had long been the Roman Empire's wealthiest province, and in Late Antiquity it was responsible for producing the grain consumed by the citizens of Constantinople. Egypt's overall dry climate means that ancient artifacts, especially textual objects like papyrus rolls and sheets, have been well preserved. As a result of this preservation, scholars today have access to an extraordinarily broad and deep pool of written evidence from Egypt that can be used to reconstruct daily life. In the case of both Sakaon and Strategius Apion II, we are fortunate to possess archives from Theadelphia and Oxyrhynchus, which include personal letters, petitions, tax receipts, census records, and work chits that illuminate the quotidian activities of these two communities.[1] Outside Egypt, our documentary evidence for daily life diminishes, but archaeological sources, inscriptions, and literary texts (when read carefully) can help us sketch a general picture of how a wide range of late ancient people lived and worked in the countryside. Readers should be aware, however, of the generally poor representation of rural affairs in the written record and that few large-scale archaeological excavations have been conducted aimed at studying late Roman peasant life. With regard to the ancient literary sources, late Roman authors were largely urban elites, whose interest in the countryside was rhetorical in nature, not sociological. To the limited extent that they discuss rural life, their descriptions of peasants, farming, and country life cannot necessarily be taken at face value. Consequently, there is a great deal that we still do not know about the late ancient countryside, though recent work is moving the conversation forward in new and exciting directions.[2]

In what follows, the chapter examines rural life in both the East and the West, taking note of differences and similarities in climate, farming practices, and living conditions. For instance, among the many changes that mark Late Antiquity is the onset of the Late Antique Little Ice Age in the sixth century, which brought cooler temperatures throughout the Roman Empire and more unstable weather. Conditions became wetter in some areas, especially in northwestern regions and Anatolia, and drier in others, such as in the Levant. Rural life, as we shall see, was likely affected by climate change alongside other factors. The chapter concludes with a section tracking the production, from farm to table, of four primary foods in the late Roman diet: bread (from wheat), olive oil, wine, and pork products.

Late ancient Romans, of course, grew and consumed many other things. Sheep and goat meat, for example, were the most commonly eaten forms of animal protein in Late Antiquity, and people also enjoyed large quantities of fish, fruits, vegetables, and legumes. Nevertheless, grains, olives, grapes, and pigs were agricultural staples for rustic laborers and their landlords. And as we shall see in subsequent chapters, these four foods also comprised the state's special provisioning system, which helped to feed both the army and citizens in its largest cities. Readers can thus follow these four products from chapter to chapter.

THE LATE ROMAN COUNTRYSIDE: A WORLD OF VILLAS AND VILLAGES

Environmentally speaking, Aurelius Sakaon and Flavius Strategius Apion II experienced the same countryside. Northern Egypt, along with most coastal regions of the Late Roman Empire, from Syria and Palestine to North Africa and Spain, enjoyed a version of a "Mediterranean" climate. A Mediterranean climate is associated with alternating seasons of dry summer heat and cool winter rain. To be sure, northern Egypt was significantly drier and received considerably less rainfall during the winter than, say, Italy. But had Sakaon and Strategius Apion II ever met Q. Aurelius Symmachus (ca. 345–402 CE), an aristocratic landowner who possessed agricultural estates in Italy and North Africa, all three could have chatted about the advantages of a Mediterranean climate for growing wheat, grapes, fruits, and vegetables. Rural inhabitants along the Mediterranean coasts of the Roman world experienced similar growing patterns and crop potential, with differences in yield noticeable between those relatively few farms with access to irrigation, such as along the Nile, and the majority that depended on water principally from rainfall. Moreover, the Nile Valley and coastal Mediterranean regions are, for the most part, flat or gently hilly, making them ideal places for farming.

When we move away from the Nile Valley and the coastal regions of the Mediterranean, we find very different physical environments and climatic conditions. Sections of the Roman Empire were mountainous, from the Pyrenees and Alps in the West, to the Atlas Mountains of North Africa, to the rocky hills of central Greece and the rugged terrain of central Anatolia in Asia Minor. Here, temperatures were far cooler, in some cases well below freezing, for parts of the year, and the topography less amenable to agriculture, especially for growing cereals. While the olive tree was a staple in some mountainous regions, in most cases rural folk focused on pasturing animals and tending smaller terraced farms. Elsewhere, in Britain, northern Gaul, and Germany, the countryside was less topographically extreme, and so long as temperatures remained relatively moderate, as they did until the sixth century, grains and grapes could be grown efficiently. The hardy olive tree did tremendously well in the dry regions of the Syrian plateau, in the mountainous rocky lands of Greece, and in the Palestinian Negev, but it did not flourish in Egypt, where it was simply too hot, and could not grow at all north of the Alps because of freezing temperatures.

The social organization of rural life also differed across the late Empire. In the East, the village was the dominant model of rustic life, and most peasants lived in small to medium-size clusters of houses and shops. A peasant village such as Theadelphia was a definite place on the map, but it and other rural communities like it had few amenities associated with ancient cities, such as temples, baths, and theaters. Rural villages were nevertheless busy places, and in some cases specialized in particular types of industry, such as textile production. A sixth-century papyrus document from Aphrodito in central Egypt, for instance, lists one dyer, eight fullers, five linen workers, a group of wool workers, and three tailors among the city's artisan population.[3] Some of these eastern rural villages were controlled, if not owned outright, by elite landowners. In many cases, for instance, peasants lived in rented housing on property owned by a landlord. We find a number of these settlements in the records of the Apiones. However, other late ancient rural villages were more independent. In Theadelphia, where Aurelius Sakaon lived, the residents exercised relative autonomy, since their village was not located on the property of a wealthy landowner. In fact, Sakaon was a recognized leader of his village, and lobbied on its behalf in a series of petitions sent to local officials, wherein he complained about the actions of nearby villages, which were siphoning off water from a common Nile-fed irrigation channel.

In the West, villages like Theadelphia and Aphrodito were less common. Many rustics lived in small clusters of housing on or close to the estates of larger landowners. Sidonius Apollinaris (ca. 430–489 CE), whom we shall meet in Chapter 3, owned a large villa in central Gaul called Avitacum. While archaeologists have not identified the physical remains of this particular estate, it was likely similar to other villas in Gaul and Spain that have been excavated.[4] Scholars hypothesize that those living around the villa were the men and women who rented land from the estate owner and hence were his tenants. They might also have worked on some of his land for wages. Here we should assume a more dependent relationship between tenant and landlord, and in fact Sidonius' letters attest to his seigneurial oversight of many men and women who lived on his estate. However, not all western rustics lived in such close proximity to a landlord. There is also material evidence for a variety of smaller, dispersed settlements, where peasants lived on their own land or as the tenants of a more distant landlord in small hamlets.

Working the Land

The Romans had few synthetic materials and no fossil fuel–powered machinery, so virtually everything that they ate, drank, wore, and used derived from the environment through physical labor. In the countryside, ancient people developed relatively sophisticated agricultural regimes and industrial processes through which they produced many of the necessary and nonessential material components of their daily lives. In many cases, cultivation and processing took place under the direction of a single landowner. Estates not only grew grapes, flax, and wheat and kept sheep and goats, but they also produced wine, linen, bread, wool, and cheese. The most important daily activities on any estate thus revolved around the planting, tending, pasturing, harvesting, and processing of agricultural products.

Both the great landlord and the peasant farmer faced ecological limitations whenever they grew a crop or pastured animals. Water was a perennial issue, and very few rural regions had dependable irrigation systems. Even in places with irrigation, such as rural Egypt, water was sometimes a problem. Sakaon, we noted, was involved in a long-term dispute with other villages over water rights. Outside these special areas, most rustics engaged in farming that was largely dependent on rainfall. The entire agricultural enterprise, therefore, was risky.

Droughts were common, while insects periodically destroyed crops or killed herds, because late ancient farmers did not have effective insecticides. According to an early sixth-century chronicle, a locust infestation ravaged the countryside around the Mesopotamian city of Edessa in the 490s CE, killing all the crops and even attacking a small child left sitting in the fields by his parents (though here the author's flair for drama may be at play).[5] The result was catastrophic for the entire region, as peasants were forced to sell what little they owned in order to buy available food, now sold at exorbitant cost, and to migrate into unaffected regions. Soil could also be easily stripped of its necessary mineral content (nitrogen, phosphorus, and potassium) by overfarming. Although many rural peasants were adept at managing the productive capacity of their land, harvest shocks were a potential experience in late ancient agriculture, which could cause irreparable harm to rural families.

In order to minimize risks, estate owners and farmers used a variety of strategies. The most fundamental was to adopt a mixed-farming regime, that is, planting a variety of crops on different plots and pasturing animals. A regime that combined cereals, legumes, and livestock helped farmers to avoid total loss from a single crop failure. A preference for mixed farming is one reason why late ancient agriculturalists owned or leased multiple fragmented holdings spread across areas. The more variety in environmental conditions, the less chance that a single household would face total ruin when a crisis hit. A mixed-farming regime also potentially increased yields, because it provided the soil with natural fertilization from manure and from nitrogen via the planting of legumes. Another key strategy was the temporary transformation of arable fields into pastures, which allowed roaming sheep, goats, and cattle to deposit manure directly onto the soil. Late Roman agriculturalists used additional tools that might strike the modern reader as less effective, namely astrology, magic, and the spiritual power of holy men. Many late ancient agricultural manuals operated on the assumption that the alignment of the moon, earth, and stars played a central role in the determination of planting and harvest times and could be used to predict yields.[6]

Some agriculturalists were also savvy about how much they farmed a particular crop, choosing small-scale over large-scale investment.

The Apion archives even show that one of the richest families in Late Antiquity pursued a "just enough" strategy when it came to growing cereals. Just enough was cultivated to pay their taxes, feed their workers and themselves, and purchase seed for the following year, with no surplus generated (at least deliberately) to sell on the market for profit. Given the significance of grain in the Roman diet and for the imperial provisioning system, this might sound odd. But cereals, unlike other crops, such as grapes and olives, were especially unprofitable: demand was effectively inelastic, but supplies fluctuated in a manner that was largely unpredictable from the grower's perspective. If a household managed to make a profit on its cereals, it was essentially by accident. It meant that somewhere else another great estate had experienced a harvest shock or a ship carrying grain had sunk – both disasters likely caused by uncontrollable environmental conditions. At this moment, grain prices might rise, but no one could predict when or where it would happen again. When it came to grain, therefore, most farmers planned for what they needed rather than for a potentially large profit.

A final strategy to mention is cooperation, especially among non-elite agriculturalists. Peasants in many cases joined forces, even across family lines, in order to dilute risk and increase their chances of success. For example, in the village of Theadelphia, a man named Kaët agreed to combine his flock of sheep with that of another man, and to oversee both jointly.[7] It was clearly advantageous to both men for Kaët to shepherd a single larger flock. Similarly, Aurelius Sakaon once took out a loan of some seventy-eight talents of silver. Late ancient farmers, in fact, often borrowed money in order to cover short-term expenses, such as purchasing seed in the spring for planting. Interestingly, Sakaon had a cosigner, one Ammonios, who was twenty years his junior. The loan agreement, which is among Sakaon's papers, shows that both men agreed to pay back the loan within three months or start accruing interest. Of course, sometimes well-intended cooperative endeavors had destructive results. We know about Kaët's oversight of this man's flock, because Kaët's wife later sued him. Immediately after Kaët's death, the owner of the other sheep repossessed not only his animals, but also those belonging to Kaët, thereby robbing his family of its property.[8]

Extracting Wealth from the Land: The Elite Landowner

Rural landownership was the basis of wealth and the primary context for labor in Late Antiquity. Consequently, it was arguably the single most important factor that distinguished one agriculturalist from another. Landowners, we have seen, came from all levels of the social order. Both the peasant Sakaon and the aristocrat Flavius Strategius Apion II were landowners, though their portfolios differed in size by several orders of magnitude. And while some sources mask female property ownership by assuming male landholders as the norm (what scholars sometimes call the "masculine neuter"), women were also landlords on large and small scales. On the Apiones' end of the wealth/landowning spectrum sat Melania the Younger (d. 439 CE), scion of a distinguished senatorial family from Rome, and quite possibly the richest individual outside the imperial family during the early fifth century. She owned estates literally all over the Empire: in southern Spain, North Africa, Italy, and Egypt. Closer to Sakaon's world was a fellow Theadelphian, Aurelia Artemis, who had enough money to purchase not one but two homes, one of which, described as a former fullery (a place where wool was cleaned and processed), cost her nine talents of silver.[9]

Yet, for elites like Melania, landownership meant something rather different. Landownership brought prestige in the late Roman world, since it was considered the only truly honorable means of accruing wealth. Elite landholders did not dirty their own hands to make their properties productive – this was a task left to the laborers, whose lives we will consider shortly. Rather, they made their fortunes on the backs of those laborers, both directly and indirectly.

Rental income was the most popular and least risky means of making money from a piece of land. Leasing out land for rental income was an extremely common management strategy, especially among those who owned multiple parcels spread over different regions. The fact that landowners typically passed the burden of farming on to tenants and did not directly work their properties does not mean that they were absentee landlords or uninvolved in the care of their estates. Q. Aurelius Symmachus, for instance, spent considerable time inspecting his properties. Symmachus' own letters show him regularly visiting his estates in Italy, checking in with his local managers and field bosses to make sure that taxes were being paid, rents collected, and crops delivered for his personal use.[10]

Landowners might also rely on slaves to provide labor on their rural estates. As scholars have shown, rural slave labor on an extensive level was no longer part of the Roman agricultural economy in Late Antiquity. The era of the large villa-estates with teams of slaves was part of the distant past. Moreover, slaves were a major capital investment for most people. Slave labor, however, was more reliable and easier to control than that provided by a freeborn tenant or seasonal employee. Consequently, slaves were still part of the rural landscape. It is possible that Melania the Younger owned anywhere between eight thousand and twenty-four thousand slaves on her agricultural properties just outside the city of Rome. Hers is undoubtedly an exceptional case, regardless of whether the high or low count is the more accurate. But other evidence demonstrates that slaves were used in some agricultural contexts, though probably more often in processing than in planting and harvesting. Slaves, of course, were central to the execution of skilled and unskilled domestic work, a point to which this book returns in Chapter 3.

The Engine of Agriculture: The Peasant Laborer

While technologies such as the plow, the yoke, the screw press, and the water wheel made agricultural work easier, the vast majority of tasks related to the cultivation and processing of goods were performed manually by peasant laborers. Seasonal migrant farm workers probably provided the bulk of the manpower during harvest seasons. They are the hardest to trace in the historical record, since they were neither tenants nor landowners, but their presence was critical to production. Some peasant laborers, we noted, were landowners in their own right. However, even freeholders like Sakaon typically rented supplemental property as a strategy to diversify their holdings. Like most late ancient rustics, Sakaon was also a tenant farmer, whose world revolved in part around a relationship with a landlord.

In social terms, the landlord–tenant relationship varied considerably. In some cases, it was steeply hierarchical, such as when the tenant was a lowborn illiterate peasant and her landlord a senatorial aristocrat like Melania the Younger or Flavius Strategius Apion II. Evidence suggests that some peasants in certain parts of the late Empire increasingly relied on their landlords for various forms of protection (legal, political, even physical), and hence became increasingly dependent upon them. In the West, where the burden of public and personal safety increasingly fell on the shoulders of private elites, peasants sought out landlords to guard them from raiders. Similarly, eastern peasants occasionally turned to their richer lords for assistance in dodging tax collectors. Less dramatic but more common, elite landlords used their personal connections to assist tenants facing legal troubles. Here the tenant clearly benefited from a close paternalistic relationship with his landlord. Of course, for some tenants this type of high-placed help came at a price. Stories abound (often exaggerated but containing elements of truth) about cruel landlords who exploited their tenants, treating them essentially like slaves.

Additionally, some rustics were legally bound to remain on the land that they leased and cultivated. This situation might sound strange, given the fact that these tenants were not slaves. How could someone have forced a freeborn person to remain a rent-paying tenant? The answer has to do with the late Roman fiscal system, as reformed by the emperors Diocletian and Constantine.[11] In some cases, the state recognized the tenant, rather than (or in addition to) the landlord, as responsible for certain tax payments and services, and required these particular tenants to register their names in the municipal tax rolls alongside the fields that they rented as their place of origin (known as their *origo*). Henceforth marked in the census as "belonging" to a certain plot of land, these registered tenants became tied to the property, were expected to work it so as to generate taxes, and were forbidden by law to leave. The children of registered tenants were also forced to remain, creating generations of tied laborers on certain late Roman estates. The practice of registering some tenant laborers in the municipal tax rolls – called the "colonate" by modern scholars (after the Latin term *colonus*, for "tenant") – existed across the late Roman Empire, albeit in multiple forms and with varying implications for the parties involved.

From the peasant's perspective, the colonate was a mixed bag. On the one hand, the colonate enhanced an existing patronage system, wherein late Roman landlords might treat their tied tenants like slaves even if they were freeborn. While the colonate was never a legal condition of quasi-servitude, it probably encouraged some landlords to see their tenants as their social dependents. There is a handful of laws, for instance, that prohibit registered tenants from selling any personal property without their owner's permission. On the other hand, rents for those tenants were fixed and landlords were legally prohibited from raising them or arbitrarily evicting tenants. In this respect, the colonate potentially benefited some tied tenants, by locking rents and creating more positive relationships of dependency for them, wherein landlords had to support specific families over generations regardless of whether they were productive workers. Indeed, the colonate was probably a drag on the economy, since landowners could not transfer tied tenants from an increasingly infertile property to one that was potentially more productive. Most scholars thus agree that the colonate emerged in Late Antiquity as a response to the Roman government's fiscal needs rather than to advantage private agriculturalists, be they landlords or tenants.

FROM FARM TO TABLE: CROPS, CULTIVATION, AND PROCESSING

Rural life revolved in large part around farming crops and creating food products that were in the greatest demand: cereals for bread, olives for oil, grapes for wine, and pigs for pork. These four commodities were part of virtually every late Roman's diet, regardless of social status or wealth. Cereals, consumed in the form of breads and porridges, made up most of a person's daily caloric intake, with fat coming mainly from olive oil and protein primarily from meats, such as mutton or lamb, goat, and, as we shall explore further, pork. Grapes were used to make the number-one beverage in Late Antiquity, wine.[12] Of course, these products were not the only foods consumed on a regular basis. Late Romans enjoyed a range of foods, especially legumes, which were rich in protein, along with fruits and vegetables, fish, eggs, cheese, and a range of flavorings, such as *garum*, a popular fermented fish sauce. But grains, olives, grapes, and pork were especially important, because they were the four products provided by the state to the army and the citizens of

Rome and Constantinople in a special provisioning system, discussed in Chapter 4. Here, we shall concentrate on the work that went into producing these four products, following their movement from farm to table.

Cereals: From Seed Corn to Bread

Cereals (wheat, barley, millet, and rye) were the most popular crops, due in large part to the ease with which they were cultivated.[13] Self-pollinating grains typically germinate over the winter months, and some (e.g., barley) are highly tolerant of extreme heat and cold. Using a scratch plow (today called an ard, but the Romans knew it as the *aratrum* or *aratron*) pulled by either animal or human, a farmer scraped the top layer of the soil, creating a furrow in which seeds would be deposited by hand or using a sieve. After sowing, the seeds were covered, sometimes by hand or with a simple hoe, in order to protect them from pests. Most of this work took place in the autumn or early winter months, with the spring bringing the wheat harvest. Reaping was done by hand with sickles (preferably in the morning, when dew on the grains limited breakage and dust), and the cut plants were then bundled into sheaves. Through these means, late Roman cultivators achieved decent cereal yields. However, without synthetic fertilizers (which were only invented in the twentieth century), the most fertile land, the most skilled farmers, and the most favorable weather conditions produced relatively little grain from the many seeds that were planted.

Workers then carried the sheaves into a space with a threshing floor, where the stalks were spread and the grain heads removed from the straw. The thresher may have used a flail, a tool made of two sticks attached by a chain that was swung at the wheat plant in order to loosen the husks from the stalks. Threshing floors attracted vermin, so cultivators spread an olive residue called *amurca* over them as a form of pest control. After threshing, the grain heads were winnowed, meaning the actual grain was separated from the chaff. Winnowing was a process of scooping and shaking the grain in a special basket using a fork. Once the grain was isolated from the chaff, it was stored on-site, ideally in raised ceramic vessels placed in cool, dry storage rooms so as to deter pests and prevent molding. On some late Roman estates, especially in the West, private granaries were actually fortified. This makes sense, given the value of cereals both on the market and in everyday lives.

Following a prearranged figure, a large portion of the grain was then handed over to the state as part of the grower's tax obligations. If there was any grain left over after taxes, the farmer would likely keep the remainder for his own household and/or hand it over to a landlord as rent. Once the grain arrived at its intended destination, it would have to be ground into flour at a mill.[14] Super-rich land-owners like the Apiones owned their own mills, but most landowners and tenants brought their grain to mills owned by others and paid on a use-by-use basis. Milling could be done by hand or in mechanical mills that were operated either by animals turning the millstone or by waterpower (Figure 1.1). Water-powered mills were typically located

FIGURE 1.1. Image of a millstone from a third-century sarcophagus found in Rome, now in the Museo Chiaramonti.
Photo by Marie-Lan Nguyen (Creative Commons license).

in cities, since they relied on aqueduct systems; hence most rustics used hand mills or animal-powered mills. Once ground, the flour was carried to the bakeries, where it was mixed with yeast and water and formed into bread loaves. On the Apion estates in Egypt, there were several settlements that had ovens and produced bread. We do not know very much about how this bread was distributed on the estates or to whom, but it is certain that it was eaten exclusively by the estates' inhabitants and not sold on the market.

Today, many consider whole-grain breads to be the most desirable, and people pay high prices for artisanal loaves made from nutty bran flour. In Late Antiquity, dark bread was the *least* desirable type, and was consumed by slaves and the poor. Bread, like Roman society, was stratified: there was high-end bread that was mostly composed of white flour. A medium-quality bread made with some bran, and a low-quality bread that was dark and fairly hard. The rich ate white bread only, as did citizens of Rome and Constantinople who were eligible for free provisions from the state. We should assume that most rustics con-sumed whatever type of bread was available, and probably only rarely ate the "good" white bread preferred by their wealthier landlords and employers. Peasants like Aurelius Sakaon and Aurelia Artemis could soften their harder, bran-based bread by dipping it in olive oil, another signature product of the countryside.

Olives: From Trees to Oil

Olive trees are known for their hardiness and longevity. They lie largely dormant in winter, but during the spring the trees bloom, and soon they produce their first fruits: the oil-rich olive. Able to sustain relatively cold temperatures and periods of little rain, the olive tree was ubiquitous in the Mediterranean regions of the Empire. Once planted and smeared with a mixture of ash and manure, an olive seedling took four years to grow to a sufficient size to bear fruit, and a mature tree might not fruit every year. It was almost always the case that an estate's olive grove did not collectively fruit at the same time, and thus production varied from year to year, some heavier than others. For much of the year, olive trees demanded little attention: a little pruning here and there, perhaps some additional fertilizer in the form of dung taken from the stables. By contrast, harvest time was highly labor intensive, since the best fruit had to be picked by hand. A faster method was to beat the tree and pick olives off the ground, but this often led to bruising. A good harvester picked between 100 and 330 pounds a day from five to fifteen trees, taking only the ripe fruit. This meant that workers had to make several trips back to the same tree in order to complete the harvest. After the olives were taken from the trees, they were sorted by size and quality.

The Romans ate their olives whole (primarily the green ones) and pressed them to make oil (usually the black variety). Olive oil was extremely important for daily life in Late Antiquity, not only as a dietary staple but also as fuel for lamps. Making olive oil was not difficult, but it took time and strength. First the olives were washed and crushed via treading, pounding with a mortar and pestle, or mashed with a stone roller. The resulting olive paste was placed in large tubs, where it was stirred with a paddle and then placed in a press. Late Romans used both lever presses and screw presses. Olive presses were less costly than grain mills, and thus appeared more frequently in rural areas. Screw presses, for instance, have been recovered from the remains of peasant villages all over the Negev and the Syrian Massif (Figure 1.2). The pressing of a single load of olive paste was arduous and could take up to twenty-four hours, even

FIGURE 1.2. Image of a screw press from an interior mosaic in the Church of SS. Lot and Procopius, Nebo (Jordan), sixth century.
Photo by Michele Piccirillo, published with permission from the Studium Biblicum Franciscorum.

with the help of a screw mechanism. The oil emitted from the paste was captured in large amphorae, where it was stored before being transported to its final destination. The Apiones do not seem to have grown olive trees or produced olive oil (they probably made their oil from pressing a special variety of radishes). But this is not surprising, since Egypt was not an olive oil–producing region in Late Antiquity. Ceramic evidence from across the Mediterranean shows that for much of Late Antiquity, a few regions – North Africa in the West and Syria in the East – produced most of the olive oil consumed around the Empire. Oil produced by a peasant from Numidia, in other words, might have made its way to a dining-room table in Rome. Again, the Roman state provisioning system was partially behind this inter-regional transportation of olive oil, since it commanded production to feed its cities and soldiers. Still, a rustic would have benefited from it insofar as any surplus (i.e., what was left over after taxes) could be saved or sold.

Grapes: From Vines to Wine

Of all the available options available to a rural agriculturalist, grapes and wine were the most intensive crop and product, but perhaps the most lucrative. Wine produced on-site went largely to fulfill the estate's needs and pay the landlord's tax bill. But it might also be sold at market, especially if the wine had a reputation for excellence. The Romans drank copious and consistent amounts of wine, something like a liter a day! They also discriminated between what they recognized as good and bad vintages. Truly bad wine, what the Romans called *posca* in Latin, was literally that: wine that had soured and turned to vinegar due to mishaps in the fermentation process. *Posca*, always mixed with water, was the staple drink among the poor and soldiers. Most Romans drank all wine mixed with water; they would have seen our custom of consuming wine neat as odd. There were higher-quality wines to purchase for those who could afford it. Falnerian, a strong wine from Italy that aged well, was especially valued, as were the numerous sweet white wines from Palestine. There were also regional specialties, like the *thalassan* wines from the eastern Aegean, which contained seawater (it apparently acted as a preservative and raised the wine's acidity level). Unfermented grape juice (*mustum*) and raisin wine (*passum*) were also popular. A wealthy family, therefore, typically had several different stocks of wine, some of which was made on premises and some purchased as a luxury item. We know, for example, that the Apiones imported Rhodian wine (a *thalassan*-style wine made on the island of Rhodes) for their personal consumption, even though they produced their own wine from locally grown grapes.

Viticulture was highly labor intensive, because the vines needed constant care and considerable amounts of water. The easiest and most popular way to grow vines in Late Antiquity was around trees, a technique known in Latin as *arbustum*. After the grapes had matured, workers cut them by the bunch with a special vinedresser's knife and placed them in baskets. The grapes were then transported for processing via cart or animal. Wine processing had three stages: treading, that is, stamping on the grapes with bare feet in large vats so they released juice, or "must"; pressing the remaining grapes for additional must, perhaps using a lever or screw press; and fermentation, which was not well understood and basically uncontrolled, at least in comparison to modern winemaking (this explains why soured wine was in large supply) (Figure 1.3). Substances such chalk or marble (to deacidify),

FIGURE 1.3. Scenes from the grape harvest and treading process, from the ceiling mosaic in the Church of St. Costanza, Rome, fourth century. Photo by Vito Arcomano, Alamy stock photos.

pine resin or myrrh (as preservatives and flavorings), or seawater (to raise acidity) could be added to the must before fermentation. Wine was typically aged in either clay vessels or wooden barrels (a technique first used in Gaul) for two or three years before it was consumed, though some, such as Falnerian, were aged for far longer.

The Pig: From Livestock to Sausage

In addition to cultivated plants, the late ancient countryside was teeming with animals. Sheep, goats, pigs, cattle, and fowl were raised by rural agriculturalists, whether in small numbers on farms or in larger herds shepherded across hills and valleys. Oxen and mules were routinely used to pull plows and wagons, whereas horses and donkeys were rarer, but hardly unheard of. Indeed, animal husbandry was an integral part of the rural economy. Animals were both owned and rented out for their milk and hair. Aurelius Sakaon, for instance, rented herds of sheep and goats, a decision that was perhaps more about risk aversion than penury: were all the animals to die from disease, he would not have lost a major investment. Skilled shepherds, men who spent their lives working for households like the Apiones', moved animals from field to field. Crop cultivation was intimately linked to pastoralism, since it was the manure from the pasturing sheep, goats, and cattle that fertilized the fields.

In fact, for the most part, animals were for working, not eating. Meat was not a predominant component of the late ancient diet. The modern love of a "meat and potatoes" dinner would have seemed odd to the Romans, not the least because potatoes are a New World food. To be sure, they liked meat and ate it frequently, but never in large amounts and never in place of wheat-based foods, such as bread and porridge. Fourth- and fifth-century recipe collections, notably those handed down under the name of a renowned first-century gourmand named Apicius, show that late Romans preferred stews to plain roasted meats, probably because meat was expensive and hard to store for more than a few days unless it was cured. Moreover, late Romans typically consumed the entire animal, with sections like the head, stomach, and even reproductive organs, such as the sow's vulva, treated like delicacies. Sausages were also popular, as was a sort of minced or chopped meat called *incisia.* The type of meat eaten varied, but the most common forms consumed up and down the social scale in Late Antiquity were sheep (lamb and mutton), goat, and pork, followed by beef (including veal).[15] By custom, the Romans did not consume horsemeat.

The popularity of pork in the Roman diet had much to do with the fact that pigs were the easiest and most efficient animals to breed. Swine could be bred anywhere, and Roman farms often had sties. The best pork, however, was thought to come from pigs permitted to range freely in forests, where they fed on acorns, chestnuts, and other nuts. Interestingly, so-called garbage pigs, which are fattened on food scraps, were not popular until the fifteenth century. Sows also have large litters, as many as twelve piglets per birth. During Late Antiquity, there is evidence of estates that specialized in breeding pigs. Excavations at San Giovanni di Routi in the southern Italian province of Lucania uncovered not only a sumptuous villa that prospered in the fifth century, but also large numbers of porcine bones, which suggests that it primarily functioned as a pig farm.[16] Pig farming at San Giovanni di Routi makes sense, given the excellent pannage afforded by the region, which was rich in oak trees. In fact, Lucania was famous throughout the Empire for its pork products. Late Romans in both the East and West loved to eat *lucania* (or, in Greek, *loukania*), a type of seasoned smoked sausage that originated in this region of Italy. Ancient recipes for Lucanian sausage suggest that it tasted like salami, seasoned with ingredients such as pepper and cumin.[17]

Whether the men and women who worked on the farm at San Giovanni di Routi produced Lucanian sausage is unclear, but there is evidence that they made a pork product resembling bacon. Given the large number of pig bones found on the site, and the higher ratio between the pig bones and the remains of whole animals, it is possible that this particular farm specialized in a cured product called *laridum.* The process of making *laridum* was fairly labor intensive, since the flesh had to be thoroughly boned before it could be salted and smoked. The fact that this Italian villa was also a butchery, and that pigs were rendered there on the spot, is highly consistent with late Roman practices. Live pigs were almost never transported over long distances, because driving them invariably led to weight loss and hence a drop in the owner's profit. Consequently, small pig farmers sold locally, while larger ones, such as the family that owned the villa at San Giovanni in Routi, had their own on-site rendering and processing facilities.

A CHANGING COUNTRYSIDE

The countryside, we have emphasized, was the seat of the late ancient economy and home to the vast majority of late Roman citizens. It was the space that connected the very rich to the very poor, where land-ownership was both a source of income and a cause of human exploit-ation. It was also tightly interconnected with cities, since it produced food and other goods that sustained dense population clusters and monumentalized spaces, as we shall see in Chapters 2 and 4. A dis-cussion of rural life in the high Roman Empire might end on this note, but during Late Antiquity developments occurred that brought change to the countryside, especially for the wealthier landowning elite. Here we must consider the very different trajectories experi-enced by eastern and western landowners and peasants, as well as the changes that united them.

For the most part, the great estates in the eastern Mediterranean flourished throughout Late Antiquity. The continued success of the Apiones is a good illustration of this trend. Archaeological evidence from Egypt to the highlands of Cappadocia in modern Turkey dem-onstrates that rural life and agricultural production in this half of the Roman Empire – the half that remained directly governed by a central state in Constantinople – continued apace into the seventh century. The eastern imperial government still demanded the production of food and rural services in order to sustain its capital and armies. In fact, some scholars have even used terms like "economic boom" to describe the eastern countryside during the fifth and sixth centuries. Peasants, too, may have directly benefited from this prosperity. As Chapter 3 shows, there were many prosperous rural villages in the East with impressive housing, which demonstrates a relatively high standard of living. In fact, the most significant changes to the eastern Roman Empire and its countryside occurred outside the parameters of this book, during the seventh and eighth centuries.

The history of the countryside in the western half of the Roman Empire is very different. Studies by archaeologists have shown that between ca. 400 and 600 CE, there was a total reduction in the number of rural settlements in the West. While the question of how to interpret this contraction remains open, there is little doubt that some people lived in the countryside rather differently in the fifth and sixth centuries than they had in the third and fourth centuries. Luxury villa homes typically either disappeared entirely or gave way to more decidedly utilitarian residences, wherein rooms once used for leisure were repurposed for dying, olive oil production, or glassmaking. (To learn more about these changes in housing, see Chapter 3.) There were, of course, exceptions. Sidonius Apollinaris lived grandly on his villa estate in central Gaul at least until his death in 489 CE. However, we should probably see Sidonius and his villa as the last of a generation. Additionally, material evidence from areas of North Africa show limited increases in settlement density as well as rising economic conditions among the rural populations. Generalizations about rural "decline," therefore, must be carefully qualified.

While the West did not experience a full-blown economic collapse, many western regions experienced an economic contraction that affected the countryside in several ways. First, there were fewer large-scale estate owners in the later fifth and sixth centuries than there had been previously, and these owners concentrated their landholdings within relatively small areas. Second, the collapse of the imperial state in much of the West during the fifth century meant that tenants no longer had to register and remain "tied" to their estates. Some scholars hypothesize a rise in peasant freeholding in this period, and perhaps even an improvement in their overall quality of life. No longer beholden to landlords or forced to grow wheat to pay their taxes, small-scale agriculturalists may have experienced a period of independence never seen before.

Third, these later landowners may have adopted different agricultural regimes from their fourth-century predecessors. While fourth-century western peasants dedicated many of their estates to cereal, oil, and wine production (their interests driven in large part by the Roman government's tax demands), agriculturalists in the fifth and sixth centuries may have preferred mixed-animal husbandry and less intensive forms of diversified farming that was more suitable to local ecological and topographical conditions. In some regions, woodlands may have increased during this period (wood, of course, remained a key form of fuel and was increasingly used as a building material), and marshlands were perhaps no longer drained, but left swampy. These changing ecological conditions were detrimental to cereal farming and grape growing, but they favored hunting, fishing, and the seasonal pasturing of sheep, goats, and especially pigs. The fact that there was no longer a strong centralized imperial state in the West demanding taxes in the form of grain, oil, pork, and wine meant that agriculturalists were freer to farm according to more local needs and conditions. Additionally, some scholars believe that the Late Antique Little Ice Age contributed to these agricultural trends, since colder, wetter conditions were not conducive to growing wheat, but they were good for growing other types of grain (such as barley), hunting, fishing, and animal husbandry.

The most significant social change to the countryside in both eastern and western regions of the late Empire was the appearance of a new major institutional landowner: the Christian church. The church had been able to own property legally and openly since the time of Constantine, and thenceforth accrued urban and rural real estate at a rapid pace. By the sixth century, the church of Rome, for example, was one of the largest landowners in West, with properties in central and southern Italy, southern Gaul, and Illyricum. The land owned by the Roman church was in large part the result of gifts, donations made by the emperor or a wealthy cleric or layperson. A church that received a landed donation benefited financially from the gift, and collected revenues by leasing it or working it directly with paid laborers. But it also meant that the church now owned slaves and estates with tenants, and that it had to collect rents from those who leased its land and was potentially obligated to pay taxes to the state. In fact, administering its properties soon became a primary duty of the bishop. Rome's Pope Gregory the Great (590–604 CE) spent hours every week writing letters and receiving petitions regarding the thousands of acres of land owned by the Roman church. As Gregory's many letters attest, he was directly involved in making decisions about livestock rearing and rendering, rent collection schedules and tax rates, and the management of agricultural overseers employed by the church, some of whom were also clerics. Christian monasteries, too, began to accrue property, and some of the earliest monastic rules expressly require monks to perform agricultural labor.

The entrance of the Christian church into the world of rural agricultural and landowning meant, among other things, that traditions and customs would not disappear even in the West. Daily life for most inhabitants of the late Roman Empire continued to revolve around the rhythms of the seasons, weather cycles, financial obligations, and rural social networks. What is more, rustics remained tied to cities, whether through urban-based episcopal landlords, seasonal labor demands, or trade. It is to the late Roman city that we now must turn.

Further Reading

The following primary sources are available in English translation and provide further insight into the topics discussed in this chapter:

Apicius, *De re coquinaria* ("On Cooking"), ed. and trans. by Grocock and Grainger (Totnes, UK, 2006).
The Archive of Aurelius Sakaon. Papers of an Egyptian Farmer in the Last Century of Theadelphia, ed. and trans. George M. Parássoglou (Bonn, 1978).
Geopontika: Farm Work, trans. A. Dalby (Totnes, UK, 2011).
Palladius, *Opus Agriculturae* ("Treatise on Agriculture"), trans. J. Fitch (Totnes, UK, 2013).
Ps-Joshua the Stylite, *The Chronicle of Pseudo-Joshua the Stylite*, ed. F. Trombly and J. Watts (Liverpool, 2000).
Q. Aurelius Symmachus, *The Letters of Symmachus,* trans. M. Salzman and M. Roberts (Atlanta, 2012).
Sidonius Apollinaris, *Letters*, trans. W. Anderson (LCL, Cambridge, MA, 1965).
The Theodosian Code, trans. C. Pharr (Princeton, NJ, 1952).

Readers interested in learning more about the Apion agricultural dynasty and their archives can peruse P. Sarris, *Economy and Society in the Age of Justinian* (Cambridge, 2006) and T. Hickey, *Wine, Wealth, and the State in Late Ancient Egypt* (Ann Arbor, MI, 2012). Those generally curious about late Roman agriculture should consult M. Decker, *Tilling the Hateful Earth: Agricultural Production and Trade in the Late Antique East* (Oxford, 2009) and P. Halstead, *Two Oxen Ahead: Pre-Mechanized Farming in the Mediterranean* (Chichester, UK, 2014). Two recommended studies of late Roman peasant communities are L. Dossey, *Peasant and Empire in Christian North Africa* (Cambridge, 2010) and C. Grey, *Constructing Communities in the Late Roman Countryside* (Cambridge, 2011). For the fate of villas and farmland in the West from an archaeological perspective, see T. Lewit "Vanishing

Villas: What Happened to Elite Rural Habitations in the West in the Fifth and Sixth Centuries?," *Journal of Roman Archaeology* 16.1 (2003): 26–74. Ancient economic history is essentially the history of agricultural enterprise and trade. See W. Scheidel, I. Morris, and R. Saller (eds.), *The Cambridge Economic History of the Greco-Roman World* (Cambridge, 2007) and C. Wickham, *Framing the Early Middle Ages: Europe and the Mediterranean 400–800* (Cambridge, 2005). And for late antique environmental and climate change, see K. Harper, *The Fate of Rome: Climate, Disease, and the End of an Empire* (Princeton, NJ, 2017) and P. Squatriti, "Barbarizing the Bel Paese: Environmental History in Ostrogothic Italy," in Arnold, Bjornlie, and Sessa (eds.), *A Companion to Ostrogothic Italy* (Leiden, 2016): 390–424. Finally, introductions to the topic of food in antiquity include P. Garnsey, *Food and Society in Classical Antiquity* (Cambridge, 1999) and J. Wilkins and R. Nadeau (eds.), *A Companion to Food in the Ancient World* (Malden, MA, 2015).

2

Urban Life

INTRODUCTION: A TALE OF TWO CITIES

Theodorus and his wife, Marta, were upstanding citizens of Brixia (modern Brescia), a northern Italian city nestled in the southernmost range of the Alps. The couple were prosperous, and they gave a sizeable sum to their preferred civic institution, the Christian church. An inscription tells us that sometime in the fifth century, Theodorus and Marta donated money to help pay for a section of a sumptuous new mosaic floor in a basilica dedicated to Saint Mary.[1] According to the inscription, the couple had paid for some seventeen feet of flooring. We do not know why Theodorus and Marta chose to be patrons of this particular church. They could have supported the city's more famous basilica, which was built in ca. 400 CE by Bishop Gaudentius (387–410 CE). Located outside the city walls in one of Brixia's major cemeteries, Gaudentius' church housed a powerful collection of relics from the East, which he had personally gathered and brought back to his hometown. Like most Christian urban residents in Late Antiquity, Theodorus and Marta probably made their decision based on social connections. The couple knew the clergy at Saint Mary's, or they perhaps lived nearby and had a stake in the church's improvement.

The church of Saint Mary was located inside the ancient walls of Brixia, but it sat at some distance from city's original Roman center, where the two largest streets, the *cardo maximus* (running north-south)

and the *decumans maximus* (running east-west), crossed. In that
ancient center, the couple's ancestors had likely worshipped in the
Capitolium, a temple dedicated to the great Roman triad of state gods,
Jupiter, Juno, and Minerva; chatted with friends and transacted business in the city's main marketplace, or *forum*; bathed in a bath complex fed by one of Brixia's two aqueducts; and enjoyed shows in its
amphitheater, which accommodated more than fifteen thousand
spectators. By the time Theodorus and Marta became active members
of their Christian church in the fifth century, the "old" Roman Brixia
had begun to change and, in places, to deteriorate. Citizens had
abandoned the Capitolium in the fourth century, likely in the wake
of successive anti-pagan legislation, and some locals started stripping
the temple of its marble, limestone, and other valuable materials.
Similarly, after the amphitheater was extensively damaged in an earthquake, Brixians repeatedly robbed its material, tossing some of the
rubble onto the seats and stage. However, neither the materials nor
the buildings were all left to ruin. Some of the marble and limestone
was reused in other buildings, and what could not be salvaged was
burned in special kilns to create quicklime, a substance used in
tanning, fertilizer, and soapmaking. Archaeologists discovered a late
Roman lime kiln inside the abandoned theater, suggesting that what
was once a place of entertainment had been transformed into a
work space.

Most significantly, sixth-century Brixians witnessed the emergence
of new city centers. Specifically, they watched the construction of two
fortified citadels, one associated perhaps with state power, the other
with the church. Walls had encircled Brixia since the first century CE,
but during the sixth century officials erected a new thicker enclosure
around a smaller area situated in the northwest corner of the city. This
fortified quadrant enclosed a large public building with three wings.
We do not know exactly who built this new space or its function, but it
may have served as the local palace for Ostrogoth rulers and later
Lombard dukes. The second citadel occupied the crest of the Cidneo
Hill in the very north of the city; it contained a church with several
episcopal burials, cisterns, workshops, and a bath complex (Figure 2.1).
The creation of these new fortifications, public buildings, production
spaces, and churches shifted Brixia's focal point away from the original center in the forum and the Capitolium toward the north and

FIGURE 2.1. The Cidneo Hill in Brixia, now Brescia (Italy), where sixth-century residents built a new fortification that enclosed a church, bath complex, workshops, cisterns, and burials. The fortification was continuously inhabited through the sixteenth century, when the surviving castle (shown here) was erected.
Photo by Riccardo Mottola, Alamy stock photos.

west, where its officials and church elites worked, and perhaps lived, behind high, thick walls.

Across the Mediterranean Sea, along the west coast of what is now Turkey, Ephesus stood out among the East's most prosperous cities. At the height of the Roman Empire, it was famous for its port, its cosmopolitan culture, and its grand Temple of Artemis, an edifice so large and adorned with such exquisite sculpture that several ancient travel writers named it one of the Seven Wonders of the World. These earlier residents and visitors could meander through Ephesus' main marketplace, or *agora*, or work out in its expansive gymnasium, which featured exercise areas and a large bathing complex.[2] They might also catch a show in the city's enormous amphitheater, which held twenty-five thousand people, or watch a chariot race in the hippodrome. One local patron, the son of a former

FIGURE 2.2. Statue of the patroness Scholastica, marking the entrance to the baths she helped remodel in Ephesus during the later fourth century. Photo by Marc Schlossman, Alamy stock photos.

proconsul named Celsus, donated money to build a major library and mausoleum to honor his father. The Library of Celsus, completed in 135 CE, contained more than twelve thousand scrolls of Greek literature, which patrons read in a large hall lit by two tiers of windows.

Two hundred years later, another Ephesian resident left her mark on the city. Sometime after the middle of the fourth century, a wealthy patroness named Scholastica elected to renovate an aging bath complex located adjacent to one of Ephesus' newer grand boulevards. Her money appears to have gone mainly to aesthetic improvements, including new mosaics for the floors and marble revetment on the walls. She added sculpture too, a series of portraits of Greek cultural heroes, including Socrates and the poet Menander. From the exterior, Scholastica's refurbished baths were immediately identifiable by a large (now headless) statue of the patroness that marked the bath's entrance (Figure 2.2).

Scholastica's patronage was deeply traditional. It associated her with generations of donors across the Roman Empire. But the city she improved was gradually becoming spatially distinct from what her second-century Ephesian ancestors had known. For one, the Library of Celsus was no longer a library in Late Antiquity. After falling into disrepair following an earthquake in 262 CE, the library was transformed into a fountain in ca. 400 CE, a renovation Scholastica may not have lived to see. Her city may also have supported a new palace for the governor of the province of Asia, replete with a private bath complex, reception halls, mosaics, and wall paintings.[3] And the street where her baths were located, which scholars call the *Embolos* (also known as Curetes Street), had begun its transformation from a road connecting the city's two primary agoras into a monument in its own right. Along with Ephesus' other major thoroughfare, the *Arcadiane* (so named after Emperor Arcadius, r. 395–408 CE), the *Embolos* functioned as the principal public space in the city. With funds from state officials, including the governor of Asia, it was lined with majestic columns, a covered colonnade, and marble pavement.[4] Cutting diagonally across the city and closed to wagon traffic, the *Embolos* was a place of bustling pedestrian activity in Late Antiquity. This was where many Ephesians lived in both grand townhouses and small apartments. It was also where they did their daily shopping in stores and workshops built into the back of the colonnade. Street lighting and the lively presence of performers encouraged evening strolls along the boulevard. As a monumental commercial space, the *Embolos* slowly overshadowed the ancient city center, which by the fifth century had become a cattle market (Figure 2.3).

Scholastica may have lived to see the erection of one of Ephesus' two great Christian churches. The Church of Saint Mary the Virgin arose in the ruins of a government building (a basilica) in the agora,

FIGURE 2.3. The *Embolos* was a major pedestrian thoroughfare in Ephesus (Turkey) dating to the fifth and sixth centuries. The street was flanked by majestic columns, shops, and housing.
Photo by gezmen, Alamy stock photos.

which had burned down in the 260s CE. The ruinous structure was rebuilt as a church in the next century, and henceforth served as Ephesus' main basilica for some time. In the sixth century, Saint Mary's significance was eclipsed by the opulent reconstruction of what had previously been a small but holy site: the church of St. John the Evangelist, built outside the city walls in the cemetery where John was believed to have been buried. Under the aegis of Ephesus' bishop Hypatius and with funds provided by the emperor Justinian (r. 527–565 CE), Saint John's was transformed into an immense imperial basilica. More than 130 meters in length, the basilica was constructed from valuable building materials sent from Constantinople, including marble capitals bearing the emperor's monogram.

The rise of Ephesus' Christian cityscape corresponds with the fall of its pagan spaces. The once magnificent Temple of Artemis was gradually abandoned in the fourth century, and may have been physically attacked in 401 CE by an angry mob of Christians. Thereafter, and far less dramatically, residents removed the temple's valuable materials, conserving some for local building projects, while sending the most beautiful pieces abroad for display in new cities.

CHANGING URBAN SPACES AND THE NEW NORMAL

Theodorus and Marta in Brixia, Scholastica in Ephesus: these three late antique urbanites experienced their respective cities during periods of transition. In material terms, late ancient Brixia and Ephesus underwent significant changes (albeit at different moments in time), some reflecting wealth and vibrancy, others a lack of resources and decay. Each city was gradually reoriented around new centers and buildings, from colonnaded, shop-lined streets to churches and official state residences. But both cities also witnessed the physical degradation of what had once been key public monuments. No example is more poignant than Ephesus' Temple of Artemis, a former Wonder of the World reduced to robbery and rubble. Yet rubble was rarely just left on the streets. Each city shows ample evidence of reuse, whether it was deliberately moving marble from one building and carefully placing it in another, or burning stones to make quicklime. Evidence from both cities also shows that the role of local patrons was diminishing. After the fourth century, the state funded the costliest and most extensive public works, projects such as the Church of St. John the Evangelist, which dwarfed Theodorus and Marta's seventeen feet of mosaic flooring. In short, cities did not wholly decline in Late Antiquity, as some scholars like to assert. Rather, urban space gradually shifted into a "new normal," where ruin, reuse, and renewal coexisted within a single cityscape.

Although they are representative cities, Brixia and Ephesus hardly tell the whole story about urban space in Late Antiquity. Rome and Constantinople, the two best known late Roman cities, offer additional histories and illustrate two very different trajectories in urban development. In many respects, Rome's late ancient history follows a path similar to the paths of Brixia and Ephesus. In it, we find areas of development and continued restoration, such as the Aurelian Walls. Built by the emperor Aurelian in the 270s, these thicker and higher walls included new guard towers and gates, which were important both symbolically and defensively. Rome also witnessed a proliferation of church building, initially with the personal funds of Constantine and his family, and later with monies from private citizens and clergy.[5] However, there were also losses in this urban new normal. Some of Rome's most famous classical monuments, such as the Forum Romanum and the Flavian Amphitheater (better known as the Colosseum), gradually lost their function as central administrative and entertainment centers, and by the late sixth century had become areas where Romans lived in rudimentary housing, labored in workshops, attended church, and even buried their dead.[6] And although Rome continued to be the West's most populous city, its population dropped precipitously in Late Antiquity, from seven hundred fifty thousand inhabitants in ca. 300 CE to fewer than ninety thousand in ca. 600 CE. The decline in human presence contributed to both the growth of green spaces within the city and the dereliction of older buildings. Late antique Rome was a busy and beautiful place, but it was increasingly distinct from the classical-era city.

In comparison, Constantinople was a boomtown in Late Antiquity. Founded by Constantine in ca. 330 CE, Constantinople was not an entirely new build (a Greek city called Byzantium was there before), but it underwent significant development following its adoption as an imperial capital. Constantine's innovations include a fortified wall enclosure; an extensive aqueduct system; new colonnaded streets, including a main boulevard called the *Mese*; an imperial palace complex; a new hippodrome for chariot racing; a grand public bath complex; a new Senate House (for a second Senate); and several new forums, such as the round Forum of Constantine near the gates to the imperial compound. Here Constantine displayed a large bronze statue of himself alongside statues imported from all over the Empire, including from the Temple of Artemis in Ephesus. These statues were mainly of pagan deities and mythic figures, such as Paris, Hera, and Athena. Nearly all late Roman emperors were Christians, but they understood the cultural meaning of pagan images as synonymous with class and historical tradition. Moreover, in Constantine's day, paganism remained tightly entwined with imperial notions of empire; consequently, when he founded Constantinople, he included a Capitolium, that is, a temple dedicated to Rome's three great imperial gods. Of course, he and his successors built churches, including the octagonal Basilica of the Holy Apostles, which was also his mausoleum. Constantine's successors continued this tradition of building and beautification, making numerous additions to the Constantinopolitan cityscape. In the fifth century, a double-wall system was erected. They were known as the Theodosian Walls (so named for Theodosius II, r. 408–450 CE), and the enceinte featured an inner and outer wall system, built in separate phases. And whereas Rome's population was falling in Late Antiquity, Constantinople's was on the rise, reaching half a million people by 400 CE.

URBAN SOCIETY

We have learned about the physical cities in which Theodorus, Marta, Scholastica, and other late ancient urbanites lived. But what about the social worlds they inhabited? All late Roman cities were places of bustling human activity, where many different people lived and/or congregated for work and play. They were also sites of considerable social diversity, where rich and poor intermingled regularly in the markets, on the streets, in the theaters, and in their residential communities. The absence of zoning laws meant that elites and non-elites lived in the same neighborhoods. Moreover, the dirt and disease that characterized all late ancient cities impacted everyone, with relatively little social discrimination, at least by modern standards. While the wealthiest lived in private townhouses with large staffs of slaves who cleaned their clothes and emptied their chamber pots, they traversed the same crowded streets, passed by the same latrines and sewers, frequented the same baths, temples, theaters, and churches, and were subjected to the same array of odors as everyone else. Needless to say, malaria-carrying mosquitoes did not distinguish between a senator and a slave.[7]

In fact, a better way to approach urban society is not by class, but by occupation and activity. Late Roman urbanites participated in a range of activities and performed a variety of services, which allowed them to earn a living or maintain their status as elites. The following discussion examines three categories of activities/occupations: official business with the government, commercial activities, and entertainment. Cities, of course, were also places for religious activities and sites of intense religious diversity. Readers interested in religion should turn to Chapter 6 for this discussion.

Official Business in the City: Law Courts, Information, and Imperial Pomp

Cities were important in Late Antiquity for many reasons, chief among them their role as spaces of official government activities. While villagers might resolve disputes among themselves, those who wished to adjudicate their cases in the law courts or present a petition necessarily traveled to cities.[8] Some cities, such as Ephesus, were also provincial capitals, meaning that the governor in residence regularly judged legal suits brought by citizens. Most cities had a range of urban officials, such as the *defensor civitatis,* the "city's advocate," whose duties involved assisting poorer litigants involved in trials. Other officials oversaw specific domains, such as the food supply and the supervision of prices. The law courts were also open to audiences. Late antique trials were public events, including proceedings that involved the torturing of witnesses. Executions, too, were open to the public, although they were usually held in arenas and theaters.

Cities had long been places where people came for important information. Most cities, large and small, had municipal archives, where individual citizens filed legal documents, such as contracts, deeds, wills, and tax records. Larger cities, especially provincial or diocesan capitals, often functioned as sites for the dissemination of imperial messages. In some cases, these messages were detailed and informational. When the emperor ruled on a legal case affecting a particular city, his response could be inscribed and displayed in prominent public places, such as forums and even churches. Similarly, lists naming high officials were inscribed on ivory plaques and publicly presented.

Cities were also places where emperors and their officials displayed more symbolic forms of power, through monumental building projects and processions. Diocletian's four imperial capitals (Milan, Trier, Sirmium, Nicomedia) were tailored for their new role through the construction of grand colonnaded streets, forums with imperial statues, and palaces for the emperor and his court. Constantinople was unquestionably the most intensely imperial space in the late Roman Empire, where emperors left their mark through projects such as new forums (e.g., the Forum of Theodosius and the Forum of Arcadius), enlarged wall circuits (the Theodosian Walls), and numerous monumental obelisks. Even in Rome, the emperor's presence was still felt in the city. Constantine commissioned a triumphal arch, still extant, that celebrates his victory over Maxentius in 312 CE; Valentinian III (r. 425–455 CE), who largely resided in the city, made numerous high-profile donations to Roman basilicas and is commemorated in inscriptions for his renovations of the Colosseum; and the emperor Phocas (r. 602–610 CE) installed the last imperial column in the Roman forum in 608 CE. Imperial processions remained part of civic life in Constantinople, Rome, and other cities the emperor visited. Ceremonial routes varied, but they typically traversed the colonnaded boulevards and new monumental centers. Depending on the nature of the procession (emperors celebrated everything from military victories to the ten-year anniversary of their reign), the emperor would ride through the city streets, visibly engaging the citizenry with his colorful apparel and gilded chariot, and perhaps tossing coins to lucky bystanders.

Commercial and Industrial Activities, and Workforce Organizations

Late Roman cities were economic centers, driven by a combination of private enterprise, collective organization, and the state. In fact, archaeology suggests that many became increasingly focused on commercial activities, whether it was lime production, glassmaking, dye processing, or simply trade. In Ephesus, and in cities across the Mediterranean, workshops and stores lined the grand colonnaded boulevards, many lit into the evening hours. Although the economic horizon of some cities shrank considerably in Late Antiquity, especially in the West, commercial and industrial activity continued to define late ancient urban space.

A good place to begin our tour of commercial life is the city of Sardis in what is now modern Turkey. Sardis' significance for historians of Late Antiquity is a bit like Pompeii's for historians of imperial Rome. In 616 CE, a devastating fire swept through Sardis (perhaps caused by a Persian attack), and the city was heavily damaged. Rather than rebuild, the citizens abandoned it, and Sardis was never extensively repopulated. This long period of abandonment allowed natural growth to cover the city in a protective layer, maintaining it largely untouched for more than a millennium. When archaeologists began to excavate in the last century, they discovered an extraordinary treasure trove of everyday items left behind by fleeing citizens. Most significantly, they recovered thousands of objects from shops that lined the city's main street, known in English as the Marble Road.[9] These included thousands of glass fragments from several different glassmaking workshops, at least one selling windowpanes; tools and vessels used for dye-making (Sardis was famous for its dyes and textiles); iron objects and tools from what appears to have been something like a hardware store; and food remains and cooking vessels from at least two structures that were almost certainly restaurants. Moreover, the finds suggest that many owners and artisans lived in small second-floor apartments over their shops. The vast number of

FIGURE 2.4. The so-called Byzantine shops at Sardis (Turkey), where locals worked, shopped, dined, and lived during the fifth and sixth centuries.
Photo © Archaeological Exploration of Sardis, President and Fellows of Harvard College.

coins found scattered throughout the shops in Sardis attests to the presence of consumers, who regularly shopped and dined along the Marble Road (Figure 2.4).

The fact that Sardis' main commercial strip included at least two restaurants is not surprising. Food was the most important commodity in the ancient world, especially in cities with large populations. As we will see in greater detail in Chapter 4, the late Roman state intervened directly in the urban food system by providing regular handouts to citizens residing in its largest cities (Rome, Constantinople, and likely Alexandria and Antioch). This system was known as the *annona*. Although the *annona* only fed a few urban populations, all late Roman cities had markets that were open to the general public and largely driven by entrepreneurial activity. In Ephesus, for instance, cattle were sold in the old agora, while stalls of fruit and vegetable sellers lined the streets of fourth-century Antioch. In Aphrodisias, another important late ancient city in what is now Turkey, residents could shop at what appears to have been something like a grocery store. Graffiti evidence from one shop on the main market square lists prices of the goods sold, which included honey, wine, oil, bread, vegetables, pulses, and a spicy-sweet balsam resin called *storax* that was a popular flavoring and preservative.

Bread, the basis of the late Roman diet, was also produced and purchased in cities. Grain was regularly transported to cities from the countryside, stored in both public and private granaries, and then sold, milled, and turned into flour. Some cities had mechanical water-mills for grinding grain into flour, such as the Juniculum mills in the west of Rome, which were powered by the aqueducts. State-financed bakers as well as private citizens brought their grain to these mills and paid to have it processed into flour. Residents could purchase loaves at professional bakeries, which were numerous in most cities and fueled by an enormous supply of firewood. Citizens of Constantinople, for instance, could buy bread at one of the city's 120 bakeries, according to one early fifth-century source. Conversely, home baking also became increasingly popular in Late Antiquity, especially in western Roman cities, as the state's involvement in food production waned in the later fifth century.

Cities were also places of heavier industry and craftsmanship. Glass and dye producers were among the artisans with workshops on the Marble Road in Sardis, as were skilled metal workers, including gold- and silversmiths. The latter worked with metals brought to them by clients and, probably because of their access to gold and silver, sometimes doubled as bankers. We know that a sixth-century silversmith in Constantinople named Flavius Anastasius loaned twenty *solidi* to four Egyptians, who were expected to repay the loan plus 8 percent interest.[10] In fact, the Latin word for silversmith, *argentarius*, also meant "banker" in Late Antiquity. Artisans who worked under more dangerous conditions, such as smelters, or those whose processing emitted strong smells, such as tanners and cheesemakers, were ideally located outside the city gates. A sixth-century treatise on urban construction from Palestine, for instance, insists that all industries whose activities risk fire or produce noxious fumes must be built away from denser urban areas.[11] However, in many cities, especially those in the West during the later fifth and sixth centuries, this neat division did not exist. Sixth-century Brixia, we recall, had several intramural lime kilns, meaning that large controlled fires were part of the cityscape.

Some members of the urban workforce were organized into collectives, known in Late Antiquity as *corpora* (Latin for "bodies").[12] *Corpora* were nothing like modern labor unions, as they did not engage in collective bargaining, lobby for better workplace conditions, or negotiate for increased pay. These modern types of workers' rights were unknown to the Romans, who regularly employed children, had slaves, and showed little regard for the dangers inherent in many working conditions. Rather, the *corpora* aimed to regularize relations between a particular skilled workforce, individual employers, and the state. Again, evidence from Sardis is illustrative. In 459 CE, a corpus of builders in Sardis drew up a general contract that was aimed at future employers. The contract, extant today thanks to an inscription, stipulated labor expectations in the event that a builder failed to complete a project.[13] For instance, the builders' organization promised that all work would be completed if the agreed wages were paid, and that if a worker refused to finish a job, the organization would replace him with another member; if the employer rejected the replacement, then the corpus had to pay him an indemnity. If the builder became ill, then the employer had to wait twenty days for him to recover. If he did not return to work, then the organization would provide new workers in his place. The inscription makes clear that all wages were settled between the builder and the employer, and that the builder had nothing like the modern concept of workers' compensation beyond what amounted to a twenty-day unpaid sick leave. Other evidence for the *corpora*, especially for workforces involved in the transport and processing of grain for the state's provisioning system, underscores the extent to which these organizations served the interests of the government rather than the workers.

Of course, there were limitations that may have made the life of a worker less grinding in Late Antiquity than in the modern era. The absence of good artificial lighting meant that most people could only work during daylight hours (sunrise to sunset), with the ninth hour (around 3 PM) as the typical time when people put their work away, went to the baths, and ended the day with their families over an evening meal. And while there was no such thing as a paid vacation, workers were prohibited from laboring on certain religious holidays.

Under pagan emperors, there were dozens of *nefas* (nonworking) days every year. Christian emperors introduced different holidays, including Sunday as a "no work" day for all Roman citizens, a law issued by Constantine in 321 CE.[14]

Infamous Workers: Prostitutes, Pimps, and Performers

Most urban workers were freeborn citizens who were somewhere in the middle socially, certainly not noble, but not the lowest stratum of society either. The lowest level was reserved for those whom the Romans designated as "infamous" workers, that is, people whose jobs warranted the legal status of *infamia*. *Infamia* literally means "unspeakable" in Latin, and the term was associated with any man or woman who willingly made an exhibition of him- or herself or others in public for personal gain. *Infamia* was an acquired status; people were not born infamous, but once they became infamous, they remained so for their entire life, regardless of whether they left the infamous profession. Those who were branded *infamous* were denied certain civic rights, from holding administrative or military office to conducting a legal marriage with a non-infamous person and representing themselves in court. Infamous people were also subject to more severe forms of corporal punishment and execution.

A range of occupations brought their members infamous status: prostitutes, pimps, gladiators, innkeepers, charioteers, actors, and dancers were all deemed infamous in the eyes of Roman law and society. While we might expect prostitutes and pimps to make the list, the others require further explanation. As prostitutes did, gladiators, charioteers, actors, and dancers subjected their bodies to what the Romans perceived as unacceptable public access, scrutiny, and violation. An honorable body should not be paraded on stage before spectators, as was the case with charioteers, actors, and dancers; nor should it be willingly subjected to physical attack or harm outside the context of war, through mutilation by animals or weapons, as happened to gladiators. And in some cases, the line between a profession and prostitution was blurred. Innkeepers, for instance, notoriously moonlighted as pimps, while actors and dancers frequently provided sexual services alongside their stage work. It was always strongly suspected that actresses were also sex workers. The emperor

Justinian's wife, Theodora (d. 548 CE), for instance, had worked as a mime for many years (see "Competitive Sports and Theatrical Shows") before marrying Justinian and becoming an empress. It was widely rumored that Theodora was also a courtesan, that is, a high-end prostitute. Regardless of whether the gossip was true, legal measures at the highest level of the land had to be taken in order to make Justinian and Theodora's marriage legal, since until that moment, Roman law prohibited actors from marrying senators.

Prostitution is without question among the oldest moneymaking activities in the world, but we should probably resist the temptation to label it the world's oldest "profession." This is because most ancient prostitutes were slaves, forced into sex work by their owners. Slaves obviously did not choose prostitution and did not financially benefit from it. An inscription on a slave collar from North Africa, which was literally bolted around the neck of its wearer, drives this point home: "I am a slutty whore; retain me, I have fled Bulla Regia."[15] Freed or freeborn prostitutes probably did not fare much better, given the fact that their pimps took at least one-third of their daily profits. Prostitutes suffered unspeakable violence in the late Roman world and received little protection from the law, despite the fact that prostitution was legal. Although prostitutes and pimps were legally disabled by their work, the work itself was not against the law. In fact, until 498 CE, the state derived revenue from prostitution through a general sales tax (known as the *collatio lustralis*). Female prostitution remained legal (except under the brief reign of the emperor Julian, r. 361–363 CE), but measures were taken against male prostitution in Late Antiquity. Following the third-century emperor Philip the Arab (r. 244–249 CE), several late ancient emperors cracked down on male prostitution. According to a law issued in 390 CE pertaining to the city of Rome, male prostitutes were to be rounded up from the brothels, tried, and burned alive for their crimes.[16]

Brothels were located in every corner of a city, but were most frequently found in or adjacent to taverns and inns as well as near places of entertainment, such as theaters and baths. A late fourth-century catalogue of buildings and businesses states that Rome had approximately forty-five brothels, a figure that is probably on the low side of reality. Ephesus, too, had at least one brothel, though its precise location is unknown, as we have only an inscription reading "brothel facilities" placed next to a latrine. According to what is almost certainly an urban legend, Constantine established a brothel in the Zeugma section of Constantinople, with a fetching statue of Aphrodite on a pedestal in front of the door. The legend claims that the Christian emperor did this in order to create a single red-light district in his new city, which would "cleanse" the other sections now free from prostitution. In truth, although some Christian leaders frowned upon prostitution, there was no such thing as moral zoning in Late Antiquity; brothels and prostitutes popped up wherever there were customers.

Entertainment in the City: Baths, Theaters, and Circuses

Cities were places of entertainment. Public shows, contests, and bathing were part of a greater Mediterranean culture shared by communities across the Empire, regardless of differences in language, religion, status, and even gender. Spending an afternoon at the baths, for instance, was a quintessentially Roman urban activity for men and women, who carried out this signature form of ancient leisure in strikingly similar ways. Costs for the general public were generally low, since local elites, and increasingly the imperial court, funded events and maintained the baths. Moreover, urban entertainment was arguably the most enduring expression of classical culture in the late ancient city. In the West, the largest cities held shows and maintained their baths through the fourth (and, in some cases, into the fifth) century, while chariot racing continued well into the sixth century. In the East, the games, theater, and baths lived on through the seventh century. In fact, the Byzantine successors to the late Roman Empire affirmed their classical heritage for centuries by holding chariot races and supporting public baths within Constantinople.

The types of entertainment available to late Romans, and their particular tastes in urban leisure, also underwent change. Most infamously, a new voice emerged in Late Antiquity that was critical of traditional forms of fun. Christian authorities from across the Empire rebuked those who attended the games instead of church meetings, and who found pleasure in watching others dishonor their bodies by offering them to the public gaze. For some late ancient Christians, the games were inherently pagan – a point that had less meaning in the later fourth and fifth centuries, when the games were no longer tied to polytheistic festivals. For others, entertainment necessarily led to erotic encounters and thoughts. The cleric John Chrysostom (349–407 CE) repeatedly attacked female actors for their allegedly pernicious influence over the men in their audience. In Chrysostom's view, the women's scandalous acting and near-naked bodies incited lust in men's hearts, causing them to sin against God. Yet, the fact that a handful of Christians repeatedly attacked the theater and the games is strong (albeit indirect) evidence for the continued popularity of these urban activities. In what follows, we shall focus on the three main forms of late ancient entertainment: bathing, theatrical shows, and competitive games.

Bathing

One could argue that it was the presence of a bath that made an ancient city Roman. There were thousands of baths throughout the Roman Empire, a figure that declined in Late Antiquity but nevertheless remained high. Sixth-century Antioch still had at least twelve, while Constantinople had more than 150 large and small baths. As we have seen, older bathing complexes were often maintained or renovated. Scholastica poured her money into improving an existing bath complex in Ephesus, while the emperor Constantius II (r. 337–361 CE) rebuilt the baths in the gymnasium near the Ephesian harbor. And in Rome, the Ostrogoth king Theoderic (r. 493–526 CE) carefully restored the imperial baths built by the emperor Caracalla (r. 198–217 CE) (Figure 2.5).

In other cities, the fate of existing baths varied. Brixia's baths, for instance, were allowed to decline in the fifth century, their materials robbed and used elsewhere. This was the trajectory, in fact, in many western cities. One new trend in bathing was the construction and use of private bathing complexes, often on the grounds of super-elite houses, such as the palace of the governor in Ephesus. Although scholars have sometimes attributed this surge in private bathing to the influence of Christian morality, the answer most likely lies in economics. Public baths demanded an enormous ongoing investment from the city, since they required huge amounts of wood and large numbers of slaves to run the furnaces that heated the water.

FIGURE 2.5. A Roman bath complex in Salamis (Cyprus) that was remodeled in the sixth century.
Photo by Dallas Deforest.

Without the direct assistance of civic officials, maintaining these large-scale facilities was challenging. Smaller baths cost considerably less to maintain, and hence became preferable.

Like their classical ancestors, late Romans had a particular way of bathing. They did it at a particular time of the day, typically in the eighth or ninth hour (around 2 or 3 PM). Baths were open all day to accommodate large crowds, however. In some cases, men and women bathed separately at different times of the day (usually women after men), but there is also evidence that in many facilities they bathed together. Bathing was done in the nude, and involved immersing oneself in a sequence of pools, each heated to a different temperature. One began in the *tepidarium* for medium heated water, and then moved into the hot room, or *caldarium*. After becoming very warm in the hot pool, one moved to the cold water of the *frigidarium*, ending one's bath there, or perhaps choosing to start the sequence again. Some bathing complexes had sweating rooms, and most had separate changing areas for men and women (at least in the larger complexes). Bathers with slaves typically brought them into the baths in order to assist with dressing and also possibly to work on their bodies after the bath. Romans liked to have their body hair plucked and skin rubbed down with oil, which was then scraped off with a special tool called a *strigil.* Additionally, through the fourth century, many bath complexes had "workout" rooms called *palestra,* where men and women exercised. Interestingly, in many cases, in the fifth and sixth centuries the *palestra* was frequently left to deteriorate, even when other parts of the complex were maintained. The late Roman baths, it seems, were no longer places for athletic activity.

Bathing remained an intensely social activity, however. One did not go to the baths primarily to get clean, or even to improve health. Rather, one went to the baths to see and be seen, to pick up the latest gossip or conduct business dealings. Late ancient bathing facilities were also like museums, because they were often decorated with colorful mosaics and marbles and contained impressive sculpture collections. In most cases, these statues were of famous pagan heroes, writers, philosophers, or even gods. Scholastica, we recall, added a whole sculpture program to her baths in Ephesus, which appears to have been selected along the theme of "great Classical writers" (Figure 2.6).

Finally, let us consider how, technically speaking, late Romans heated their baths. Architects often tried to take advantage of topography to maximize a building's exposure to sun and shade, but all baths used a hypocaust heating system that circulated hot, warm, or cold air under the flooring of the pools and in the walls of the sweating rooms. The floors of a Roman bath were supported by short brick pillars, which raised it off the ground by about a meter. This was the space in which the heated air circulated. To heat the air, the Romans constructed wood-burning furnaces against the exterior walls of the bath buildings, which generated heat beneath the floors and heated the rooms to the desired temperature. The furnaces also heated large bronze boilers for the water, which connected to the *caldarium* pool by lead pipes controlled with valves. The cold pool was fed directly from its own tank of cold water, which could be mixed with the hot water to create the warm water of the *tepidarium.* It would be interesting to know more about the precise temperatures bathers liked in their pools, but the Romans did not have thermometers or

FIGURE 2.6. Classical-era statues from the Salamis (Cyprus) bath complex located in the *palestra* (exercise area), which was no longer in use after the fourth century.
Photo by Dallas Deforest.

any kind of temperature gauge. Scholars have experimented with modern Turkish baths, and found that they typically have floor temperatures between 107 and 111 degrees Fahrenheit (suggesting that visitors needed to keep their sandals on!), and hence room temperatures between 98 and 100 degrees.[17] It is also important to remember that behind the scenes, and beneath the floors, of every functioning Roman bath were workers, who continuously fed the fires with enormous quantities of wood (Figure 2.7).

Competitive Sports and Theatrical Shows

Throughout Late Antiquity, public competitions and shows continued to define the urban experience. During the first half of the fourth century, citizens of Rome enjoyed 177 days of events a year, 101 of which were theatrical shows. At this point in time, private patrons, typically important elites and local officials, funded the majority of

FIGURE 2.7. Remains of a late Roman hypocaust heating system installed at the Villa Romana La Olmeda (Spain). Note the raised flooring, under which heated air circulated.
Photo by Valdavia (Creative Commons license).

spectator events in most cities. The costs of putting on shows were enormous, since they involved not only hiring performers and paying for sets and arena maintenance, but also importing exotic animals and feeding horse teams. The fourth-century Roman senator Q. Aurelius Symmachus, for instance, claimed to have spent two thousand pounds of gold on games to inaugurate his son as a magistrate. In the early fifth century, another Roman senator reputedly spent twice as much. To be clear, the games were never designed to *make* money. Spectators either watched for free or paid a small admission price. Rather, the games and shows were designed to display the largesse of the patron. For private citizens, this was a way to underline duty to the city and their personal, and familial, honor. For emperors and kings, who funded the most extravagant shows in Rome and Constantinople, the games were also venues for controlled public expression, where the crowds could voice approval or disapproval of their leader, (usually) without succumbing to mob violence. In fact, emperors and imperial officials gradually became sole patrons of the games as costs rose and the relative wealth of private civic elites fell. This change from local/private patronage to state oversight meant that there were fewer places where games and shows were held in Late Antiquity than in previous times, since only major cities received imperial and/or regal attention.

Constantinople, Rome, Antioch, and a handful of other cities continued to host games and shows throughout Late Antiquity. When Constantine created his imperial capital at Constantinople in 330 CE, he built an enormous racetrack adjacent to the palace complex, which could hold a hundred thousand spectators. In so doing, he deliberately mirrored the imperial topography of Rome, where the Circus Maximus, with a capacity of two hundred thousand, sits just below the Palatine Hill, the traditional home of the emperors before the western capital was transferred to Milan and then Ravenna.[18] Amphitheaters were maintained in some cities into the sixth century. In Rome, fifth-century emperors and early sixth-century kings made a string of repairs to the Colosseum, the city's famous round amphitheater, which could hold nearly ninety thousand people. And while Brixia's theater was no longer used for shows after the fourth century, the Ostrogoths renovated Pavia's amphitheater as late as 529 CE, undoubtedly so that they could hold games in their new capital city. Across the Mediterranean, Ephesus' amphitheater held shows and competitions until Arab armies destroyed the city in the seventh century. Similarly, Antioch and its suburbs boasted several theaters, as did the city of Gerasa (now in Jordan), all of which were actively used through the end of the sixth century. In the main, however, archaeology tells us that circuses stayed in use far longer than theaters, especially in the West, where amphitheater maintenance declined rather rapidly in the fifth century in all but a few cities (Figures 2.8 and 2.9).

What did late ancient people watch in amphitheaters and at circuses? Until the early fifth century, gladiatorial combat remained popular, and audiences across the Empire cheered for their favorite "net fighter" (*retiarius*) or "pursuer" (*secutor*), to cite two of the different types of gladiators. Contrary to many modern depictions of gladiatorial combat as a sort of armed free-for-all, professional gladiators competed in highly structured, regulated events and were trained to use specific sets of weapons. It was not the case, as is often portrayed in Hollywood films, that gladiators improvised with whatever weapons

FIGURE 2.8. A Roman amphitheater in Arles (France). The theater, built in the late first century and in use through the fourth, held up to twenty thousand spectators. During the fifth and sixth centuries, citizens reclaimed the structure for habitation and began to fortify it with towers.
Photo by Paul-Louis Ferrandez, Société Mepros (Creative Commons license).

FIGURE 2.9. A hippodrome (or circus) in the city of Gerasa (Jerash, Jordan). Built in the second century for chariot racing, the space remained in use perhaps until the sixth century.
Photo by EmmePi Images, Alamy stock photos.

FIGURE 2.10. Detail from the famous "Gladiator Mosaic" dating to the fourth century, now at the Borghese Museum in Rome.
Photo by De Agostini Picture Library/G. Dagli Orti/Bridgeman Images.

might be thrown at them. Moreover, they did not always fight to the death. Regardless of whether they were freeborn or enslaved, gladiators were expensive athletes, and the people who trained and/or owned them viewed their fighters as valuable investments. Consequently, gladiators more often competed to exhaustion or against wild animals, which they slaughtered before delighted audiences. Some gladiators became famous and achieved something like a glamorous lifestyle despite their sociolegal branding as "infamous" persons (Figure 2.10).

In fact, some high-status men and women sought out gladiatorial combat despite the social and legal repercussions of *infamia*. This social trend seems to be the primary reason why fourth- and fifth-century emperors passed legislation regulating the status of those who took up gladiatorial combat, a move that contributed to the gradual end of the sport in the fifth century. Cost, too, was undoubtedly behind the sport's demise in Late Antiquity, especially when it involved expensive animal hunts and baiting, wherein exotic animals such as lions were imported from Africa. In 499 CE, staged animal hunts (called *venationes*) were banned in the eastern Empire, in part on ethical grounds. However, as late as 523 CE, spectators in Rome's Colosseum still watched hunting shows involving combatants performing acrobatic-like feats, jumping over animals and using screen-like contraptions to shield themselves from the blows of wild lions and bears.

In addition to gladiatorial combat and this newer sport of hunting acrobatics, late Romans enjoyed watching weaponless athletic competitions. Ancient Greek-style games involving running races, the pentathlon, boxing, wrestling, and the *pankration* (a sort of ancient form of mixed martial arts) were still held in cities across the Mediterranean through the early fifth century, after which interest and funds waned. The famous games at Olympia, the eponymous ancient site of contests that inspired our modern Olympics, were held until the fifth century. Generally speaking, late Roman tastes for competitive games gravitated toward a high-speed and extremely dangerous event: chariot racing.

Chariot racing was an old sport, with origins in the Greek world during the eighth century BCE. It rose to prominence in the high Roman Empire, gradually surpassing all other forms of athletics in popularity. Chariot racing involved multiple teams of either two or four horses, which were hitched to a light cart driven by a single charioteer. The race began at the starting gates (called the *carceres*) and consisted of five laps around an oblong track that was divided longitudinally by a central pillar, or *spina*. Unlike modern harness racing, ancient chariot racing was chaotic and extremely dangerous for the drivers and horses. The carts were small and easily knocked over. The horses could run at any speed, and the rules permitted physical contact between teams on the course. Drivers thus simultaneously endeavored to knock over their competitors while avoiding crashing themselves. Of course, crashing was highly exciting, and fans cheered when their favorite teams caused others to flip over. Prizes were awarded to the winning charioteers, not to the horses, since the race was more a test of driving skill than equine speed.

Chariot racing drew fans from all walks of life. Graffiti from the ancient theater at Kom el-Dikka near Alexandria, for example, refers to nine different charioteers who drew crowds and fans from the region. The most famous charioteer in Late Antiquity was arguably Porphyrius Calliope, who was something of a household name in the cities of the East during the early sixth century. Porphyrius was so great that he won major prizes for both of Late Antiquity's major fan clubs: the Blues and the Greens.

Just as European cities have their dedicated soccer clubs and American colleges their revered football teams, late ancient Romans had their circus factions, fan-based organizations that revolved initially around chariot racing. Circus factions had long been part of the Roman entertainment world. Originally, each Roman city with a racetrack had four circus factions: the Reds, the Whites, the Blues, and the Greens. By Late Antiquity, the Blues and the Greens dominated the scene. Graffiti covering Aphrodisias attests to their presence and popularity: "The fortune of the Greens triumphs!," "Up with the fortune of the city!," "The fortune of the Blues triumphs!," declare three from the city's agora.[19] Members of both clubs could be found in almost every major city, but their numbers were relatively small, perhaps no more than a thousand in any given urban center. Everyone knew who the fans were, however. Circus supporters wore distinctive bright-colored clothing to races and usually sat together in designated areas of the racetrack, in a kind of rabble-rousing section that was probably very intimidating for outsiders. Anyone who has attended a European or South American soccer game and accidentally sat with the hardcore fans will have a good sense of what their presence at races was like. For one thing, the Blues and the Greens were known to chant loudly, in sync, for their favorite team. Sometimes their shouts bled into politics when they called out the emperor. In fact, there is evidence that the circus factions participated more formally in civic ceremonies where the emperor was publicly acclaimed. Occasionally their intense support for an emperor or, more often, a charioteer became physical and riots ensued, an urban phenomenon to which we will return.

It is not hard to understand why late Romans loved circus racing, as it fits our modern stereotype of the ancient world as dangerous and masculine. It might come as a surprise to learn, therefore, that late Romans also enjoyed, and perhaps even preferred, pantomime, a late ancient dance form. There is no modern western equivalent to pantomime, a solo act featuring a male performer using gesture and dance to tell a story, typically one drawn from Greco-Roman tragedy and myth, which was well known to audiences.[20] The pantomime never spoke, but his dance was always accompanied by a distinct form of music, performed by musicians with pipes, flutes, cymbals, and a percussion instrument played with the feet called a *scabellum*. The solo male pantomime played all roles in the narrative, including the female parts. According to Cassiodorus, a sixth-century statesman from Italy, "the same body represents Hercules and Venus, presents a woman in a man's body, makes a king a soldier, shows an old man and a young man so that there were many different people."[21] To play the various roles, the pantomime wore long, flowing robes and used wigs and masks to heighten the drama. Pantomime performances were intense experiences, and the actors drew devoted followings. Fans would fiercely debate who was the "best" performer. As we will see shortly, pantomime devotees were often identified as the inciters of urban riots. In fact, by the fifth century, the circus factions were intertwined with the theater and supported actors as well as charioteers.

Mime, the comedic counterpart to the drama of pantomime, was the other major form of popular theatrical entertainment in Late Antiquity. Mime was typically performed by groups of male and female actors who combined scripted lines with more improvisational slapstick. It thus approached our modern concept of physical comedy. In nearly every mime show there was a character known as the *stupidus*, a sort of clownish figure who was the target of abuse in the play. The narratives that mimes performed were often crude and inappropriate, centering on themes of sexual and social debasement. The most popular storyline featured a husband's "discovery" of his wife's affair, and the derisive responses to his cuckolded status. (Typically, the *stupidus* played the husband of the adulterous wife.) Mime performances could also veer into cultural mockery. In some mime shows, Goths were lampooned for their barbaric habits, Jews for their poverty and miserliness, and Christians for their claims of "rebirth" following baptism. The fact that Christian rituals were comedic targets in popular performances is an important correlative to the disparaging views of Christian authorities like John Chrysostom, who rejected the dramatic arts as pernicious and sinful. Then, as now, even the most solemn moments could be used as the butt of a joke.

WASTE, WATER, AND WARFARE

Living in a late Roman city brought residents a variety of advantages: access to commercial goods and markets; proximity to the law courts and, in some cases, to seats of state power; availability of relatively good-quality housing, especially in the East; the benefits (for some) of the *annona* food distribution network; and open participation in popular leisure activities, such as bathing, chariot racing, and the dramatic arts. To this list we can add access to a greater diversity of both health care and education (see Chapter 5) and spaces of religious community and worship (see Chapter 6). Scholars today thus no longer accept the proposition that cities wholly declined in Late Antiquity, or that the importance of urban space for the expression of power and commercial exchange disappeared.

However, even the most optimistic historian of Late Antiquity concedes that urban life embraced new challenges, which were largely unknown to urbanites in earlier periods of Rome's history. We have already noted the ways in which the physical space of many late Roman cities was characterized by a mixture of ruin and renewal. Old monumental buildings, especially pagan temples and defunct entertainment spaces (like the gymnasium at Ephesus and the amphitheater at Brixia), were systematically robbed of their valuable materials and left, for the most part, to fall apart. Consequently, sections of buildings, and perhaps even entire zones of cities, became structurally unstable over time, causing potentially dangerous conditions for residents and pedestrians. In cities such as Brixia and Ephesus, where there was uneven building maintenance, citizens had to learn where to walk and what to avoid.

Daily life changed in other ways, too, especially with regard to our last three subjects: garbage removal, water access, and the frequent threat of siege warfare.

Waste and Water

Even with smaller populations, late antique cities produced garbage: organic waste from cooking, humans, and animals; commercial waste from industrial activity; and building waste from the ruinous structures in the city, which in some cases created hazards that demanded clearance. As we have already noted, late ancient urbanites recycled and reused on an extensive level, and in this regard were much like their classical-era counterparts. Metal and glass were remelted, and slag, a byproduct of smelting and refining, was reused for street construction. Human and animal excrement was the best available fertilizer, while urine was an important component of the fulling process (it was used to clean wool). Building materials might be collected, burned into quicklime, and/or incorporated into new structures.

Yet however far Romans went in their recycling efforts, they could not reuse everything. Dumps and garbage removal were still needed. Through the end of the third century, Roman cities had workers, typically slaves, who regularly collected and deposited waste, generally in dumps located outside the city walls. Street cleaners were employed to pick up the food and biowaste that city residents tossed into the streets, a common habit for quick disposal. In some cases, landfills for certain types of garbage were created inside city walls. In Rome, for instance, people deposited ceramic vessels that had contained imported olive oil in a large mound near the Tiber River known today as Monte Testaccio. When it was abandoned in 268 CE, Monte Testaccio held the remains of more than fifty-three million clay vessels. Large cities also had public latrines, which undoubtedly helped contain the human waste and, to a certain extent, cut down on the spread of disease (Figure 2.11).

FIGURE 2.11. Public latrines near the baths of Scholastica in Ephesus (Turkey). Photo by Carole Raddato (Creative Commons license).

In Late Antiquity, cities continued to organize their waste disposal, but they followed new patterns. Rather than removing all the organic waste outside of the city walls, residents and officials created new intra-mural dumpsites, some ad hoc, some planned, that mixed different types of waste. In many cases, the new dump sites were located inside ruinous abandoned buildings. For example, in Sagalassos, a city in southwestern Turkey, citizens periodically dumped domestic waste into an unused room within a still functioning Roman bath complex. While they diverged rather dramatically from earlier Roman habits, these new dump sites reflected some form of waste management. To be sure, ancient urban dwellers had always lived in smelly, squalid conditions, but many late Roman cities were almost certainly dirtier and more odoriferous than their classical counterparts. Of course, the decrease in population during Late Antiquity may have alleviated the severity of these conditions.

Access to fresh running water also became increasingly restricted, again particularly in the West, where a weakened state had fewer resources to maintain the Empire's famed aqueducts. On the one hand, a large number of late Roman cities in both the West and the East remained connected to at least part of the original Roman aqueduct system, which transported fresh water for use in baths, fountains, latrines, community spigots, and, in limited cases, for pri-vate use in homes. On the other hand, the aqueducts could and did fall into disrepair, and they could also be deliberately sabotaged. In areas affected by extensive periods of warfare, such as sixth-century Italy, armies cut aqueducts as a tactic during sieges. However, even under these sorts of pressures, it was unusual for an army to be able to destroy a city's entire water system, and in many cities (such as Rome), repairs quickly followed. Nevertheless, in places where there were no officials with the power or funds to maintain the aqueducts, residents learned to rely more heavily on cisterns and wells. The shift from aqueducts to cisterns and wells became the pattern through the Middle Ages.

Many late Roman cities, especially in the East, had working sewer systems. Roman technology had developed to the extent of installing separate pipes: one for the transport of sewage out of the city, typi-cally into a nearby body of water (such as the Tiber in Rome or the Sea of Marmara in Constantinople), and another for the transport of fresh water into the city. Most sewer systems had a network of smaller

terracotta pipes leading from homes, shops, and latrines that fed into
a larger barrel-vaulted sewer, such as in Rome, with the famous Cloaca
Maxima, or in Constantinople, with twin sewers beneath the *Mese*, the
city's main street.[22] The main vaulted sewers were large enough for an
adult to crawl through, and size was an important technical feature,
because the sewers needed to be cleaned periodically. Sewer workers,
who were typically slaves, given both the danger (from methane
buildup and vermin) and overwhelming stench, would crawl down
through manholes to remove blockages caused by fecal material,
stones, hay, dead animals, and other objects. But without this constant
maintenance, and the funds to support it, sewer systems became
increasingly unusable, especially in western cities.

Violence in the City: Warfare and Rioting

The fact that cities were valuable places where food was likely available, goods easily procured, and large numbers of bodies readily
commanded made them prime military targets. Cities were invaded
both by armies of warring nations, such as the Persians, and by
internal war bands, some little more than small-scale bandits, others
more disciplined troops led by ambitious generals such as Alaric
(d. 410 CE) and Ricimer (d. 472 CE), both of whom besieged and
sacked Rome. Urban sieges were relatively common events in Late
Antiquity: both Brixia and Ephesus endured them.

A typical siege was a long, drawn-out form of warfare, which caused
more deaths from starvation and disease than from armed engagement.
Sieges could last anywhere from a few days to several years and, as noted,
could involve the cutting of aqueducts, hence stopping the flow of fresh
water into a city. More detrimental to the army and citizens inside, the
besieging army also routinely blocked all entrances and exits, thus
preventing the transport of food into the city. Having an enemy stationed just beyond the city walls made it dangerous for starving inhabitants to sneak out in order to forage. Additionally, diseases took hold
more easily when people were worn down from fatigue and hunger, and
spread quickly through contaminated water that was no longer being
flushed by fresh streams supplied by the aqueduct.

There are numerous accounts of urban sieges in Late Antiquity; in
fact, they present something of a literary form. Common assertions

include acts of cannibalism committed by famished citizens and the consumption of other extreme types of famine foods, such as nettles and leather shoes. Despite the rhetorical nature of these particular details (they appear in descriptions of sieges across time and space), the accounts nevertheless provide some insight into what it was like for civilians to experience a military siege in all its grinding horror. In other words, while we should not assume that all late ancient sieges ended with people eating one another, we can be certain that many led to periods of extreme hunger and acts of desperation.

In his account of the siege of Amida during a war with the Persians in 502–503 CE, the Christian chronicler known as Pseudo-Joshua the Stylite offers the following account.[23] Situated along the Tigris in the far eastern province of Mesopotamia, Amida was fortified during Late Antiquity by a set of enclosure walls with square towers. As we noted, the presence of thick, fortified enclosure walls was a hallmark of many late Roman cities in both the East and the West. In Rome, the emperor Aurelian embarked on a massive building campaign in 271 CE to construct a new set of walls that enclosed the entire city. The Aurelian walls, at nineteen kilometers long, eight meters high, and three and a half meters thick, dwarfed Rome's preexisting enclosures. They also reflected a new interest in defensive posturing and included a series of square towers. Later, the emperor Honorius undertook extensive renovations between 401 and 403 CE, when he doubled the wall's height and added a new upper level to the towers for easier use of projectile weapons. In the East, Amida's late antique walls fit this larger pattern.

Amida's fortifications stopped the Persian army for some time, and required them to use siege devices and to build a mound up against the walls – a tactic that the Roman defense countered by raising the wall's height and digging under the mound to destabilize it.[24] The Amidenes, we are told, continued to defend their city for days, hurling rocks down on the Persians and their shelters beneath the wall. This reported cooperation between citizens and soldiers is most likely not literary artifice. Amida had a Roman garrison stationed inside to help protect it from the Persians (there was a war going on), but the garrison was probably no larger than five or six hundred men, making it essential for civilians to participate directly in their city's defense. The siege at Amida was also typical in its duration. It lasted for approximately three months before the Persians gained access. At this moment, the author writes, "[the Persians] ransacked the city and plundered its property; they also trampled on the consecrated elements, broke up its church service, stripped its churches, and led into captivity (all) its inhabitants except the old and the disabled and those who were in hiding. ... The number of those they took out through the North Gate was more than 80,000, excluding those whom they led out alive and stoned outside the city."[25] The extremely high figure provided by Pseudo-Joshua warrants skepticism, though the Persians were uniquely adept at mass captivity, and the general details about the siege mesh with other evidence.

The threat of an external enemy was a concern in Late Antiquity, but so was internal violence precipitated by rioting. Rioting was a relatively common feature of urban life in Late Antiquity, especially in larger cities. Citizens rioted for all sorts of reasons, but the most violent urban unrest can usually be traced back to the circus factions and the theater. In Antioch, the famous "Riot of the Statues" in 387 CE, which culminated in attacks on imperial images (a crime legally tantamount to treason), was largely instigated by theater claques, that is, groups of supporters of particular pantomimes whose role was to stir up applause and other responses from the audience. Ideally, devoted fans of pantomimes and charioteers were peaceful in their enthusiasm and conveyed their preferences in a public manner without resorting to violence. Usually they did little more than shout at one another. "Burn here, burn here! Not a Green anywhere!" and "Set alight, set alight! Not a Blue in sight!," chanted the Blues and Greens of Constantinople in 561 CE. However, as happened in 561 when the Blues and Greens moved from shouts to fists and a full-on riot ensued, aggressive chanting could escalate into physical violence.

The deadliest riot in Roman urban history, the Nika Riot of 532 CE in Constantinople, similarly began with the reaction of circus factions. Following a clash between Blues and Greens after a race, the government arrested two fans from each club and sentenced them to death. However, the state botched the executions and the fans escaped, seeking asylum in a Christian church. What happened next was unprecedented: the Blues and the Greens joined forces and demanded that the emperor Justinian spare their friends. When Justinian refused, violence erupted on the streets as the fans set fire to several of

Constantinople's most prominent buildings, looted its markets, and killed innocent bystanders. At one point, a mob broke into the city's prison and freed all the prisoners. The entire situation deteriorated further when politics entered the mix. A group of anti-Justinian elites voiced their support for a usurper, and Justinian responded with a massive show of force: he ordered his general Belisarius to lead several thousand soldiers into the hippodrome, where most of the rioters remained. The army swiftly attacked the largely unarmed fans, killing as many as thirty thousand people.

The Nika Riot in Constantinople was an extreme case of urban rioting, but it reminds us that cities were potentially dangerous places. This sort of internal danger was often heightened during periods of severe political stress and economic instability. The Riot of the Statues in Antioch, for instance, was precipitated in part by the announcement of a tax increase. Rome was frequently rocked by riots over rising food prices and shortages. In 365 CE, enraged citizens surrounded the townhouse of a senator during the height of a wine shortage. The rioters had heard a rumor that the senator said he would rather use his wine to quench his lime kilns than sell it at a reduced price to alleviate the shortage and lower prices. Spurred by gossip, the enraged crowd burned the senator's house to the ground. Religious quarrels, too, sometimes escalated to violence. Around the same time that senator's home was burned down, two factions representing opposite sides in an episcopal election in Rome clashed in front of a church. According to one eyewitness account, 137 people died in the rioting over a new pope.[26] Apparently the fighting was so intense that the city's urban prefect had to flee the city. The story is a good reminder that ancient cities did not have an urban police force prepared to deal with large-scale unrest. If a riot did not die down on its own, city officials had no other choice but to flee or bring in the army, as Justinian did during the Nika Riots in 532 CE.

***

The late ancient city increasingly differed in physical terms from its classical counterpart, but it remained a site of intense social and economic activity. Brixia, we noted, underwent a gradual spatial contraction and reorientation to the north beginning in the early fifth century. Despite physical shrinkage and having been besieged twice in the fifth century Brixia remained an inhabited city, replete with industry, housing, and an official government presence. It went on to thrive in the medieval and early modern periods, when it was among the wealthiest cities in Italy. While not all western provincial cities developed along the same path (some seem to have disappeared altogether), Brixia's fluid urban landscape and continuous living conditions are representative of the West. Similarly, Ephesus underwent physical changes that reflected a new concentration of wealth and activity along large colonnaded streets, in churches, and in state palaces. Its post-Roman history began in 614 CE, when a major earthquake destroyed half the city. After being sacked by Arab armies in the later seventh and eighth centuries, Ephesus became a small Byzantine village until its partial rejuvenation under the Ottomans in the fifteenth century.

Moving now from the city to the household, we shift our attention from public society and space to the private world of families, slaves, and domestic work. As we shall see, the household was hardly marginal to the city or countryside; rather, it was central to all aspects of late Roman rural and urban life, from the economy to personal social relations.

Further Reading

Ammianus Marcellinus, *The Later Roman Empire (AD 354–378)*, trans. W. Hamilton (London, 1986).

Cassiodorus, *Variae*, trans. S. Barnish (Liverpool, 1992).

Collatio Legum Mosaicarum et Romanarum, trans. R. Frakes, *Compiling the Collatio Legum Mosaicarum et Romanarum* (Oxford, 2012).

Ps-Joshua the Stylite, *The Chronicle of Pseudo-Joshua the Stylite*, trans. F. Trombly and J. Watts (Liverpool, 2000).

Julian of Ascalon, *Treatise on Urbanism* is only available in French translation: *Le traité d'urbanisme de Julien d'Ascalon*, trans. C. Saliou (Paris, 1996).

Readers interested in general studies of urban change in Late Antiquity can consult J. Rich (ed.), *The City in Late Antiquity* (London, 1992) and the introduction and first chapter of H. Dey, *The Afterlife of the Roman City: Architecture and Ceremony in Late Antiquity and the Early Middle Ages* (Cambridge, 2015). An especially detail-oriented reader will appreciate the comprehensive study by I. Jacobs, *Aesthetic Maintenance of Civic Space. The 'Classical' City from the 4th to the 7th c. AD (Orientalia Lovaniensia Analecta 193)* (Leuven, 2013). Anyone interested in the changing symbolic meaning of cities will enjoy C. Rapp and H. Drake (eds.), *The City in the Classical and Post-Classical World. Changing Contexts of Power and Identity* (Cambridge, 2014).

Scholars of Late Antiquity typically focus on individual regions or cities, or even specific urban buildings or spaces. For Constantinople, see S. Bassett, *The Urban Image of Late Antique Constantinople* (Cambridge, 2004). For Rome and Italy, see R. Krautheimer, *Rome: Profile of a City, 312–1308* (Princeton, NJ, 1980), along with B. Ward Perkins, *From Classical Antiquity to the Middle Ages: Urban Public Buildings in Northern and Central Italy, AD 300–850* (Oxford, 1984). For Sardis and Ephesus, see C. Foss, *Byzantine and Turkish Sardis* (Cambridge, 1976) and *Ephesus After Antiquity* (Cambridge, 1979). For Alexandria, see C. Haas, *Alexandria in Late Antiquity: Topography and Social Change* (Baltimore, 1997). For North Africa, see A. Leone, *Changing Townscapes in North Africa from Late Antiquity to the Arab Conquest* (Bari, 2007). Unfortunately, there are no English-language publications on late Roman Brixia, but readers who know a little Italian can consult the museum catalogue entitled *Brixia, scoperte e riscoperte. Museo Santa Giulia* (Brescia, 2003). On baths and bathing, see F. Yegül, *Bathing in the Roman World* (Cambridge, 2010). On early Christian churches, see R. Krautheimer, *Early Christian and Byzantine Architecture* (London, 1981) for a broad introduction.

A good general introduction to urban labor and economics is P. Garnsey and C. Whittaker, "Trade, Industry, and the Urban Economy," in *The Cambridge Ancient History*, vol. 13 (Cambridge, 2000), 312–337. For prostitution, see T. McGinn, *The Economy of Prostitution in the Roman World. A Study of Social History and the Brothel* (Ann Arbor, MI, 2004) and K. Harper, *From Shame to Sin: The Christian Transformation of Sexual Morality in Late Antiquity* (Cambridge, MA, 2013). Readers interested in urban entertainment may consult S. Remijsen, *The End of Greek Athletics in Late Antiquity* (Cambridge, 2015), C. Rouché, *Performers and Partisans at Aphrodisias in the Roman and Late Roman Periods* (London, 1993), and A. Cameron, *Circus Factions* (Oxford, 1975). For the theater, see R. Webb, *Demons and Dancers: Performance in Late Antiquity* (Cambridge, MA, 2008).

3

The Household

An Urban Household in Rome. The wedding had been in the works for months, possibly even years. The bride and groom were the shining stars of their illustrious fourth-century families. Proiecta, the bride, came from a blue-blooded Roman family that counted consuls and prefects among its men. Her father, Florus, was a high-ranking official in the Roman government and perhaps a distant relative of the emperor Theodosius I (r. 379–395).[1] The groom, Lucius Turcius Secundus, was a perfect match for such a highborn girl, and as was often the case with aristocrats, the two may have been related. Moreover, Proiecta and Secundus were Christians, perhaps the first of their generation to be raised from childhood in the faith. Precisely how old they were when they wed is unknown. If this was the first marriage for both, and evidence suggests that it was, Secundus was likely in his early twenties and Proiecta in her mid-teens, perhaps fourteen or fifteen, but the law permitted girls as young as twelve to marry. Regardless of when the marriage took place, the two were betrothed far in advance of the actual union, perhaps when they were small children.

As far as the wedding event itself, Roman law did not require any ceremony or ritual to consecrate a marriage. This is because the consent of the couple and their fathers was all that the law demanded. But late Romans loved to celebrate marriages, whether through parties or rites. Proiecta, for instance, may have donned a flame-red veil on her wedding day, while Secundus' friends may have gathered around the couple and sang bawdy songs while they processed to the groom's home for their first night together. And despite the fact that both were Christians, a priest did not officiate at their wedding, as would happen routinely in the Middle Ages. Rather, the two simply feasted with family and friends, who showered them with song, praise, and gifts. In fact, Proiecta and Secundus are known to us today primarily through their wedding presents and silver collection, which archaeologists discovered among the remains of a large late ancient home on the slopes of the Esquiline Hill in Rome. These sumptuous objects underscore the extent to which a marriage was ultimately about the transmission of wealth from one generation to the next (Figure 3.1a,b).

After the wedding, the couple moved into a house of their own, perhaps a mansion on the Esquiline where their silver was found. There, Secundus conducted morning business with colleagues and clients, maybe while seated in a high-backed chair, the fittings from which were discovered along with the wedding gifts. Like all aristocratic landowners, Secundus probably left Rome regularly to inspect his many agricultural estates scattered throughout Italy and abroad. Proiecta was also certainly a property holder in her own right, and she would have brought slaves, valuable objects, and land to the marriage. She likely spent her days dressing and having her hair done, weaving brightly colored textiles, paying visits to lady friends in the city, managing the household slaves and larders, and overseeing the care of any children the couple may have had (evidence suggests that they were childless). Together, Proiecta and Secundus threw lavish dinner parties at the evening meal called *cena*, where diners would have savored delicacies like dormouse and shaved ice and sipped high-quality imported wines, such as the sweet white from Palestine that was all the rage in the late Empire. They enjoyed live entertainment as they dined, reclining on couches (the traditional Roman style of eating) while watching performances by musicians and mimes.

While our evidence is sketchy, it appears that this storied union ended earlier than expected, when Proiecta died at the age of sixteen in December of 383 CE. The cause of her death is unknown. Perhaps she passed during childbirth, a leading cause of death for women in Late Antiquity. Alternatively, Proiecta might have fallen victim to

(a)

(b)

FIGURE 3.1. (a) Silver items from the Esquiline Treasure. Discovered among the ruins of an elite house on the Esquiline Hill in Rome, the high-quality luxury objects date to the fourth century. Photo © The Trustees of the British Museum. (b) Silver gilded furniture fittings from the Esquiline Treasure, Rome, fourth century. Photo © The Trustees of the British Museum.

disease, which was especially rampant in the Empire's largest cities such as Rome, where dense population growth and poor sanitation encouraged the spread of pathogens. Florus, her father, celebrated his daughter's life and death on a marble tombstone, which is extant today. Whether Secundus celebrated his late wife in similar fashion is unknown. It is possible that he, too, commissioned an epitaph for Proiecta that accompanied her parents', but it has been lost to history.

Two Rural Households in Gaul. The two young lovers met furtively at first, knowing that a path to marriage would be difficult. She was the daughter of a much-loved *nutrix*, or wet nurse, who helped raise the children of a former imperial statesman, landowner, and local bishop named Sidonius Apollinaris (d. 489 CE). Her mother must have been either freeborn or a freedwoman (most wet nurses were slaves or freedwomen), because the girl was freeborn. She likely grew up on one of Sidonius' lavish agricultural estates either in the Auvergne or near Lyons (central France) and was considered part of his household. Her boyfriend, also the son of a wet nurse, came from a neighboring estate belonging to another elite landowner named Pudens. However, her boyfriend's legal status was rather more complicated, because he was the son of a tenant tied to Pudens' property by law. The colonate, we recall from Chapter 1, was a peculiar facet of the late Roman tax system.[2] It obligated renters of certain properties to remain on those properties for generations in order to work them and pay tax. Generally speaking, the two lovers had a great deal in common, as they were both non-elite members of large aristocratic households, and were tied to their respective householders (Sidonius and Pudens) through social, economic, and, in the boy's case, legal bonds. However, late Roman law prohibited men and women with different socio-legal statuses from forming legal marriages. Even if both kids and their parents assented to the union, it would not be seen as legitimate in the eyes of the law, because the boy was a *colonus* and the girl untied to the land.

Despite these legal impediments, the two eloped. While we may see this as a romantic turn of events, their families, as well as Sidonius and Pudens, were dismayed by the development. For one, their parents had apparently not consented to the liaison, and consequently the elopement was tantamount to bride theft. In fact, the very concept of a legal elopement did not exist in Late Antiquity: without the explicit permission of both sets of parents or legal guardians, a secret union was considered an "abduction marriage" and was thus categorically illegal, with heavy punishments for the parents for not stopping the "theft." Moreover, from Sidonius' perspective, the fact that the two did not have the same legal status was a serious problem. It was not right, he insisted in a letter to Pudens, for a freeborn girl to wed a man who was legally tied to the land and under the strong authority of his landlord.[3] Perhaps Sidonius was also concerned that any children born to the couple would not only be illegitimate, but also have the same legal status as their father, i.e., a *colonus*, and be hence bound to Pudens' land. In fact, an imperial law of 419 CE stated that all children born to fathers registered as tax-responsible tenants must remain tied to that same rental property.[4] Perhaps, too, Sidonius had strong personal feelings for this wet nurse and her daughter, who may have been nursed side-by-side with the aristocrat's own children.

Fortunately, all signs point to a happy ending for this domestic crisis in rural fifth-century Gaul. In the letter to Pudens, Sidonius requested that his neighbor convert the man's status from being Pudens' tax-obligated *colonus* to his client. We'd like to think that Pudens agreed to Sidonius' request, and that the young couple were subsequently able to enter into a legal marriage, move into a single household (likely on Pudens' estate), and carry out their hard lives as domestic laborers. Under Pudens' patronage, they might have received extra food during periods of lean harvests and physical protection from bandits. He could have also been a source of loans and legal help. Of course, now that the man was freed from his tax obligations to Pudens' estate, he might have attempted to scrape out an existence as an independent farmer. Such freeholding peasant households were common in the East, but less usual in the West, where poor rural workers tended to live in close proximity to large villas, working rented property and/or remaining bonded to larger, more powerful householders like Pudens and Sidonius.

As these stories demonstrate, the late ancient household was a complex social unit that stretched across different physical spaces (urban townhouses, rural villas, agricultural properties, humble peasant abodes) and human relationships (parents, children, spouses, slaves, freedmen, clients, *coloni*). In fact, the Latin word *domus* (from which we derive our modern adjective "domestic") and the Greek words *oikos* and *oikia* (from which we derive our modern term "economy") connote both the physical house and the social community that lived within it. Whereas English speakers use two different terms ("house" for the place, "household" for the social community), Greek and Latin speakers had a single word. What does this linguistic fact suggest? Among other things, it tells us that ancient people closely associated property with social relations; in many respects, the two were inseparable. The purpose of having a family was to beget heirs who could inherit the family property, burnish its reputation, and/or provide vital labor and income. Moreover, in Roman society both men and women could own property, meaning that female heirs were as important as male heirs when it came to property transmission.[5] Female property ownership was rather unusual in the premodern era, and is perhaps best explained by high mortality rates. For Romans, it was essential that both sexes had the legal capacity to own and transmit property to the next generation.

As we shall see, late ancient household members did not experience domestic life as a form of seclusion from the demands of work, politics, and religion. Rather, the household was an alternative venue for all of these activities. Moreover, the household was never disconnected from the economy, community, or state. As we saw in Chapter 1, private households largely generated the state's revenues and services, and hence were linked to the government through closely monitored obligations. Additionally, households produced statesmen and soldiers, and were seen as the cornerstone of the well-functioning state. It is important always to keep in mind when studying the household that the domestic sphere was Late Antiquity's most central social institution and the engine of the late Roman economy.

HOUSEHOLD ROLES AND RELATIONSHIPS

To an extent, the size and composition of the late Roman household looked a great deal like the typical American household. It was usually organized around a nuclear core, with one or two parents (depending on variables such as death and divorce) and their children. Late ancient Romans did not practice polygamy or sibling marriage, and they did not demand that newly wedded couples live with the parents of either the bride or the groom. Divorce and remarriage were common, and this meant that stepparents and stepchildren were also a regular feature of late Roman households. And while married children remained closely bonded to their natal families (recall Florus' epitaph for Proiecta), they did not necessarily live with their parents.

Beyond this nuclear core, many late ancient households included additional members: grandparents, unmarried siblings, aunts, and uncles; slaves and freedmen; clients and tenants. Moreover, some residences might have been large multi-building estates that housed hundreds of people. For example, Sidonius' nurse and her daughter were a family, but they were also part of Sidonius' household, just as Pudens' nurse and her son were part of his. The dependence of these extra-family members on the householder (whether Sidonius or Pudens) illustrates how different people were embedded within complex social and legal webs that linked household members both vertically (Sidonius and his nurse) and horizontally (the two young lovers who eloped).

Research suggests that many rural households relied on seasonal labor. This meant that at certain times of the year (e.g., harvest in the fall and sheep shearing in the spring), households included individuals who were not related by blood, marriage, tenancy, or patronage. Similarly, urban households often took in boarders for extra income. In crowded apartments, these men (and perhaps women) would have had little choice than to sleep, cook, wash, and use the chamber pot alongside their landlords and fellow tenants. Although temporary household members were probably not treated the same as blood and marital relations, or as clients, for that matter, they nevertheless formed part of the household. Their temporary presence also reminds us that the composition of the late ancient household was remarkably fluid. It changed not only with the marriage of a child, but also with the hiring of seasonal laborers and the letting of space to boarders.

Marriage

At the center of many late ancient households was a married couple. Generally speaking, marriage was highly desirable, and most men and women were married at least once in their lives. As we have seen, the marrying process began in any number of ways: two youths meet and fall in love; a father decides that his teenage daughter is ready to wed and searches for an appropriate match; a widower is introduced through mutual acquaintances to a divorcée. Both elite and non-elite parents sometimes used matchmakers to help them select an appropriate bride or groom. From our modern perspective, which sees marriage as an emotional bond built on already established mutual love, late ancient matchmaking seems cold and calculating. But for many late Romans, an arranged union was to be expected, since marriage was both a business transaction and an intimate personal relationship. On the one hand, a marriage was about uniting two households with the goal of maintaining or expanding their social, political, and/or economic standing within the community. On the other hand, marriage was a close sexual, personal relationship that at best was built on bonds of affection, mutual obligation, and fidelity. There is no reason to conclude that in all cases, arranged marriages were always loveless. In fact, concord between couples was the ultimate ideal when it came to marriage.

Following the selection of a spouse, the two families negotiated a betrothal agreement. The agreement was both material and temporal: gifts were exchanged, a marriage contract was written up, and a time was set for the wedding. There was no set limit on the length of a betrothal; it could be a few weeks or years. Legally, a girl had to be at least twelve and a boy fourteen to enter into a marriage. Betrothals had long been part of the ancient Roman marrying process, but during Late Antiquity they took on increased significance. Starting in the fourth century, new rituals connected to the betrothal emerged, such as the fiancé's presentation of engagement gifts to the bride's family in addition to the traditional dowry from the bride's household to the groom's, and the limited involvement of Christian clerics in engagements. Evidence from North Africa shows bishops overseeing the signing and sealing of marriage contracts, while sources from Italy reveal a new form of blessing for the couple, wherein clergy veiled the bride in a church, most likely to publicize the betrothal agreement. This was not a consecration of the marriage itself, however. Marriage did not become a holy sacrament until the twelfth century.

After the engagement period, the couple wed. In Late Antiquity, neither law nor custom demanded brides and grooms to undergo any particular rite. As mentioned earlier, a marriage was predicated on the principle of mutual consent: if the bride and groom agreed to be married along with their respective families, then the bride and groom were married. Additionally, the couple had to be free Roman citizens (freeborn or freed) and of the same socio-legal status (the restriction that initially separated our two Gallic peasants), and they could be distantly related by blood (as was likely in the case of Proiecta and Secundus).[6] Slaves could not form legal marriages with other slaves, freedmen, or freeborn citizens.

Although families did not need to hold lavish wedding events or engage in specific rituals to make a marriage, late Romans nevertheless liked to mark and publicize their unions through a range of rites and practices. In some cases, the bride donned a red veil or listened with her groom to personalized wedding poems, known as *epithalamia*, written and performed by guests. Sometimes the couple participated in a ritual procession from her parents' house to the groom's home, called the *deductio ad domum* in Latin. The *deductio ad domum* was often a raucous event, as it involved the singing of lewd songs by friends and family while the couple walked through the city or village. Christian bishops tended to disapprove of this particular ritual, for obvious reasons perhaps, but their objections did little to curb the tradition.

Late Roman marriages were of a type that did not legally subjugate a wife to her husband. Unlike earlier Roman forms of marriage, wherein the bride became her husband's legal dependent, wives in Late Antiquity remained legally tied to their fathers through a mechanism called *patria potestas* (see "Children and Childhood"). Among other things, this meant that husbands did not automatically possess their wives' property upon marriage, and marital property was treated as separate in the courts. Culturally speaking, however, wives were expected to be subservient to their husbands, and husbands typically acted as unofficial guardians of their wives, even if they could not exercise legal control over their independent wealth.

Divorce and Widowhood

Not all marriages lasted, of course. It is impossible to estimate divorce rates in late ancient Rome, but they were likely roughly equivalent to those in modern western countries. In cases where both spouses wanted to end a marriage, divorce was extremely easy in Late

Antiquity. If marriage was simply the consent to be wed, then divorce was the removal of this consent. Some spouses formalized a divorce by sending their wife or husband a written declaration of withdrawal, but this was not required. Most often, the separation happened and the property was divided according to the arrangements set forth in the marriage contract, which typically required the return of the dowry to the wife's family. To be sure, disputes frequently arose over dowries and other property, but the legal prohibition against joint marital property probably helped reduce them. On child custody, see "Children and Childhood."

Throughout most of Late Antiquity, bilateral divorce (meaning both parties wished to end the union) remained legal and easily attainable, and there were no penalties placed on couples who mutually agreed to split up. However, several late ancient emperors, including Constantine (r. 312–337 CE) and Valentinian III (r. 425–455 CE), sought to curb unilateral divorce (that is, when only one party desired to end the marriage). They did this by limiting the circumstances under which one spouse could dissolve the marriage. Restrictions were especially harsh for women in the western regions of the Empire, which were governed separately from the East.[7] In the West, it remained legal for a man to divorce an adulterous wife (in fact, they were legally required to do this) or a wife who was thought to be otherwise unchaste, unable to produce children, or a sorceress. A wife, however, could only divorce her husband and receive back her dowry if he had committed murder or treason. In the East, more liberal imperial rulings allowed women to divorce husbands who committed murder or treason, brought prostitutes into the home, whipped them, or had an affair with a married woman. With one exception (Justinian, r. 527–565 CE), no late Roman emperor ever prohibited bilateral divorce, by far the most common form. Couples routinely split up in Late Antiquity, despite the emerging Christian views against severing the marriage bond (on which, see Chapter 6).

Given the fact that many girls wed older men, and that many women died in childbirth, widows and widowers were ubiquitous in the late Roman world. For most widows and widowers, and especially for young ones, remarriage was the desirable next step. Of course, some preferred to remain unmarried, not only for religious reasons (as explored in Chapter 6), but also for social ones. A widow over the age of twenty-five (the legal age of majority for men and women) whose father was deceased was legally independent; this meant that she could make her own financial and personal decisions, including whether to remarry.[8] For wealthy widows in this situation, there were undoubtedly many reasons why a new husband was less than appealing. Although independence is highly relative, such widows arguably enjoyed more freedom than their married counterparts. There were fewer reasons for men to remain unmarried, especially since pervasive Greco-Roman cultural norms allowed married men to have sexual relations with certain people to whom they were not married. As we shall see in the section on slavery, men had various socially acceptable, legal outlets for satisfying their sexual urges. However, the strong double standard that governed ancient gender norms refused these same options for women.

Common-Law Marriages (Concubinage) and Adultery

The fact that there were legal restrictions governing marriage eligibility in Late Antiquity did not prevent some late Romans from forming lasting sexual and emotional relationships with partners whose status denied a legal union. These relationships were identified as "concubinage" (*concubinatus*), and the woman, who was typically the social inferior of the couple, was seen as a concubine. Concubinage, regardless of its length or commitment, carried none of the benefits of legal marriage. Any children born of such a relationship were considered illegitimate and could not inherit property from their father. Moreover, the children's sociolegal status necessarily followed the mother's. A famous case of concubinage involved the Christian bishop Augustine (354–430 CE). Before becoming a bishop, Augustine had a long-term monogamous relationship with a concubine. The relationship produced a son named Adeodatus, who was illegitimate, since his parents were not married in the eyes of the law. However, Augustine did not abandon his son. There is evidence from his own writings that Adeodatus remained part of his father's life, and was baptized with Augustine in 387 CE. Augustine had the option of legally adopting Adeodatus, but there is no evidence that he did so.

Augustine was unmarried during his long relationship with a concubine, but some men were married when they coupled with other women. While today we label an unfaithful husband as an adulterer, Roman law did not recognize male adultery. By definition, adultery was a crime involving married women who had sexual relationships with men who were not their husbands. Although the man with whom she cheated faced penalties (typically a reduction of his inheritance), the married woman was punished far more severely. According to a law issued by Rome's first emperor Augustus (r. 31 BCE–14 CE), wives guilty of adultery were exiled from Rome and denied their inheritance.[9] Augustus' law remained active in Roman society through Late Antiquity, though the penalties became harsher and now included execution.

Cultural forces, mainly those influenced by the rise of Christian morality, introduced some change to the sexual landscape. Beginning with the apostle Paul, a handful of Christian moralists and preachers emphasized the importance of sexual fidelity for both spouses. For the first time, men were chastised for extramarital liaisons as well as women. Later in the fifth century, Roman law permitted women in the East to unilaterally divorce a husband who had sex with a married woman. Yet, the definition of adultery as a crime involving a married *woman* having sex with another man remained unchanged, and the double standard that defined sexuality in classical antiquity continued to orient law and practice.[10]

Children and Childhood

For many years, scholars believed that ancient people had no concept of childhood and that children were treated as mini-adults. Historians used to argue that the ancients were so accustomed to high mortality rates among infants and young children, and were so inured to the ubiquity of child labor, that they failed to forge affective bonds with their children, as parents do today. Recent research has debunked these myths. Epitaphs, literature, and archaeological evidence show that late Romans viewed their children as children, whom they loved and cherished, even when they died too soon. One grieving mother, whose son Boethius died in 577 CE, proclaimed on his tombstone: "Because of your death, your mother wanted to die: she would have been happy if she could have joined you."[11] Our sources clearly attest to the fact that late ancient children played with toys, in some cases went to school, enjoyed eating sweets and cakes, and were spanked and rewarded. Of course, childhood in Late Antiquity was rather different from what children and parents experience today. The following discussion highlights some differences and similarities.

While late Romans identified age categories, including childhood, they did not observe rigid boundaries between them. Childhood effectively began at around one month of age, when (at least until the fourth century) married parents participated in a naming ceremony, wherein the father ritually recognized the child as a family member. Adolescence is harder to date with uniformity; in one text it encompasses the lengthy period of ages fourteen to thirty. For most people, however, adolescence probably coincided with the ages of ten to fourteen. The shift from adolescence to adulthood was identified in multiple ways. The Roman age of legal adulthood was twenty-five years for men and women, but there were other equally important cultural markers. For girls, marriage, perhaps as early as age twelve, characterized their transition to adulthood. For boys, marriage or joining the army at age eighteen could have marked them as adults. Until the fifth century, elite urban Roman families participated in a ritual involving the presentation of a toga to a son when he reached the age of fourteen. The rite, called the *toga virilis*, marked the boy's transition from childhood to manhood. In parts of the late Empire that were increasingly inhabited by non-Roman peoples, such as Gaul, the transition to adulthood may have been measured differently. A study of burial goods suggests that manhood arrived as late as age twenty-five or even thirty, long after these young men left their homes for training in the courts of Merovingian kings. It seems that they were not considered adults in the eyes of the community until they married and had children.

Significantly, infant and early childhood mortality rates were exceptionally high in the late Roman Empire. Life expectancy at birth was twenty-five to thirty years. This figure is so low because up to 35 percent of newborns did not survive beyond the first month of life, and only 50 percent reached the age of ten. Of these, half might live to the age of fifty, with a third reaching sixty. The absence of vaccines is the primary culprit, along with poorer hygienic standards and a lack of antibiotics. In order to maintain the entire population of the late Empire at a steady level of around fifty million, women had to have four to six live births in the course of their lifetime. One Italian couple in the third century lost six children, an extreme but not unique example. Most parents had at least one child die in their lifetime, and virtually all kids lost a sibling and/or playmate while growing up. Death, in other words, was a common experience for children in Late Antiquity.

Equally if not more startling for the modern reader is the fact that dire straits forced some poor late Roman families to expose their infants (meaning that they abandoned them), to sell their freeborn children into slavery, or to use them as collateral for repaying a debt. This was not a decision taken lightly, or something done regularly, since children provided essential labor within the home. Most children born to non-elite households worked from an early age, helping to cook and clean, tend crops and animals, and/or assist in workshops. When parents exposed or sold their children to slavers, it was as a last resort to save the rest of the family from starvation, often during periods of severe crisis, such as a famine. Parents also exposed newborns with noticeable birth defects, in the belief that they would not survive infancy. Some emperors attempted to regulate these practices, and it was always technically illegal to enslave freeborn persons.[12] But the late Roman government did little to curb them.

Conversely, some children lost their parents and became orphaned. Under Roman law, a boy or girl under the age of twenty-five (the age of legal adulthood) had to have an official guardian, who, in the case of very young children, might act as a surrogate parent. Typically, this guardian was the oldest living male relative, usually an uncle or cousin. Adoption was also sometimes an option. In most parts of the late Empire, there were no orphanages, which meant that orphaned children without responsible guardians or other forms of help were rendered homeless. For most of Roman history, no institutions, governmental or religious, offered assistance to orphaned children, but during Late Antiquity this began to change slowly. Sometime in the second half of the fourth century, the Empire's first orphanage, the Orphanotropheion, was established in the city of Constantinople. This institution for homeless and destitute children was closely associated with the Christian church. It was funded privately, with land and money from wealthy donors, including the emperor. Children appear to have received some education at the Orphanotropheion, primarily in music (the children's choir was well known). The first documented orphanage in the West, in the city of Rome, did not appear until the late seventh century.

One final point about children and childhood underlines the difference between modern and late Roman experience. Under Roman law, all children were under the authority of their oldest living male relative on the direct paternal line. This figure, known in Latin legal sources as the *paterfamilias*, was typically was the child's father, but he could have been a grandfather or even a great-grandfather. The *paterfamilias'* legal power over his children or grandchildren, called *patria potestas*, or "paternal power," was extensive. It included legal ownership of any property a child might earn or acquire, control over selecting a marriage partner (his permission was legally necessary for a marriage to be valid), and the right to discipline his children physically. What made *patria potestas* so extraordinary even in the ancient world was the fact that it remained in force for the duration of the older male relative's lifetime. This meant that, theoretically, an adult man with a house, wife, and children of his own was legally under the power of his living father. In reality, however, relatively few adult men and women would have been subject to *patria potestas*. For one, child emancipation was a common legal tool in Late Antiquity, which freed a child from *patria potestas* (though it, too, required the *paterfamilias'* permission). More important, demographic realities mitigated this situation, because few men and women over twenty-five years old had a living father to lord over them. The existence of legal concepts such as the *paterfamilias* and *patria potestas* meant that children "belonged" to their father and his family and not to their mother's. In cases of divorce, child custody would automatically go to the father, although we should assume that in many situations arrangements were made that gave mothers access to their children.

In many other ways, late ancient childhood bears similarities to its modern form. All late ancient babies were breastfed. Formula did not exist, and ancient medical authorities advised against feeding infants non-human animal milk. Ancient medical experts prescribed breastfeeding until the child developed his or her first tooth (around seven months), and then full weaning at around two years. Not all infants were breastfed by their mothers, however. Wealthier families employed wet nurses, like the *nutrix* in Sidonius Apollinaris' household. An ancient profile of the ideal wet nurse describes a woman between the ages of twenty and forty who has had several births, and who is morally upright and in good physical health. Moral qualities were important in a wet nurse, because the Romans believed that breast milk transmitted character as well as nutrients. Poorer families would likely not have had wet nurses, though a mother who breastfed her own infant may have actually improved the baby's chances of survival, since she could give it colostrum, which transfers immunities. (A wet nurse likely could not.) Consequently, babies from poor families may have been more likely to survive early childhood diseases than babies from rich families. Nevertheless, elites were discouraged from breastfeeding their own children and wet nurses were ubiquitous, at least until the late sixth century. At that time, the Roman Pope Gregory the Great (d. 604 CE) criticized mothers who relied on wet nurses instead of breastfeeding their own children.[13] It is hard to say whether Gregory's statement represents a shift in attitude or simply the personal views of the bishop, who, one should add, never had children of his own.

For elite children between the ages of six and ten, a typical day began by being aroused by a slave or *paedagogus*, a sort of male governess-like slave, who would wash and dress them and make sure they ate their breakfast. Children went to school starting at six, though this happened largely with the *paedagogus* at home.[14] Lunch (*prandia*) would follow a requisite handwashing, and many elite children bathed before dinner (*cena*), which they often attended with their parents.

Playtime was also part of an elite child's daily life. Archaeology has provided many examples of toys and games. Dolls were typical toys, some with articulated limbs, but all of our extant examples physically represent adult women, not babies. Some dolls even had clothing and accessories, such as jewelry. Miniature tableware sets and chests have also been found, which suggest that children played "house." Kids also loved games involving knucklebones, marbles, and hoops. Of course, children then, as now, often improvised with whatever they could find. Pottery shards, sticks, rocks, and mud could all become fun toys. There were no designated playgrounds in Late Antiquity, so children played wherever they could: in the courtyards of their homes or apartment buildings, in the street, or out in the fields. We should remember, however, that the fun ended for elite girls at least in

FIGURE 3.2. A fourth-century female doll with articulated arms and gold earrings from Egypt.
Photo by the Princeton University Art Museum/Art Resource, NY.

their early teens, when they married and were henceforth expected to manage large households and start producing children of their own (Figure 3.2).

Non-elite children certainly enjoyed playtime and liked to have dolls and sweets. However, their day would have looked rather different, and their access to toys would have been extremely limited. Days were spent not in school, but working in the home, field, factory, or workshop. While some would have received limited homeschooling (perhaps enough to learn their letters and numbers), most worked and/or learned a skill that would contribute to their family's income. Older children, especially older girls, were tasked with minding their younger siblings while their parents worked at jobs that were too difficult for kids to take on. In fact, girls in non-elite homes probably married somewhat later than their elite counterparts, precisely because they were essential members of their households.

Slaves and Slavery

Sometime in the mid-sixth century, a young Roman slave named Andarchius became the personal attendant to Felix, a Gallo-Roman boy living with his senatorial family in the environs of Marseilles. We do not know whether Felix's parents bought Andarchius at one of the slave markets still active in Gaul. If Andarchius was a new purchase, Felix's parents paid a pretty sum for him: ten *solidi* if Andarchius was younger than ten, and twenty *solidi* if he was older. Alternatively, he may have been a "homebred" slave (what the Romans called a *verna* and the Greeks a *threptos*), meaning that Andarchius' mother was a slave already owned by the household and had given birth to him in the home. A child born to a mother who was a slave automatically became a slave owned by his or her mother's master. Felix's parents ordered Andarchius to look after Felix, although in reality Andarchius may have been only a few years older than him. When Felix began his schooling, his slave accompanied him to lessons, carrying Felix's codices, stylus, and tablets, but in the meantime, the slave soaked up everything taught to his master. Andarchius not only learned how to read and write Latin, but also mastered the poetry of Virgil and soon the more demanding subjects. When Felix moved on to study law (a more advanced subject) in his teenage years, Andarchius studied with him.

Andarchius' education, though not a primary consideration for Felix's parents, may nevertheless have been seen as a good investment. A literate, highly educated slave could serve subsequent children in the household as a *paedagogus*; *paedagogi* were teachers/child minders who played crucial roles in the upbringing of elite children. Moreover, Andarchius could be sold at a profit. Skilled male slaves fetched thirty *solidi* or more on the market. Yet, according to Gregory of Tours (ca. 538–594 CE), who relates Andarchius' story in his history of sixth-century Gaul, Felix's parents did not enjoy much of a return on their investment.[15] For Andarchius also demonstrated a quality that was unacceptable in a slave: ambition. Under unknown circumstances, Andarchius left Felix's household and secured the protection of even more powerful patrons, first a duke loyal to the Frankish king Sigisbert and then Sigisbert himself, who reportedly sent Andarchius on royal missions. Gregory's account of Andarchius' life – a rare vignette about a real-life slave that has many rhetorical flourishes – does not describe the conditions under which Andarchius received his freedom, or whether he remained a slave with new owners. (Did Felix's parents offer him to the duke as a gift, perhaps thankful to get an uppity slave off their hands?) Regardless, Gregory portrays Andarchius as a con artist, ultimately murdered by an elite whose fortune he stole and whose daughter he attempted to marry.

For late ancient readers, Gregory's story had an obvious moral: slaves should know their place within the household. Simply put, slaves were property, belonging to the householder or a family member. While recognized widely as human beings with minds and souls, slaves were denied any rightful ability to exercise their will, since their bodies were owned, and hence completely controlled, by other people. Slavery was the most despicable status for any Roman man or woman. It placed you outside of the Roman honor system and meant that you were denied all the civic rights of free people. A slave could not run for office, legally contract a marriage, own and bequeath property, or exercise paternal power over a child. The fact that another man or woman owned a slave's body meant that the slave could be shackled, raped, and beaten.[16]

Late Romans did not associate slavery with any particular ethnic or racial group. Consequently, the specter of enslavement was not easily discounted as something that happened to "other" people deemed inferior because of their skin color or origin. In this respect, Roman slavery differed from the race-based system developed by early modern Europeans, who largely enslaved darker-skinned, non-Christian people from Africa and South America. While Roman law expressly prohibited the enslavement of freeborn people, in reality, anyone could become a slave if she or he were in the wrong place at the wrong time. However, slavery was not necessarily a lifelong status, even for those born into it. Manumission, the legal freeing of a slave, was common in Late Antiquity, and slaves in some cases actually purchased their own freedom. Masters and mistresses could become emotionally close to slaves, and decide to free slaves during their own lifetime or in their will.

Although the attitudes of individual owners toward their slaves ranged enormously, no one in the late Roman Empire questioned, much less condemned, slavery as an institution. Slave owners could be found at virtually every level of Roman society, from peasants living in humble Egyptian villages to wealthy Roman nobles like Sidonius Apollinaris. In fact, true poverty was often associated with people who owned no slaves at all. Moreover, a person's religious or philosophical views never stopped him or her from owning slaves.

Stoic philosophers, Christians, and Jews owned slaves and never apologized for it. While moralists sometimes criticized a slave owner for failing to control his or her anger toward a slave, they were unbothered by the effects of brutal discipline on the slave herself.

Sometime in the late fourth century, John Chrysostom (d. 407 CE), then a Christian priest in Antioch, delivered a sermon to his congregation on the importance of household order and calm. In it, he singled out the excessive abuse of slaves as an example of the kind of clamor and chaos that disrupted his ideal of domestic bliss. The sermon focused on hypothetical female slave owners, who supposedly yelled at their slave girls so loudly that the neighbors could hear, and who "lash their slaves [so harshly that] the stripes don't dissipate within the day. They take off the girls' clothes, call their husband in for it, and tie them to the couch." As horrifying as this image is to us, Chrysostom makes clear that the slaves' welfare was not his concern: "'But slaves are an evil tribe,' you [the audience] say, 'and reckless and shameless and incorrigible.' Yes, I know this. But there are other ways to maintain order – fear, threats, words – that are more effective and rescue you [the slave owner] from shame."[17] For Chrysostom, the problem was not with the slaves' physical and emotional abuse, but with the slave owner's moral health: excessive discipline, even if aimed at a lowly slave, was a dangerous sign that she or he had lost self-control, and thus honor. In short, while slaves were welcome to become Christians, Christianity did little to improve the conditions of slaves, nor did Christians oppose slavery. The most we can say about Christianity concretely improving the daily lives of slaves is that in the sixth century, some Christian churches in Gaul declared Sunday to be a day of rest for slaves as well.

In Late Antiquity, most slaves were created via "home-breeding," that is, by natural reproduction. As noted, a newborn's legal status followed the mother, meaning that any child born to a female slave was automatically a slave who belonged to the mother's owner. Although slaves could not legally marry, they often formed partnerships that were the emotional equivalent of marriage, and these unions frequently produced offspring. To be sure, some home-bred slaves had freeborn fathers, possibly the householder himself. As John Chrysostom hinted in his sketch of slave discipline, freeborn men in a household were accustomed to using their slaves for sex.

The offspring of these encounters were slaves, since legal status always followed the mother, and might actually belong to their own fathers.

Had Andarchius been purchased for Felix, he was likely procured at a local or regional slave market, such as the one that was held annually in the countryside of southern Italy as part of a larger fair marking the feast day of St. Cyprian. According to a sixth-century witness, this fair included "the loveliest of market-stalls," as well as "boys and girls … on display marked out by their differences in sex and age, brought on the market not as captives but by freedom: their parents are right to sell them, since they benefit by slavery itself."[18] Slave markets have been identified in cities across the Mediterranean, and may have been especially common in North Africa and the East, where the economy remained more buoyant through the end of the sixth century.

What were the sources of slaves sold at markets? As stated, some were sold into slavery by parents or guardians. It was illegal to sell any freeborn persons into slavery, including children, but some desperate parents did so anyway. Others skirted the law by "leasing" their children as indentured servants, though it is unlikely that their lives differed significantly from a slave's. Infant exposure was another source of slaves, since abandoned babies were often picked up, and then sold, by slave traders. Slaves were also procured by capture, both in war and during raids. Wars often concluded with the enslavement of soldiers from the losing side, perhaps along with their families. Barbarian slaves were thus common in the Roman slave supply, and Roman military commanders, especially those stationed along the Danube frontier, sometimes moonlighted as slave dealers. Roman citizens, however, were also at risk for capture and enslavement. John Chrysostom spoke proverbially when he warned his congregation about slavers who kidnapped children by enticing them with cakes and dice, but the fear that slave dealers might ride into town and kidnap residents was grounded in experience. Another Christian observer we met earlier, Augustine, described how teams of slave dealers regularly swooped into rural North African villages, sometimes pretending to be invading barbarians, seized the locals, and then sold them at slave markets. Augustine shared more stories of individuals, like that of an unnamed woman in Hippo (Augustine's city) who apparently lured people into the countryside on the pretext of buying wood, only to beat them and sell them into slavery. Even a worker at Augustine's monastery in Hippo had fallen prey to predatory slave dealers, though he was among the fortunate: Augustine managed to purchase his freedom.[19]

The cost of a slave is hard to determine with precision, since we have relatively few ancient sources that present systematized pricing. Our two most important documents are Emperor Diocletian's "Edict on Maximum Prices," section 29, an imperial law given in 301 CE that fixed a ceiling on prices of numerous goods and services in the (unsuccessful) attempt to arrest inflation; and Justinian's administrative price schedule of 530 CE, found in the *Codex Justinianus* 7.7.1. From these two documents, we may draw a few preliminary conclusions about slave prices in Late Antiquity. First, male slaves were more expensive than female slaves, at least until the sixth century. (Justinian's schedule does not differentiate between the sexes.) Second, skilled slaves fetched far higher prices than unskilled slaves. Third, age was a factor in pricing, and slaves between twenty and forty years of age were the costliest. Eunuchs (castrated male slaves) were also especially expensive, in large part because castration was illegal in the late Roman Empire. A skilled eunuch on Justinian's schedule cost seventy *solidi*. Finally, slaves were cheapest when purchased along the frontiers, where supplies were greater, and more expensive in regions such as Egypt and Italy, which were relatively stable and where demand typically exceeded supply.

One technique that Roman slave owners used to discipline their slaves was to offer cash and other gifts in return for good work and obedience. This property, known as a *peculium* in Latin, legally belonged to the master, who could demand its return at any time. However, most slaves were permitted to keep it and, depending upon its value or form, use their *peculium* to accrue further wealth and perhaps ultimately purchase their freedom. But it is important not to lose sight of the primary function of the *peculium*. It was a disciplinary tool used by slave owners to extract labor. Similarly, slave owners might have held out the promise of manumission so as to motivate their slaves to work harder. To be sure, some slave owners formed deep emotional bonds with their slaves, which inspired them to free the slaves either during their own lives or after they died. But good will and economic interests can coincide: a well-treated, richly rewarded slave was a more obedient and industrious slave.

If the *peculium* and manumission were the carrots in the slave owner's toolbox, then his fists, shackles, and whips were the sticks. We should assume that all slaves in the late Roman Empire were physically disciplined, if not seriously abused, at some point in their lives. Chrysostom's hypothetical story about the Christian mistresses refers to several disciplinary techniques that were undoubtedly all too familiar to his audience: heavy verbal abuse, emotional humiliation (being stripped naked before a man may have felt as demeaning to a slave girl as it did to a freeborn lady), physical beatings, and forced sexual encounters. Today we would call those sexual violations rape, but the Romans did not have a concept of rape when it came to sex with slaves. Remember, what Chrysostom found distasteful was the excessive intensity of the owner's behavior; he posed no objection to the violation of a slave who deserved it.

In Late Antiquity, slaves never rebelled in large numbers, but individual slaves performed small acts of resistance. They deliberately underperformed, and they spread malicious rumors about the sex lives of their masters or perhaps the masters' wives, turning the masters into the dreaded cuckold. Sometimes they stole from their owners, and sometimes they simply ran away. Fugitive slaves were ubiquitous, and the absence of a permanent police force made the recovery of fugitive slaves challenging. Their numbers likely increased during periods of political instability and war, which were increasingly common during the fifth and sixth centuries.

Slave owners used various tactics to deal with the perennial problem of fugitive slaves. The remains of shackles and chains are a stark reminder that humans were literally bonded in Late Antiquity. In a recent study of several villas in Gaul, scholars noted a disturbing number of iron shackles all dating to the third and fourth centuries. We must not assume that such devices were used exclusively for slaves (prisoners, too, were sometimes shackled), but they offer a chilling reminder that brutality sometimes went hand-in-hand with the management of labor. Some masters marked their slaves physically so that in the event of flight, the slaves could be returned to their owners. Until the early fourth century, slaves were sometimes tattooed on their foreheads, the *stigma* or mark a means to distinguish a runaway slave from a free person. In 315–16 CE, the emperor Constantine ruled that this practice was inhumane, and decreed that slaves could be tattooed only on their calves or hands.[20]

Iron slave collars were another means of identifying fugitive slaves. Archaeologists have uncovered some forty-five slave collars, mainly from the western provinces (Italy, Sardinia, North Africa), all of which date to the late Roman period. These collars fit tightly around slaves' necks and were permanently fastened by soldering or riveting. Most carried inscriptions, some etched along the collar itself, others inscribed on a round pendant, or *bulla*, that would have hung between the slave's clavicles, like a modern dog tag. Some inscriptions were simply generic statements, like "Hold me lest I flee" (*TENE ME NE FUGIA[M]*), while other collars were personalized, identifying the slave by name and/or by the name of the owner; some even gave specific directions for return (Figure 3.3).

FIGURE 3.3. An iron slave collar with an inscribed bronze pendant that reads: "I have fled, take me to my master Zoninus and you will receive a *solidus*." Zoninus and his slave, whose name we do not know, apparently lived in Rome during the fourth century.
Photo © 2012 by Fotosar/MIBAC/Sopritendenza Speciale per i Beni Archeologici di Roma.

Slaves, of course, were not thought to possess dignity, for they existed in a realm apart from the code of honor that so tightly structured late Roman thought and behavior. This is why men and women could undress, defecate, and have sex in front of their slaves without feeling the shame of another person's eyes. Slaves typically slept in the same rooms as their masters (and not in separate slave quarters), where their presence went unacknowledged unless their assistance was required. Slaves simply did not count in the high-stakes game of reputation building. To what extent slaves internalized these feelings of irrelevance, passivity, and baseness is impossible to know, since we do not possess a single slave narrative from Late Antiquity. Some probably never questioned their lot in life and looked askance at their fellow slaves who caused trouble. However, even if Andarchius' story is more fiction than truth, it reveals a fear among elites that under the right conditions, a slave might exercise the very same reason and agency as his owner.

HOUSING

Housing in the late Roman Empire varied enormously in terms of size, functionality, decor, and location. In cities, one encountered opulent urban townhouses, replete with private baths and large reception halls, alongside squalid multifamily apartment complexes with no running water and communal cooking facilities. In the countryside, there were enormous, richly decorated villas with peristyle gardens as well as single-room farmhouses shared by humans and animals. There was also a great deal in between these extremes of luxury and impoverishment.

Late Antiquity witnessed something like a housing boom, and there is archaeological evidence for new construction and substantial renovations all over the Empire. In the West, the housing boom took place largely in the late third and early fourth centuries, and typically involved the construction of giant luxury townhouses and rural villas. In the East, the boom occurred somewhat later, toward the end of the fourth century and during the fifth, and involved more middling housing, too. Both housing booms coincided with periods of economic expansion and concentration in the hands of fewer elites, and they ended when the economy contracted and the geopolitical structure of the Empire shifted, first in the West and later in the East.

Urban Housing: From Mansions to Apartment Blocks

If the location where archaeologists discovered their wedding gifts and silver is any indication, the Esquiline Hill in Rome was home to Proiecta and Secundus. Although rich and poor lived side-by-side in Rome, the city had its share of luxury neighborhoods, and the Esquiline was among them. Scholars have identified 116 single-family elite homes in Rome (originally there may have been nearly 1,800). Most of these homes were built in the late third, fourth, and early fifth centuries, typically by renovating, and vastly enlarging, existing buildings. In some cases, large multifamily apartment blocks were bought up and converted into single-family mansions. In other cases, private householders cannibalized preexisting buildings, including public administrative spaces, and their materials (e.g., marble) to expand square footage and beautify their homes.

The houses of the late Roman elite shared many features with earlier homes (e.g., an open-roofed, colonnaded garden inside the house, called a peristyle; indoor and outdoor fountains), but on average they were larger and more ornate. Many had an enormous reception hall accented by an apse, a semicircular recess with a hemispherical dome, or several of them. Apses were not originally used in housing. They more typically appeared in monumental public buildings, such as law courts, in order to accentuate the power of the magistrate who sat within the apse. However, late ancient rich people liked to show off their wealth and status to each other, and so incorporated this hieratic architectural feature into their private homes. Indeed, housing for the wealthy was often about one-upmanship, and hence about out-building or out-decorating your friends. A neighbor of Proiecta and Secundus on the Esquiline, for instance, had a home with an extraordinary reception hall with six apses, and the whole house was built over cisterns used for the still functioning baths of Trajan. The owners of this house did not have their own private baths, but a few urban mansions in Rome and elsewhere did, such as the "House of the Hunt" and the "House of Amphitrite," both in Bulla Regia (modern Tunisia). Most urban townhouses also had specialized dining rooms, typically accented with apses and mosaics. In Apollonia (modern Libya), the "Palace of the Dux" featured a tri-apse dining room, an architectural form for a dining area that was fairly

FIGURE 3.4. Archaeological remains of a *stibadium*, or semicircular dining couch, from the Villa di Faragola in Foggia (Italy). The *stibadium* dates to the fifth or sixth century.
Photo by Giuliano Volpe and Maria Turchiano, with permission from the Sopritendenza Archeologia, Belle Arti e Paesaggio di Barletta-Andria-Trani e di Foggia.

FIGURE 3.5. A modern reconstruction of the *stibadium* and dining area at the Villa di Faragola in Foggia (Italy).
Photo and reconstruction by Giuliano Volpe and Maria Turchiano, with permission from the Soprintendenza Archeologia, Belle Arti e Paesaggio di Barletta-Andria-Trani e di Foggia.

common throughout the Empire. In a handful of cases, the remains of dining furniture show that late Romans liked to eat in a reclining position on three-sided or semicircular couches called *stibadia*. The couches, typically made of wood (and hence movable), were sometimes placed on raised platforms around a semicircular table, meaning that diners ate on what must have looked and felt like a stage (Figures 3.4 and 3.5).

Needless to say, most city dwellers did not live in mansions with apsidal entrance halls, semicircular dining tables, and private baths. Rather, they lived in multifamily apartment blocks called *insulae*, where they rented one or more rooms. Typically, an *insula* was home to several different households, which shared cooking facilities in a central courtyard, and very occasionally had joint access to water. While the poorest families would have crammed themselves into single-room units, middling households likely lived in multi-room apartments. For instance, in Utica (modern Tunisia), an *insula* built around a thirteen-meter-long corridor had a single locked doorway to the street outside, suggesting there was one owner for the entire building. On the street side of the *insula*, there were three ground-floor shops, the largest of which connected to a spacious unit with four rooms, and there was a second three-room apartment in the rear. A wellhead for a cistern suggests that the building's residents had access to water. Here we can imagine two families, perhaps related, living in the *insula*, with additional persons residing in the two smaller shops. In fact, many craftsmen and merchants lived in their storefronts, that is, in the same rooms in which they worked and traded. In Sardis, we recall from Chapter 2, archaeological remains suggest that the second floor of the shops along Marble Road was dedicated to residential use, with each apartment perhaps inhabited by the merchant or craftsman working below.

Rural Housing: Western versus Eastern Empire

Like all mega-wealthy landowners, Sidonius Apollinaris almost certainly possessed a city home, and at one point in his career resided in Rome. But he focused his energies on his rural Gallic estates, where

he lived in grand style as a country gentleman and bishop. The same
housing boom that produced the stunning townhouse with the hex-
agonal apsidal hall in Rome generated a range of newly renovated
country homes in Gaul and elsewhere. Within the context of the
countryside, however, we find more pronounced differences in housing choices between eastern and western residents. As noted in the
discussion of Flavius Strategius Apion II in Chapter 1, wealthy landowners in the East preferred to live primarily in cities, and visited their
country estates intermittently. Consequently, they did not build large,
sumptuous villas, because they spent most of their time in urban
townhouses in cities like Constantinople, Alexandria, and Antioch.
Alternatively, in the West, landowners invested much of their sizeable
wealth in renovating older farmhouses and transforming them into
elaborate, multi-building villas. In them, landowners like Sidonius and
Pudens could accommodate a larger household and provide for all of
their personal needs as men of culture and leisure. Multiple bedrooms offered rest and relaxation; heated baths aided health, exercise, and grooming; libraries provided books and study; colonnaded
peristyles gave bright sunny spaces in which to calmly contemplate;
and giant, ornate reception halls were available to entertain and
impress guests.

Perhaps the most famous late Roman villa that is still visible today
is the Villa Romana del Casale at Piazza Armerina in Sicily. Built in
phases during the first quarter of the fourth century, this single-story
villa features a large central peristyle, several enormous apsidal halls
and corridors, as many as two dining rooms, multiple bedrooms and
storage areas, latrines, and a small heated bath complex (Figure 3.6).
A visitor would have been struck not only by the size of the villa, but
also by its ornate decorative features: multiple apses accented the
halls, corridors, and even latrines, while polychrome mosaic floors
featuring geometric patterns and figurative scenes covered most of
the rooms. One reception space, for instance, had three apses and
opened onto a long corridor with a detailed hunting scene laid in
mosaic on the floor (Figure 3.7). In many ways, the sprawling villa
at Piazza Armerina epitomizes the grandeur of late ancient rural
housing, and similar (if not smaller) houses were constructed all over
the western Empire.[21]

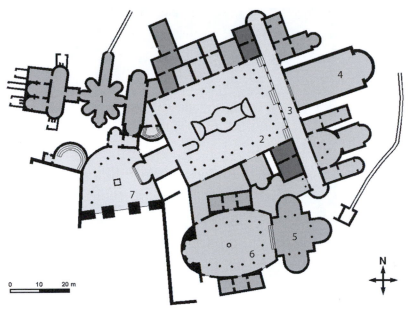

FIGURE 3.6. A plan of the Villa Romana del Casale in Piazza Armerina, Sicily, built in the late third or early fourth century. (1) Bath complex, with *frigidarium* (cold pool) and *calidarium* (hot pool). (2) An open-air peristyle, surrounded by colonnades. (3) Hall of the Great Hunt. (4) Apsidal audience hall. (5) *Triclinium*, or dining room. (6) A second, oval-shaped peristyle. (7) Main courtyard entrance to the house. Plan drawn by Bernhard J. Scheuvens (Creative Commons license), with key provided by the author.

There were variations in rural villa types that heralded new trends in elite residential building. For example, the villa at San Giovanni di Ruoti, the southern Italian pig farm we encountered in Chapter 1, was built in phases during the fourth and fifth centuries, and thus reflects construction dating a century later than the villa at Piazza Armerina. While the villa at Piazza Armerina had a broad, axial layout with a central peristyle (classical features of a Roman house), the villa at San Giovanni di Ruoti is more compact, with narrower corridors, a possible second story, and a tower at the northeast corner – an architectural element that came to emblematize early medieval elite housing. Nevertheless, the villa at San Giovanni di Ruoti had elements that would have marked its owners

FIGURE 3.7. Polychrome mosaics along the floor of the Hall of the Great Hunt, so named for the images' main theme, inside the Villa Romana del Casale in Piazza Armerina, Sicily.
Photo by Rafi Hodges.

as cultured, wealthy landowners. These include an apsidal reception hall and a small bath complex.

Significantly, the wealthy did not use their country estates exclusively for leisure. Along with the lavish rooms inhabited by the owner and his family, called the *pars urbana*, or "urban part," since city living was associated with sophistication, villas like San Giovanni di Ruoti had areas that were used for work, production, and storage. The *pars rustica*, as these areas were collectively known, was hardly an afterthought. It included rooms or, in most cases, separate buildings where various industrial activities took place, such as ceramic and brick production, bread making, glassblowing, grape and olive pressing, or, in the case of San Giovanni di Ruoti, pork processing.

The architecture and quality of non-elite rural housing ranged enormously, from masonry buildings with tiled roofs and sculpted lintels to what were essentially earthen shacks. The latter type of residence is notoriously difficult to identify in the archaeological record, because it was built largely of organic materials like wood and mud bricks, which decompose quickly. In the West, housing for non-elites tended to cluster together around the estates of wealthy landlords, suggesting that they lived in a more dependent relationship with the elites as renters. Most of these peasant dwellings were one- or two-room abodes made of wood and/or mud bricks with thatched roofs. In many homes, farm animals lived with their owners. Of course, some western peasants possessed their own land, and in places such as North Africa, they were prosperous enough to purchase roof tiles.

In the East, we have considerable evidence of more substantial non-elite housing. In the Syrian Limestone Massif, a fertile region to the north of Antioch (now known as the Aleppo Plateau), archaeologists have uncovered the remains of more than seven hundred rural settlements, what are known today as the Dead Cities. Most of the houses in the Dead Cities were constructed between 350 and 550 CE. They typically had two floors, with two or three rooms on the ground level and a courtyard, which usually abutted a neighbor's yard. Families who lived in these homes likely slept on the top floor, and used the ground level and courtyard for working (olive presses have been found in some areas), cooking, and stabling animals. It is clear that some of the residents invested their money in home-improvement projects, for many have decorative features such as carved moldings, relief sculpture, and colonnades. These Syrian peasant homes were not cheap investments. An inscription states that one of the more substantial houses in Methane (modern Imtan in southern Syria) was built in 486 CE for forty *solidi*, and took a team of workers three hundred to four hundred days to construct (Figure 3.8).

Furnishings and Home Decoration

By today's standards, late ancient homes were sparsely furnished, but many had some form of decoration. A piece of high-quality pottery

FIGURE 3.8. Serjilla, one of the Dead Cities of Syria, reached its acme of development in the fifth and sixth centuries.
Photo by Julian Love Photography, Alamy stock photos.

imported from North Africa, for example, could have accented a humble home in Marseilles or Antioch in much the same way (though on a far smaller scale) as an elaborate mosaic or piece of furniture in a grand mansion. Nevertheless, our evidence for home decorating is heavily weighted toward the wealthy end of the spectrum. The most durable form of decoration was the mosaic, a sort of miniature brick-work created from thousands of small pieces of colored marble or stone called *tesserae*. Domestic mosaics from villas and urban town-houses reveal an extensive and relatively homogenous taste for color and images within the home. Rich late Romans, regardless of whether they were pagan, Christian, or Jewish, liked to decorate their walls and floors with mythological figures (Dionysius was especially popu-lar in dining rooms), astrological signs, geometric patterns, and self-referential inscriptions. They also liked large visual scenes featuring their favorite pastimes, such as dining, hunting, and chariot racing (see Figures 3.7 and 6.2). Less durable but no less colorful were the tapestries, curtains, and screens that adorned elite homes. In many cases, rooms were enclosed not by doors, but by curtains and screens.

FIGURE 3.9. The "Hestia Tapestry" was almost certainly created for and used within a domestic setting, and is a product of sixth-century Egypt. It features the image of a female figure identified in Greek as Hestia Polyolbos, or "Hestia full of blessings," a distinctly pagan motif decorating what was likely a Christian household.
Photo © Dumbarton Oaks, Byzantine Collection, Washington, DC.

Very few of these items remain, but the extant fragments of hangings suggest that they could have been extraordinary (Figure 3.9).

Chairs, wooden tables, and lockable cupboards for storing household objects existed in most homes, but the number and quality of such items depended entirely on wealth. Secundus, we recall, was the owner of elaborate sculpted silver furniture fittings, each representing the guardian spirit of the Empire's four major Christian cities (Rome, Constantinople, Jerusalem, and Antioch; see Figure 3.1b). These fittings presumably decorated a wooden chair, which was surely on permanent display and perhaps even used by Secundus when he greeted his clients. It is unclear whether the couple's silver was regularly displayed in the home or only brought out on occasion to impress guests. Given the value of such objects, their owners probably locked them away for safekeeping most of the time.

Changing Domestic Space: The End of the Housing Boom

The housing boom, experienced at virtually all levels of late Roman society, gradually came to an end during Late Antiquity. In the West, the boom was largely over by the late fourth century, while in the East, housing construction remained robust into the sixth century. What follows is a general description, meant to convey a trend that first hit the West and later the East.

In the western countryside, the great monumental villas typically suffered one of two fates: they either were abandoned entirely or were repurposed to accommodate residents with different lifestyles and interests. In many cases we find various signs of industrial work in what were once grand reception halls and dining areas. For example, in a formerly sumptuous Spanish villa (Torre Llauder in Iluro, modern Mataró), eighteen *dolia* (storage tanks) were set into a mosaic floor, with additional tanks built within what had been the central peristyle. The mosaics are still visible, despite the obvious change in the room's function (Figure 3.10). Similarly, parts of a villa in northern Italy (Calderara di Reno in Bologna) were converted into a glass

FIGURE 3.10. Floor mosaic with cut-in *dolia* (large ceramic vats) inside the former late Roman villa of Torre Llauder (near Barcelona, Spain). The villa's mosaics date to the third century, while the *dolia* were added in the fifth century, when the villa was partially abandoned and some rooms were made to serve more strictly industrial uses.
Photo by Kimberly Bowes.

factory. On other western rural estates, archaeology tells us that churches were established and/or burials dug within the walls of former houses. In eastern rural areas, there were few expansive villas to abandon or divide, but the more middling housing for the villagers of the Syrian plateau show signs of progressive deterioration and abandonment during the seventh century.

Urban housing followed a similar pattern of change. In Brixia, sixth-century residents of what had been a substantial house (itself the product of an early fourth-century renovation project) drilled into the sumptuous mosaic flooring to install posts and build new wooden roofed structures within the former peristyle. Garbage was now thrown into unused rooms. Again, the history of housing in the East follows the same trajectory at a later date. In Ephesus, for instance, the glamorous homes along the city's two main colonnaded streets were well maintained through the early seventh century, when the entire city suffered substantial damage from an earthquake and invasions.

Although scholars used to interpret these changes as evidence of total decline and depopulation, they now believe that the repurposed villas and urban homes demonstrate the continued vitality of everyday life and new forms of economic activity, albeit at a contracted level.[22] Evidence shows that people still lived in many of these houses (including those with graves), even if they inhabited smaller, partitioned rooms and poorly constructed wooden structures. In fact, in some regions, a switch to more insulating organic building materials and a movement away from stone and brick may have occurred in response to cooling temperatures during what scholars call the Late Antique Little Ice Age. What does appear to have changed was how status was determined: industriousness and labor seem to have become more significant in measuring social position and wealth than expensive decorations.

DOMESTIC ACTIVITIES

People in Late Antiquity used their houses for all sorts of activities, many of which were related to the larger economy. In fact, we have already learned a great deal about domestic activities in the countryside from Chapter 1, which examined agricultural production and other forms of industry. Here we will briefly explore some of the activities that took place within the house that directly involved the care and maintenance of the household, such as cooking, cleaning, and sleeping. Readers should also keep in mind that the house was a space of regular religious practice. Chapter 6, on religion and daily life, explores the important topic of domestic piety.

Eating and Cooking

As emphasized throughout this book, how one experienced daily life in Late Antiquity was largely determined by socioeconomic status. This dictum especially holds true for cooking and dining. What people ate varied across social strata more in terms of available quantity and quality than in terms of types of foods consumed. As we saw in Chapter 1, grains were the primary ingredients in meals, and they provided 75 percent of the daily calories. A typical breakfast for late Romans, for instance, consisted of bread dipped in oil or wine. A wealthier person would consume finer-quality bread with good-quality wine, while a poorer person or slave would eat lower-quality bread with *posca*, soured wine. At the second daily meal (*prandia* in Latin, *ariston* in Greek), which happened mid-morning (late Romans typically awoke at dawn), most ate cold food: sausages, cheese, eggs, fruit, nuts, and more bread, with olive oil for dipping. The largest meal of the day, *cena* or *deipnon* ("dinner"), was eaten in the early afternoon, starting at around three o'clock. Dinner might be a lavish affair with multiple courses or a simple repast, but it normally involved warm cooked foods. Households consumed porridges and legume-based pulses that were seasoned with oil, spices (pepper was an especially popular flavoring), salt and occasionally with other flavorings, such as onions, leeks, or garlic. At this meal, Romans especially enjoyed heavy soups and stews, often milk-based, with meats, legumes, and vegetables. Depending upon availability, fish might be on the menu, seasoned with salt, oil, and *garum* (also known as *liquamen*), a fermented fish sauce that was something like the ancient equivalent of ketchup in terms of its popularity. Readers interested in cooking can examine late Roman recipe collections handed down to us under the name of a first-century gourmand, Apicius.[23]

There was such a thing as dessert in Late Antiquity (called *secundae mensae*), though it typically meant fruit and nuts. On special occasions, a household might serve fresh fruit with a sweet syrupy sauce called *sapa* or *defructum*. Cooks prepared *sapa* by boiling down unfermented grape juice in a lead vessel. Unaware of lead's poisonous properties, late Romans enjoyed the metallic taste that the lead brought to the grape syrup, which they liberally poured over their fruits and cakes.

Sleeping, Bathing, and Human Waste Disposal

Sleep is a necessary part of everyday life for all humans across time and space, but it is also a cultural practice, meaning that sleeping habits are not universal. In Late Antiquity, people awoke at dawn or before, regardless of whether they lived in the city or countryside, or were rich or poor. There was nothing in the bedroom to keep them there, for these were often simple chamber-like rooms, with a small single bed and perhaps a chest. Bedrooms were never personalized or decorated in an age-appropriate manner; in fact, it is often hard to distinguish in archaeological remains between a bedroom and a storage closet. Moreover, people who could afford larger homes typically alternated where they slept, depending on the season and climate. Of course, people who lived in one or two rooms slept wherever there was space, likely on a floor mat made of reeds or grass. Beds were largely for the rich. The bed itself was a wooden frame held together by strips of webbing, which supported a relatively thin mattress. Late Romans used bolster-like pillows to rest their heads. The pillows of the wealthy were stuffed with wool, and were considerably softer than the cheaper versions filled with straw or reeds. Shutters would have kept out light and drafts, and some luxury Roman houses even had central heating, which rose up through a hypocaust system beneath the floor. But no one had fireplaces in their rooms, and in the winter months a blanket was all most people had to keep warm (see Figure 2.7 for a floor heating system).

Most people went to sleep soon after nightfall (remember, dinner usually started at three o'clock in the afternoon). However, lighting, typically either oil lamps or tallow candles, allowed people to stay up later. Of course, the lighting from oil lamps was dim by modern standards, and the smoke these lamps emitted would have further darkened the room. People who did manual labor undoubtedly welcomed the rest and slept through the night, but elites prided themselves on their lucubrations, that is, late-night work on literary

FIGURE 3.11. A ceramic oil lamp from Cyprus dating to the fifth century. This sort of lamp was ubiquitous in Late Antiquity.
Photo by the Metropolitan Museum of Art (Creative Commons license).

endeavors. As we will see in Chapter 6, monks were often required to awaken several times during the night to worship (Figure 3.11).

Most late Romans did not bathe in their homes. Among those who did, the vast majority washed in water from small basins or buckets. Most urban and rural homes did not have running water, and so water had to be carried in several times a day. Given the labor-intensive nature of water use in the average home, all but the richest would have seen body washing as a wasteful activity. However, this is not to suggest that late Romans did not bathe at all. Many regularly visited public bathing facilities with heated pools, especially in towns and cities. These baths were easily accessible, relatively inexpensive, and well maintained, as we saw in Chapter 2. Similarly, few Roman houses had latrines. Generally speaking, at home, human waste went first into a chamber pot and then was either dumped out or reused as fertilizer (excrement) or as a treatment for textile processing (urine for cleaning wool).

Domestic Work and Leisure

Someone, of course, had to collect this waste and wash out the chamber pots. In a time before automatic dishwashers and washing machines, electric ovens and food processors, electric heating, vacuum cleaners, disposable sponges, flush toilets, and readymade cleaning solutions, taking care of a house was a dirty, laborious, and time-consuming endeavor. Whenever possible, late antique Romans delegated these highly undesirable tasks to slaves. Unskilled domestic slaves spent much of their day cleaning pots and pans, washing linens, moving furniture, preparing food, chopping and hauling wood, and, most important, carrying water to and around their master's home. The fact that relatively few houses had running water and all depended on wood-burning stoves meant that slaves had to transport clean water into the house every day, along with cords of firewood. Of course, many poorer families had a single slave or no slave at all, which meant that children and other household members were expected to help regularly with these backbreaking chores.

Elite masters and mistresses who did not perform manual labor still "worked" inside the home, though for them work was closely intertwined with leisure. For centuries, weaving, spinning, and other textile work had been viewed as the quintessential labor of the virtuous Greco-Roman woman. Material evidence of loom weights and spinning needles confirm this image: matrons and their daughters spent part of their day doing needlework and weaving. In most cases, their handiwork would have been enjoyed or worn solely by the family, but we should not discount the possibility that some of it was sold. For the gentleman, there was no direct counterpart to weaving as a suitable household activity, but rich male householders kept busy through literary study (reading and/or listening to their friends read their compositions aloud) and writing letters. If the letter collections of Q. Aurelius Symmachus are representative of epistolary activity, the average senatorial householder spent hours each day corresponding with friends, clients, patrons, estate managers, and tenants. These gentlemen also enjoyed hunting expeditions on their properties, along with board and dice games. According to Sidonius Apollinaris, the Visigoth king Theoderic II (r. 453–466 CE) was far likelier to grant a petition to a visitor if he had just beaten him in a game of dice.[24] As this anecdote shows, business was often mixed with pleasure in elite homes. It was customary for clients to approach patrons with requests and information (often for legal advocacy) in the early morning hours. We should imagine Secundus seated in his ornate silver-accented chair and greeting his clients and other business acquaintances with an air of authority and entitlement. Or at least this is how he may have wished to appear.

***

The household was the center of late Roman social and economic life. It was never experienced as a "refuge" from public life, since elites and non-elites alike used their homes for an enormous range of activities, from sleeping and dining to business negotiation and industrial production. Although the household was legally a form of private property owned and/or overseen by an individual, it was hardly disconnected from the world of the Roman government. Moving into the next chapter, we shall examine many ways in which the state was part of daily life in Late Antiquity.

Further Reading

Augustine, *Letter* 10*, trans. R. Eno, *Letters*, Vol. 6 (*1–*29), *Fathers of the Church*, Vol. 81 (Washington, DC, 1989).

Cassiodorus, *Variae*, trans. S. Barnish (Liverpool, 1992).

The Codex of Justinian: A New Annotated Translation, 3 vols., trans. F. Blume (Cambridge, 2016).

John Chrysostom, *Homily 15 on Ephesians*, full translation in *The Nicene and Post-Nicene Fathers*, vol. 13, available online: www.newadvent.org/fathers/230115.htm.

Gregory the Great, *Letter* 11.56a, also known as the *Libellus responsionum*, is most easily accessed in English through translations of Bede, *History of the English People* 1.27.

Gregory of Tours, *Ten Books of History*, trans. L. Thorpe as *The History of The Franks* (London, 1974).

Sidonius Apollinaris, *Poems and Letters*, 2 vols., trans. W. Anderson (LCL, Cambridge, MA, 1965).

The Theodosian Code, trans. C. Pharr (Princeton, NJ, 1952).

There are numerous excellent studies on the late Roman household as a social institution. See, for example, K. Harper, "Marriage and Family in Late Antiquity," in *The Oxford Handbook of Late Antiquity*, ed. S. Johnson (Oxford, 2012), 667–714, G. Nathan, *The Family in Late Antiquity* (London, 2000), and G. Clark, *Women in Late Antiquity: Pagan and Christian Lifestyles* (Oxford, 1993). On the history of late ancient childhood, see J. Evans Grubbs et al. (eds.), *The Oxford Handbook of Childhood and Education in the Classical World* (Oxford, 2013), and M. Harlow and R. Laurence (eds.), *A Cultural History of Childhood and Family in Antiquity*. Vol. 1 (Oxford, 2010). For slavery, see K. Harper, *Slavery in the Late Roman World, AD 275–425* (Cambridge, 2011) and K. Bradley and P. Cartledge (eds.), *The Cambridge World History of Slavery*, Vol. 1: *The Ancient Mediterranean World* (Cambridge, 2011).

For the archaeology of late ancient domestic space, see L. Lavan et al. (eds.), *Housing in Late Antiquity* (Brill, 2007) and K. Bowes, *Houses and Society in the Later Roman Empire* (London, 2010).

4

The State in Everyday Life

Flavius Abinnaeus joined the army in 304 or 305 CE. He was probably around eighteen years old at the time, the minimum age for new recruits. He began his career as a member of a mounted unit called the Parthian Archers (*Parthosagittarii*). Their name likely originated with the unit's founding in the East, when it was composed largely of Persian men from the former Parthian Empire. When Abinnaeus signed on in the early fourth century, however, the unit was made up of Romans and stationed in Egypt, a critical economic region. After serving with the Parthian Archers for thirty-three years, Abinnaeus retired from the unit. Because of his excellent service, he was then promoted to the office of commander (*praefectus*). Until his retirement in ca. 351 CE, Abinnaeus commanded a garrison unit stationed at Dionysias (modern Qasr Qarun), an Egyptian city located in the Fayoum oasis.

Life for Abinnaeus at Dionysias was busy and complex. The garrison was located far from the active frontiers, so the unit's main military role was to protect the region from brigands and suppress smuggling, especially the sort that undermined the Roman state's grain interests. Yet, much of Abinnaeus' time was devoted to more mundane administrative demands. He expended considerable effort insuring that his garrison was supplied with food and other goods, and was known to intervene if a requisition was not quickly filled. He labored, too, over personnel decisions, such as whether to grant an indefinite leave for one soldier or excuse a potential recruit from service because his mother was a widow and relied on the boy for her livelihood. He was also responsible for helping local veterans with private matters, such as when the honorably discharged Priscus and his wife, Alia, were the victims of a home invasion. Sometimes Abinnaeus was called on to provide muscle for local tax collecting or resolve legal disputes between soldiers and civilians. And if commanding a garrison of several hundred troops was not burdensome enough, Abinnaeus was married, living in Dionysias with his wife, Aurelia Nonna, several children, and a household of eight additional members. Because he and his wife were both property owners, the commander's attention was frequently drawn to managing their personal affairs, including her messy relationship with her siblings, who fought over an inheritance.

Abinnaeus' career and his daily experiences as a garrison commander in Egypt are known to us because he kept meticulous records of his official activities – records that are still extant, thanks to the same dry climate that preserved the personal archives of Aurelius Sakaon and the Apion family explored in Chapter 1.[1] What is arguably most striking about the Abinnaeus archive is the extent to which it reveals regular interactions between the Dionysias garrison and civilians in the neighboring villages. We find similar levels of interaction between the army and civilian life elsewhere, from the military sieges that imprisoned urbanites for months to the quartering of soldiers in the homes of peasant freeholders. And if we widen our lens to consider other government activities, such as tax assessment and collection, the provisioning of food to citizens in the largest cities, the meting out of justice in courts, and the management of roadways, we find an even broader basis for seeing the role of the state in the lives of ordinary late Romans.

In some ancient societies, the state was a distant entity, an institution that had little impact on the daily lives of men and women outside elite society or the army. This was not the case with the late Roman Empire, however. Its civil government and military directly touched – we might even say intruded into – many aspects of everyday life.

ARMY AND WARFARE

Before turning to some of the details provided by the Abinnaeus archive and other late ancient sources on the military and daily life, a brief introduction to the size and structure of the late Roman army is needed.

Organization of the Late Roman Army: A Brief Synopsis

The late Roman Empire supported a large and well-organized standing army, which received pay and other benefits for service. The size of the late antique army at its largest was between five hundred thousand and six hundred thousand men. The figure drops perhaps as much as one half, to about three hundred thousand troops, after the fifth century, when many western regions of the Empire ceased to be directly governed by the Roman state. This means that until the fifth century, more than 1 percent of the Empire's total population was soldiers – a figure all the more impressive, considering it represents only men between the ages of eighteen and forty-five.[2] Soldiers joined one of three main divisions: the emperor's bodyguard (*schola palatina*), stationed in the imperial capitals; the mobile field armies (*comitatenses*), which originally accompanied the emperor into battle and were assigned to particular regions; and the non-mobile armies (*limitanei*), which were stationed along the major frontiers (e.g., the Rhine and Danube Rivers) and in Egypt. Readers familiar with the early imperial army will not recognize these terms or divisions, because they were inventions of two late antique emperors, Diocletian (r. 284–305 CE) and Constantine (r. 312–337 CE).

The commander in charge of a particular field army was called a *magister militum*, while the leader of frontier forces within a particular region was called a *dux*. In the East there were five field commanders, but in the West only one. These generals also had their own private bodyguards, known as *bucellarii*, or "biscuit men," a name given to them from the hardtack issued to soldiers. The size of the individual combat unit in Late Antiquity was also different from earlier times. While the early imperial army had legions of approximately fifty-two hundred men, the late Roman army was built around a larger number of smaller units, perhaps with as few as a thousand troops in each.

The early imperial Roman army also included units of entirely non-Roman troops, such as the Parthian Archers. Originally, foreign contingents were annexed to the army through treaties, and they fought on behalf of Rome while being led by their own commanders. Over time, the constitution of non-Roman or federate units became increasingly heterogeneous, as men from many different backgrounds, including Romans, joined them. By Late Antiquity, federate units were not necessarily composed entirely or even mainly of non-Romans, though they could be. What made these federate units different from the three others described was the fact that they were not part of a permanent standing army, but were called up on an ad hoc basis.

Over time, the late Roman state increasingly relied on federate troops, and distinctions between them and other types of units became less clear. Barbarian soldiers often rose to the ranks and became leading officers; some even attained the top post, *magister militum*. Ricimer, for instance, was of barbarian heritage and commanded the western army as its sole *magister militum* from 456 to 472 CE. Occasionally, hostile armies formed within the Roman Empire and marched through the countryside besieging Roman cities, with the intent of obtaining gold and human prisoners. In 378 CE, for instance, an army of Goths who had been settled in Thrace defeated the Roman army at Adrianople and killed Emperor Valens (r. 364–378 CE). Later, the Goth Alaric, who had risen through the ranks of the Roman military, led a federate army westward to Rome, which he besieged for nearly two years before sacking the city on August 24, 410 CE. However, while popular history likes to highlight these barbarian victories over Rome and their alleged role in the Empire's "fall," scholars have shown that they were few in number. Most of the time, barbarians were welcomed and essential members of the late Roman army who fought for Rome, not against it.

Recruitment and Pay

In the early sixth century, a teenage boy from Hermopolis (Egypt) named Heracleon joined the local army unit. According to the document recording his enrollment, Heracleon came from a military family, did not belong to an excluded citizen rank, and was able-bodied.[3] This single papyrus sheet preserves traces of a common phenomenon in Late Antiquity: the recruitment of young men into the army. In order to qualify for service, boys had to be at least eighteen years old and meet a minimum height requirement (five-foot-seven in Roman feet, which is approximately equivalent to five-foot-five, or 1.65 meters, in modern standard measurements). And as Heracleon's record shows, certain groups with heavy civil obligations were exempt from military duty, such as those of the curial class and members of the colonate. Generally speaking, slaves could not enlist, nor under any circumstances could women. And in addition to being relatively strong (or, as Heracleon's papers put it, "not of weak physique"), the recruit's body could not be maimed or disfigured in any extreme manner.

What Heracleon's enrollment papers do not tell us, however, is whether the boy actually wanted to serve. This is because the consent of the recruit was never a requirement for enlistment. While some men clearly enrolled voluntarily, others were forced into the army, whether through heritage (sons of soldiers were inscribed on the registers of their fathers' units for future service, as Heracleon likely had been) or through the pressure of a patron or landlord. In fact, the state obligated cities and landowners to furnish recruits, and they could comply with bodies or with cash. An individual or municipality could substitute a tax payment, called the *aurum tironicum* ("recruit's gold"), for an actual person if that person's labor was deemed more needed on the farm or in the factory than in the army. But not everyone went willingly. Stories abound in Late Antiquity about the press-ganging of citizens. While forced enrollment was something of an urban legend, it was an experience grounded in reality. The Abinnaeus archive, for example, records the difficulties faced by one civil administrator who, for three days, could not get a single resident of the village of Karanis to volunteer. Finally, the villagers gave him cash in lieu of men, but we can easily imagine other scenarios where the village or landlord could not pay up.[4] Some citizens attempted to avoid enrollment through self-mutilation, while others resorted to emotional and economic pleas. Abinnaeus once received a letter asking that the only son of a widow be spared military service on the grounds that his departure would cause the widow's ruin.[5] It is unclear if the petition was successful, but it suggests that a recruit's personal situation might be taken into consideration. Desertion was also a

steady problem, and deserters faced stiff penalties. One deserter from
Dionysias named Paul tried to obviate punishment by asking a local
Christian cleric to beg Abinnaeus' forgiveness; whether the com-
mander acquiesced is unknown.

Of course, many men willingly joined and profited from army life.
While the residents of Karantis wanted to avoid military service at
all costs, those in Syene (modern Aswan) in southern Egypt flocked
to the army in such large numbers that there were waiting lists for
admission. The biggest draw was the regular pay and the opportunity
to acquire significant financial rewards as a veteran. Soldiers received
money from two different sources: cash grants and donatives (at set
intervals or to celebrate the emperor's birthday), and regular salaries,
which for cavalry units included fodder for their horses. Rates of pay
varied from region to region, but they ranged in general from four to
five *solidi* a year (for a simple soldier) to twenty to twenty-five *solidi* (for
officers), with up to eight *solidi* provided to cavalry troops for fodder.
To put these salaries into perspective, a peasant laborer in Egypt made
about six *solidi* a year.

The relatively low pay for noncommissioned soldiers meant that
many had to work additional jobs to make ends meet, especially if
they had family members to support. War booty was theoretically
distributed equally among the soldiers, but officers controlled the
process and hence the shares. Plundering, though discouraged, was
a constant facet of late ancient warfare, since it provided yet another
source of income for soldiers. Even garrisoned soldiers in peaceful
areas exploited their power over civilians to reap financial benefits.
A village leader wrote an angry missive to Abinnaeus, in which he
complained about the "many outrages committed in the village" by
Abinnaeus' men.[6] In addition to looting a house where residents had
stored their valuables for safekeeping, the soldiers drove off their
cattle, and then retreated to the garrison with the booty. The leader
threatened to take the case to the regional military commander if
Abinnaeus did not send the guilty soldiers back to the village for
questioning.

Upon finishing his career, a veteran could expect a handsome
payout and other financial privileges. After twenty years of field
service or twenty-four years guarding the frontier (the obligatory
terms for a full and honorable discharge[7]), a soldier would receive

retirement benefits, which included a bonus and numerous tax exemptions. Other rewards included a gift from the state as a start-up grant or, for the soldier interested in farming, an allotment of land, two oxen, a hundred *modii* of seed corn, and cash for initial expenses.[8] Veterans, however, were also sometimes asked to work for the state after initial retirement. Abinnaeus, for instance, became a garrison commander after thirty-three years in service, though it was an appointment from which he obviously benefited.

Soldiers, Marriage, and Family Life

Abinnaeus, we noted, was married to a woman named Aurelia Nonna. We know that they had at least three children, since Nonna possessed *ius liberorum*, a legal right granted to women who had given birth to three or more children that exempted them from mandated legal guardianship. Nonna was clearly a woman of some substance, owning properties in both Alexandria and the Fayoum. She and Abinnaeus together managed a large household, which included at least eight additional people. Abinnaeus' busy domestic life was, in many ways, usual for a military man. During the early Roman Empire, soldiers were prohibited from marrying. However, the emperor Septimius Severus (r. 193–211 CE) lifted this ban, permitting soldiers to wed legally for the first time. This does not mean, of course, that all soldiers in the late Roman army were married men with families.

Married field troops (*comitatenses*) typically left their wives back home when sent on campaign. The prolonged separation was undoubtedly difficult for many couples. The poor state of communications made it hard for wives to acquire information about their husbands' safety, or even death. Wives could spend years wondering: Is he still alive? When will he return? Should I assume he's dead and remarry? In fact, Roman law dealt expressly with the problem of marriages that had been severed due to soldiers' disappearance in combat. Wives had to wait at least four years before they could assume their husbands were dead and remarry. The emperor Justinian (r. 527–565 CE) extended the waiting period to ten years, and required wives to get a signed affidavit from their husband's commanding officer confirming his death. And for those wives awaiting the return of a spouse, late Roman lore offers disturbing images of immoral soldier-husbands taking advantage of the distance to have extramarital relationships. A fifth-century saint's life featuring a young Christian girl named Euphemia, for instance, portrays her marrying a Gothic soldier billeted in her mother's home. The tale of love at first sight quickly turned tragic, however, when Euphemia traveled with the soldier to his homeland, only to discover that he was already married and intended Euphemia to serve as his slave. In real life, soldiers on prolonged campaigns were just as likely to desert as to become bigamists, especially if they believed that their families were in danger. In Italy during the Gothic War (535–554 CE), Roman units recruited from Illyricum suddenly abandoned a siege to rush home after learning that the Huns had attacked their towns and enslaved their women and children.[9]

Occasionally, wives accompanied their husbands into the field. According to the biographer of the Christian holy man Sabbas, the saint's mother accompanied his father to his post in Alexandria, leaving their small son with relatives back in Cappadocia.[10] There were obvious dangers in this choice. One soldier from Constantinople who had taken his wife and two children on campaign to Italy during the Gothic War found them captured by the Goths after his unit retook Rome. To be sure, accompanying one's husband to a post in Alexandria was hardly as dangerous as traveling on campaign during active warfare. Nevertheless, we should probably assume that most field soldiers, married or not, carried out their service without their families in tow.

Alternatively, garrisoned troops may have lived with their spouses and families in nearby settlements, in some cases owning local property. We do not know precisely where Abinnaeus and Nonna lived with their bustling household, but the family clearly owned property throughout Egypt. As the Abinnaeus archive shows, marriage and family life complicated military command, but they were hardly incompatible with it.

Military Housing: Forts and Billeting

Most soldiers, we noted, lived as singles, whether in temporary camps, purpose-built fortresses, or the homes of civilians via billeting. Diocletian and subsequent fourth-century emperors constructed forts and fortifications along the Empire's frontiers (e.g., the Danube and the

Rhine or just west of the Tigris and Euphrates along the Persian border) and in other strategic locations, including Egypt. Unlike early imperial fortresses, which were highly standardized in terms of size and design, late Roman fortresses came in various forms (circular, square, rectangular) and were often architecturally distinct. But they shared certain features, namely enormous exterior walls (on average seven to eight meters high and three to four meters thick) and multiple towers. Towers became increasingly important in Late Antiquity as a means to survey the surrounding area in case enemies attempted to scale the walls and as a vantage point for launching projectiles. The fortress that Abinnaeus commanded at Dionysius, for example, centered around a square-shaped fort and had several towers, along with imposing walls measuring seven meters high and three meters thick. Another structure stood nearby containing fifty-two small rooms (possibly barracks) as well as a large apsidal hall flanked by two small rooms, likely spaces where Abinnaeus undertook his administrative duties. Late ancient fortresses tended to be smaller than early imperial models (with the smallest referred to as "forlets" in the scholarship), and had fewer gates and fewer clearly differentiated internal rooms. Some late ancient fortresses were constructed within preexisting military structures, a sort of fort-within-a-fort architecture, though with only the newer inner buildings used. Gone, too, were the workshops common to earlier Roman fortresses, since soldiers now received their weapons and uniforms from state-owned factories (Figure 4.1).

Not all soldiers were housed in fortresses. While on campaign, field troops, the emperor's imperial guard, and temporarily garrisoned soldiers could be billeted in private homes. The state required citizens to surrender one-third of their house to assigned military "guests" (as they were called in Roman law). Certain privileged categories of people were exempt from billeting (e.g., clergy, teachers, doctors), but most citizens were required to provide rooms for soldiers and even space for their animals. They were not legally obligated to offer food, bedding, or other supplies, such as wood for heating or oil for lamps. Nevertheless, soldiers often demanded additional resources from their hosts, including a *cenaticum*, or "free supper." Given the fact that their guests were armed, hosts probably had little choice but to comply.

Needless to say, billeting was highly unpopular with civilians. Arguments broke out over which "third" of the house was to go to the

FIGURE 4.1. A reconstruction of the late Roman fortress at Durostorum (Silistra, Bulgaria) erected in the fourth century. The walled fortress was situated along the lower Danube, a major frontier of the Roman Empire. Image reproduced with permission from the Regional History Museum in Silistra, Bulgaria.

soldiers, and landowners complained that troops illegally grazed their animals. Some sources paint rather disturbing pictures of extortion and mistreatment. According to a sixth-century chronicle from Syria, the citizens of Edessa near the eastern frontier suffered regular abuse from their billeted soldiers, who were stationed in the city during a war with the Persian Empire. The chronicle presents a litany of crimes: throwing people out of beds, stripping clothes off their backs, stealing cattle, verbally and physically assaulting citizens, preying on old ladies for supplies, and raping women.[11] Reports of excessive drinking by billeted soldiers also appear frequently in our sources. The same Syriac chronicle, for instance, describes inebriated troops falling out of windows.

Consequently, people went to great lengths to prevent billeting in their homes. Some tore down notices affixed to their doors identifying their residence as a billet to incoming troops, while others bribed officials to pass over their residence when assigning housing. The people of Edessa went further still. According to the chronicle, the citizens posted public notices critical of the soldiers' commander in an attempt to embarrass him into action. Their tactic apparently worked and the abuses stopped.

Of course, relations between soldiers and civilians were not always dysfunctional. Soldiers might become interconnected with the surrounding community through marriage, or they might enter into business arrangements with civilians. There is evidence that both peasants and large landowners employed soldiers in a sort of "moonlighting" arrangement, the former to protect them from overzealous tax collectors and the latter to guard their estates and resources. The Abinnaeus archive shows military officers functioning as important patrons in local communities and assisting in business transactions. For example, a civilian named Demetrios, head of the regional natron monopoly, expected Abinnaeus to seize the products of his competitors so that he could maintain his hold on the industry; apparently the two had a long-standing cooperative relationship.[12]

In short, the relations between soldiers and civilians differed from region to region and were highly contingent. They were undoubtedly the tensest during wartime, when field troops, worked up by the fear and adrenaline of a live campaign, were forcefully imposed on people's lives. Permanently garrisoned troops would have had altogether different relationships with civilians, though these relationships would have been structured around the army's two main duties, assisting with policing and collecting taxes.

Experiencing Warfare

What did war feel like for the average soldier in Late Antiquity? Emotional experiences are notoriously difficult to reconstruct, especially for people who lived more than a thousand years ago. But we can try to understand what warfare was like by examining the types of combat that were typical of the period, the conditions soldiers were subjected to on marches and in camps, and the sorts of weapons they used to inflict injury and death.

Historians of the late Roman military emphasize that warfare in Late Antiquity was largely focused on low-intensity engagements, which included raids, skirmishes, and ambushes. For the most part, Roman soldiers were involved in defense, whether of traditional frontier regions or of interior areas that became increasingly unstable over the course of the fifth and sixth centuries, such as North Africa, Italy, the Balkans, Britain, and northern Gaul. Moreover, most were infantrymen, armed with spears, swords, and shields. As in classical Roman battle formations, the infantry fought in the center, flanked on either side by cavalry wings, and were followed by archers, including some on horses. Calvary troops became increasingly central in Late Antiquity, especially the heavily-armed mounted "shock troops" (the *cataphracti*), whose initial contact with an enemy was more about inciting psychological terror than inflicting physical injury.

As discussed in Chapter 2, late ancient campaigns typically revolved around sieges rather than open warfare. While the classic "pitched battle" remained part of the late Roman military experience, most operations were sieges, involving either the defense of a city or an attack on one. There are many reasons for this, but most important is the fact that pitched battles were especially risky, and were not attempted unless the Romans were certain that they held an advantage in numbers or position, or could surprise their enemy. Moreover, in comparison to most of their enemies, the Romans were especially good at sieges; their only true competitors were the Persians.

Roman field troops (*comitatenses*), we mentioned earlier, were the mobile units of the army that moved around the Empire from front to front. Marching, in other words, was a major component of a field soldier's daily life. The basic load each soldier carried weighed around twenty kilos (about forty-four pounds). The kit included twenty days of rations, their arms and armor, personal items (e.g., extra uniform pieces, such as boots, a woolen tunic, trousers), a canteen, and blankets. Tents, pickaxes, and palisade stakes used to set up camp, along with additional rations, were typically conveyed on mules or in carts, but in some instances the soldiers would have carried these items, too. A day's march usually lasted eight to ten hours, and at regular speed covered twenty miles (a unit could cover about twenty-four miles in a day). What most soldiers would have noticed on these marches was the intense heat of the day and the enormous amount of dust raised by the troops and animals. Combat season ran from spring to fall, the warmest and driest part of the year. At the end of an exhausting ten-hour march, the soldiers were expected to set up camp, a duty that required them to endure more physical labor, such as ditch digging.

When possible, troops were moved over long distances by ship, but the physically demanding march in the heat and dust was still a central part of the soldier's experience.

During a siege or on campaign, a soldier would live at first from his rations, which were consumed on a three-day rotation: bread for one day, *bucellatum* (hardtack) for the next two days, salt pork for one day, mutton for two days, with sour wine (*posca*) at each meal. Other foods (e.g., fish, cheese, oil) were eaten depending on availability. Field soldiers typically carried a twenty-day supply of rations. If a siege lasted for more than a few weeks (many went on for months), then the attacking Roman troops could expect to be resupplied. Troops defending a city or garrison, however, were perhaps the most imperiled when it came to food supply. They (along with any remaining citizens) would have to live off internally stored supplies, lest they risk foraging beyond the walls, where enemy forces might strike them down. During especially long sieges, soldiers sometimes consumed "famine foods," such as acorns (ground into flour), nettles, horsemeat, dog and cat meat, mice, rats, human excrement, and even old leather shoes.

Fighting in battle, whether during a siege or in open battle, was typically a close, hand-to-hand experience. Infantry troops carried spears and, as a secondary weapon, usually a sword. They wore some body armor (usually mail) and a helmet, and carried a large oval shield that measured just over a meter high. Troops in the front typically had more armor, including greaves, while those in the back had less, especially if their main duty was to throw projectiles or shoot arrows from bows and bullets from slings. It was hard to see during battle, especially for the men in the back. (This is why units carried flags and standards: this was the primary means of identification and direction.) During a battle, infantrymen fought extremely close together, in a highly disciplined formation. The less experienced soldiers were always placed in the center of the pack, with junior officers stationed around them who could prevent flight and push them back into formation. When in range of the enemy's missiles, the infantry formed a shield wall by locking their shields together. In late antique texts, this arrangement is called a *fulcum* or *foulkon*, and it is similar to (but not identical with) the old Roman *testudo*, or "turtle" formation. Casualties occurred frequently, when people were struck by projectiles or cut down by a handheld sword or spear (Figure 4.2).

FIGURE 4.2. A sixth- or seventh-century helmet of the type called the Spangenhelm. This particular helmet was discovered in Trévoux, near Lyon (France). It may have once belonged to a Frankish soldier.
Photo by the Metropolitan Museum of Art (Creative Commons license).

We do not have death rates for soldiers, but they were likely a great deal higher than for civilians. We must remember that even a relatively superficial wound could cause death if it became infected. It was likely uncommon for a field solider to survive a full twenty-year career, especially if he saw actual combat, and the relatively short life expectancy of soldiers perhaps explains why the Roman state was so generous to its veterans. Frontier units (*limitanei*) and garrisons, such as the one Abinnaeus commanded in the fourth century, typically had less stressful and less dangerous experiences. However, as the old frontiers began to crumble and the centers of engagement moved into the center of the Empire, the careers of permanently stationed soldiers became equally perilous. A chilling story from Eugippius' *Life of St. Severinus,* the account of an early sixth-century saint's life portraying an ascetic leader named Severinus from a western province on the Danube frontier, describes how one of the last frontier units in the region had gone for months without pay.[13] Desperate to survive, the unit sent a few soldiers across the Alps into Milan to collect money and rations. However, before the soldiers could reach their destination, a local war band attacked and killed them. When their mutilated bodies washed up on the shores of the Danube, their fellow soldiers abandoned their posts for good.

THE LAW COURTS

On December 12, 321 CE, Quintus Iper, governor of a province (or *nome*, as it was known in Egypt) in the Nile Valley called Arsinoites, was visiting a city in his jurisdiction. In his role as governor, adjudicating disputes among citizens and casting judgment on criminals were among his official duties, and Iper frequently made the rounds to hear legal cases. His docket in this particular city included a fairly common case involving an illiterate peasant (whose name we do not know) and some aggressive creditors, who were hounding the poor man for land that his deceased wife had inherited. (Apparently it was the father-in-law who had incurred the debt.) The plaintiff, despite his low status, had decent representation. We learn from the court records that two men, Sotarion and Horion, pleaded with the judge to protect the plaintiff from the constant harassment of the creditors. Apparently, this was not the first time they had petitioned the governor to intercede on the peasant's behalf. "Your majesty offered help," they stated, "ordering that the harassment against him be put to an end through the intervention of the *praepositi* [local military commanders]. Nonetheless these men have neither ceased their harassment nor produced anyone here in court – on the contrary, they are hounding our client with their pressure. We beg your majesty that the harassment against these men be formally repelled."[14] Iper then asked that their client point out the creditors and promised that the man would not suffer further trouble.

As this case shows, the Roman legal system was part of everyday life for many citizens. A functional legal system available even at the village level was among the hallmarks of the late Roman Empire, and the ability to resolve disputes through mediation, rather than violence, was a key element of Roman life that connected citizens to one another, to the emperor, and to the Empire as a whole. The barbarian rulers of the western successor kingdoms deliberately preserved the late Roman legal system, both its logic and many of its specific laws, precisely because of its utility and symbolic resonance.

As these kings understood, access to courts, judges, and a legal system maintained across the realm was a powerful tool that helped keep citizens loyal and unrest relatively under control.

Of course, access to the legal system was never truly equal in Late Antiquity. The costs of a court case were high enough to shut out the very poor. Moreover, patronage links often played a role in determining outcomes. Sotarion and Horion, for instance, may have been the unnamed peasant's patrons as well as his lawyers, though the precise relationship of the three men is not clear from the text. Nevertheless, the Roman legal system was a place where ordinary people, like our anonymous peasant and his two country lawyers, routinely interacted with the state, with both positive and negative effects.

The enforcement of laws and rulings was obviously important. Indeed, it is hard to imagine people buying into a legal system that lacked mechanisms for carrying through its commands. However, as we noticed in our discussion of urban life, the Roman Empire did not support local or regional police forces. To be sure, governors like Iper had access to armed retinues and could call upon local military forces, of the sort that Abinnaeus commanded, to help quash civil disturbances. They might also call upon the army to help arrest fugitives charged with serious crimes or corral defendants into hearings. Some cities even had small corps of *stationarii*, bands of lightly armed low-ranking soldiers, who enforced writs on litigants and brought defendants to court. Yet, in truth, the state took a far more active role in tax collecting than it did in enforcing its own laws. Consequently, it is impossible to say whether Sotarion and Horion's client was ultimately protected from the creditors.

Additionally, while the late Roman legal system was highly functional, it was hardly immune to corruption. For one thing, judges were known to take bribes from litigants to hear a particular case, sway a verdict, or refuse to render judgment at all. In the last case, litigants were essentially stuck, since a case could only be appealed if a judge had actually delivered a decision. "The chamber curtain of the judge shall not be venal; entrance shall not be gained by purchase, the private chamber shall not be infamous on account of the bids. The appearance of the governor shall not be at a price; the ears of the judge shall be open equally to the poorest as well as to the rich."[15] The emperor Constantine issued this ruling in Constantinople in

331 CE, clearly in response to corruption in that region of the Empire. The fact that this law (and many more like it) was retained a century later in the *Theodosian Code*, a legal compendium issued by the emperor Theodosius II in 438 CE, reminds us that corruption in the courts was a routine and persistent issue, which undoubtedly impacted the poor far more than the rich.

Resolving Disputes in Late Antiquity

Let's say a shepherd agrees to watch over another man's flock in addition to his own sixty animals. While roaming, the goats and sheep get mixed together, but the shepherd is able to distinguish his property from his partner's. Let's then imagine that the shepherd dies suddenly, and his partner swoops in and takes not just his flock, but all the animals, effectively stealing the shepherd's property. Now let's envision the shepherd's widow and her children with little left on which to survive, since the wool and milk from those sheep were their primary sources of income. What are her options? In fact, the widow, whose name was Aurelia Artemis and who lived in Egypt during the late third century, had several, including the use of the court system.[16]

Late Romans had several options for resolving disputes with other citizens, regardless of whether it was a civil case or a criminal matter (on which, see the next section).[17] The first was to use the formal state system and have the dispute judged by a Roman official.[18] This process typically began at the local level, with the case brought before a town magistrate. We know from extant documents that Aurelia Artemis elected to take the formal route and began the process of suing the partner for the return of her late husband's flock. We also know that she hired an advocate, a man named Isidoros, who was ostensibly literate and familiar with the many complexities of the Roman-Egyptian legal system. He spoke on her behalf before an official, demanding the animals' return. However, the case seems to have stalled there, because the defendant refused to appear in court. Perhaps he bribed the judge as well, another common occurrence that could stymie a legitimate complaint.

Depending on the judge's decision and the litigants' responses to it, the case could end at the local level. However, very often an appeal followed, which brought the litigants to the next level: the governor's court, located in the provincial capital. Aurelia Artemis seems to have attempted to move her case to this higher level, given the defendant's initial refusal to comply. A letter addressed to the governor of the province in Artemis' name (but ostensibly produced by Isidoros) implored him to take pity on the poor widow and return the animals for the sake of her young children. It was probably not an easy decision for Artemis to pursue her case this far. At this higher judicial level, more strictures applied in terms of the process. The letter to the prefect would have cost her additional money to draft, and had she decided to move her case to trial, she would have had to pay for the drafting and issuing of a formal summons. The costs for these services were relatively moderate, but still out of reach for some. On top of the fees, litigants were expected to pay "tips," called *sportulae*. These were effectively unregulated and may have driven up court costs considerably. And, of course, perhaps at this stage it was Artemis who resorted to bribes to move her stalled case forward. Nevertheless, we have no evidence that Aurelia Artemis' case went to trial, suggesting that the prefect's interventions brought the animals' return or that she dropped the case.

Finally, if the governor's decision was not to the litigants' liking, they had one more level of appeal: the imperial court. Again, further costs were involved, as more paperwork had to be generated and visits made to capital cities, where the highest-ranking imperial officials resided. If the case went forward, the emperor's officials would hear the litigants' testimony and make a final, binding decision. This decision, not incidentally, was considered the emperor's pronouncement and hence law.

If Artemis was frustrated by the state court system, she had alternative paths to consider. The late Roman state recognized two other options for resolving disputes between citizens. Litigants could simply agree to have an informal arbitrator decide the case, and swear an oath to respect the decision. The arbiter could be anyone in the community, but typically would be a person of high local social standing, such as the largest landowner. The only requirement was that both parties agreed to that person's authority to decide the case. Women could be arbiters as well. A law issued by Justinian in 531 CE expressly forbade women from acting as informal arbiters in civil disputes; this ruling only makes sense if women had been performing this crucial civic role in the recent past. Informal arbitration was probably the most common form of dispute resolution in Late Antiquity, because it was free or low cost, and was by far the most accessible system for non-elites.

The third option available to late Roman litigants was an ecclesiastical court, where a Christian bishop would judge the case. Bishops had long acted as informal arbiters in local disputes involving Christians (remember, any citizen could be an arbiter), but their role was defined more clearly in late imperial legislation. All religious-oriented suits, including civil and criminal cases involving clerics as litigants, would automatically fall under the aegis of a church court. Additionally, in some cases, lay parties involved in disputes of a nonreligious nature could elect to have their case heard by a bishop. If both sides agreed to this course of action, then the bishop's decision was binding. And while bishops might expect "tips," ecclesiastical court costs would have been substantially lower than the state system's costs.

Experiencing a Criminal Case

Unlike our modern system of criminal justice, where the state prosecutes men and women accused of crimes like murder and theft, the Roman legal system observed few procedural differences between civil and criminal cases. Just as in a civil case, where the plaintiff registered the complaint and personally brought the defendant to court, a criminal case also involved a plaintiff (typically the victim of the crime, or the victim's family) who pursued the defendant before a judge. In other words, the state bore no responsibility to pursue justice, regardless of whether it was a property crime or serial murder. This is why Aurelia Artemis, and not government officials, brought the case of the stolen sheep to the magistrates' attention. Even accusations of treason (the highest form of crime in Roman law) had to be presented to the state, usually through paid informers acting as plaintiffs. In both criminal and civil disputes, therefore, the state only resolved the case and determined the relevant awards and penalties, and only if this was the course chosen by the litigants. Informal arbitration or ecclesiastical courts were also possible venues for settling some criminal cases.

There was one major difference between civil and criminal cases. In a criminal case, the judge orchestrated a special form of "questioning" of the defendant and witnesses. The *quaestio,* as it was known, often involved the use of torture. While it sounds odd and counterintuitive to us, the Romans believed that for certain classes of people, truth could only be elicited under torture. For much of the Empire's history, the testimony of slaves and noncitizens was gathered through sessions involving beating, torture devices, and starvation. During the late Empire, the use of torture in the *quaestio* component of criminal cases continued, but physical abuse during the evidence-gathering stage was further extended to virtually all sociolegal statuses, including elites (though this was, admittedly, rare). Perhaps the only justice in the *quaestio* tradition lay in the fact that the accuser would be subjected to the same tortures if she or he were unable to prove the validity of the charges.

As for punishment, the decision rested with the judge, who was expected to enforce any preexisting legislation that laid out specific penalties for particular crimes. Punishments were meted out not only in accordance with the nature of the crime, but also in relation to the social status of the criminal. High-status people were typically punished by loss of property or civilian rights, exile, or heavy fines, while low-status people were beaten, sent to the mines for hard labor, or executed. Generally speaking, ancient prisons were not institutions for rehabilitating criminals, though the fifth and sixth centuries witnessed the use of the Christian monastery in this precise manner. Most of the time, prisons were used to detain people accused of crimes before their court appearance, or, in the case of debtors, to hold them until they rendered payment. The Romans thus did not construct prisons as distinct spaces, as we do today. Instead, they relied on preexisting buildings, typically private homes, to incarcerate men and women.

PAYING TAXES: AN EVERYDAY ACTIVITY

As in many large states, the late Roman government obligated its people to support its programs financially. Taxes were its primary source of revenue, which it used to pay for its enormous military expenditures (the largest item in the annual imperial budget), its expanding civil administration, its investment in infrastructure and urban activities like the games, and its extensive food-provisioning program for citizens in the largest cities.

To pay for these programs, which cost millions of *solidi* a year, the state extracted taxes on a regular basis, in some cases three times a year. Although taxes were collected from certain commercial transactions, the vast majority were property-based. In fact, many late Roman landowners were taxed twice: once for their property (a land tax, *tributum soli*) and once for the people and animals associated with their land (a head or poll tax, *tributum capitis*), both of which might be passed on to their less well-off tenants. It also demanded services as a form of tax. The state obligated skilled workers, for instance, to provide labor-intensive services, such as bread baking and textile weaving. It also required some urban elites to provide capital-intensive services, such as tax collecting and public building/infrastructure repairs. In short, the state's most obtrusive but constant interaction with the daily lives of Romans was through its pervasive and oppressive tax system. Arguably, taxes were *the* central facet of daily life, the one quotidian experience that most late Roman men and women shared.

Late Roman Taxation: A Short History and Explanation

During the high Roman Empire, each imperial province had its own system for assessing and collecting taxes, because there was no single, centralized program directed by the emperor from the capital. In most cases, taxes were levied not on individuals but on municipalities, which made their own decisions about how to divide the burdens among their citizens. So long as the town council paid what the government claimed that it owed, all was well. As one might imagine, however, there were many inefficiencies inherent in a tax system that differed from place to place. Following the crises of the third century, the emperor Diocletian determined that the haphazard nature of the Roman tax system was a key problem, and so embarked on some of the largest fiscal reforms in Roman history. Most significant among them was centralization: from the time of Diocletian, the imperial government directed a single empire-wide system for the assessment and collection of taxes. This centralized system supplanted, or attempted to supplant, the traditional regional systems used for centuries. What Diocletian devised was a government-directed, top-down system with tighter controls that replaced the more "laissez-faire" system of the earlier Empire. These changes applied both to the general tax pool and to the *annona* obligations, which, as we will see, were collected for the two government-run provisioning programs, one for the citizens of Rome and Constantinople, the other for imperial soldiers. Let's look at the major features of the new system, developed largely under Diocletian, with important amendments by Constantine and subsequent emperors.

Assessing Tax Liabilities

The late Roman government drew up tax schedules for individuals based on expected income. Previously, land taxes had been assessed purely on the size of the holding. From the late third century, projected productivity or income was the key variable. This figure was determined by a number of factors: the types of crops grown on the land, the general conditions of the land in a particular province (an estate in the Nile Valley would be taxed at a higher rate than one in the rocky hills of Macedonia), and the specific quality of the holding in question.

Assessment began with the moment of land purchase or inheritance. The new owner was legally required to register his or her name on the tax roll, or *census*, which was an actual document typically located in the nearest municipal archive.[19] Next, the numbers and names of all laborers and tenants on land belonging to the landowner were registered, including those who were legally tied to the estate. The Roman government did not have the equivalent of an Internal Revenue Service, but it did appoint imperial officials, called *censores*, to assign values to land and any persons/animals on it. These assessments were performed every fifteen years, which the Romans called an indiction.[20] All *censores* throughout the Empire now used the same abstract units of measure: *iugum* to denote productive land and *caput* to denote persons and livestock. Declarations of tax assets were known as *iugationes*. However, it is interesting to note that local traditions died hard, and conversion tables were still used to help late imperial officials translate local assessment units into standard imperial units.

Despite Diocletian's interest in centralizing the Roman fiscal system, neither he nor any Roman emperor instituted a universal tax code. In other words, while the assessment system was universal, its rates and application were not. Not all provinces were expected to pay both land and head taxes, for instance. Moreover, fluctuating budgets meant that the amount levied changed from year to year, thus so did tax rates. Consequently, we have limited knowledge about how much people were actually taxed. One important exception that provides some insight into the land tax is the *Syro-Roman Law Book*, a fifth-century Syriac translation of an earlier Greek compendium of Roman law that pertains to eastern provinces. It contains one of the few existing tax conversion charts from Late Antiquity, which shows how many units of specific types of land translated into a single *iugum* (the tax unit). As far as tax rates, we can provisionally assume that individuals paid one *solidus* per 20 *iugera*, a Roman unit of area. Also note that the figures apply only to eastern provinces, and perhaps only to Syria.[21]

Type of land	Land per *iugum*
First-class arable	20 *iugera* per *iugum*
Second-class arable	40 *iugera* per *iugum*
Third-class arable	60 *iugera* per *iugum*
Vineyard	5 *iugera* per *iugum*
Olive grove ("old")	225 trees per *iugum*
Olive grove ("mountain")	450 trees per *iugum*

Tax Collection

Once landowners received their fiscal declarations from the *censor*, they were expected to hand over the taxes in either cash or kind, with the form of the payment determined on an ad hoc basis. Land tax payments were made three times per annum. The late Roman government relied largely on local officials to collect and deliver the assessed amounts. Some municipalities were granted the right to pay their taxes corporately. However, the government typically looked to individual landowners, who, in their role as magistrates, were obligated to collect taxes not only from their tenants (who typically paid both rent and a share of the landlord's taxes), but also from other freeholders in the region. These wealthier local landowners, in other words, were often the very same officials who oversaw *all* tax collection for their particular city or region, including their own.

Needless to say, possibilities for noncompliance, corruption, and evasion existed at all levels of the process. The state had really only one mechanism to enforce compliance, the military, which it used regularly in this capacity, as Abinnaeus' records show. We recall the letter about the drunken soldier who became a bit too aggressive with his collection tactics. What was probably unusual about this situation is the fact that the village complained to a commanding officer, not that a soldier used force to extract payment. Despite the threat of violence, landowners could and did refuse to pay taxes. In some cases, they bribed assessors to underestimate their payments, and in others they hired armed guards to keep the collectors away. Sometimes villagers simply attacked the taxman. Abinnaeus' archive preserves one letter recounting the beatings sustained by the grandson of a local official from residents whose taxes he was sent to collect.[22] And, of course, there was always the option of patronage. If you were a small or middling freeholder, becoming the client of more powerful land-owners might reduce or eliminate your tax burden. It was just as likely, however, that clients made up for the evasion of their wealthy patrons by paying the difference.

In short, the burden of the tax system fell unequally in Late Antiquity, weighing more heavily on those who could least afford it. Local officials burdened with collecting taxes often complained that they were forced to make up the difference when revenues came in below the levied amounts, and that this left them in financial ruin. However, others clearly made a profit from tax collecting, especially those who were adept at evasion and extraction, or who could profit from service obligations, such as some shippers did on the *annona*, to which we now turn.

The Annona: *Rome's Great Provisioning System*

While the state collected taxes for numerous expenditures, they were principally focused on funding its two enormous provisioning pro-grams, one for feeding the populations of its largest cities, the other for supplying its soldiers and officials. The Romans (and modern scholars) denote these two provisioning programs respectively as the *annona civilis* (the civilian *annona*) and the *annona militaris* (the mili-tary *annona*).[23] The *annona civilis*, we noted, was offered exclusively to registered citizens in Rome and Constantinople, and perhaps in Alexandria and Antioch, though inclusion of the last two cities is debated. The principal food provided by the state was bread, but the late ancient *annona civilis* also included rations of wine, oil, pork, and salt. The *annona militaris* was more extensive, since it involved provisioning of not only food to the soldiers, but also weapons, uniforms, and fodder. Civil bureaucrats (who were included in the military *annona*) also received goods and services as part of their pay. Significantly, late Romans did not view the *annona* as welfare or an entitlement. Rather, those who received the *annona* saw it as a privilege, a mark of status that underscored their citizenship within a great city or service to the Empire.

By all accounts, the *annona* was a major economic dynamic in the Roman Empire, since it required the state to create and maintain massive interregional infrastructures for the collection, processing, and transporting of goods across large distances. Egypt, for instance, was the major source of grain distributed in Constantinople, while North Africa supplied Rome until the mid-fifth century, when relations with its Vandal rulers broke down. Thereafter, Rome's grain *annona* came largely from Sicily and Campania (Italy).

On the one hand, the *annona* rested on the backs of individual citizens, who were obligated by the government to contribute cash, foodstuffs, transport vehicles, animals, storage space, and/or labor toward provisioning the Empire's largest cities and army. For many, it was simply another tax. All landowners and those who labored on the estates of others contributed to the *annona* directly and indirectly. The Egyptian Apiones, for instance, contributed to the *annona* by handing over to the state set amounts of grain and other goods. In fact, they may have grown wheat solely to pay their taxes and derived no profit from the grain market. Equally obligated was the fourth-century Egyptian peasant Aurelius Sakaon, who paid his share of *annona* taxes by supplying set amounts of wheat each year, as did rural villagers recorded in the Abinnaeus archive. These taxes were sometimes oppressive and could push subsistence farmers over the edge, especially since growing grain was dependent on favorable weather conditions and regular water. When Sakaon and his fellow Theadelphians complained to local official about their water dispute (see Chapter 1), they underscored the impact that water loss was having on their fiscal contributions. Even great estates could fail to fulfill their quotas or even feed themselves. A devastating crop failure on one of his Gallic estates forced a senatorial aristocratic named Ausonius (310–395 CE) to ask a friend to ship him an emergency grain supply. Services were also obligated, since grain and other supplies had to be delivered to their point of use and processed (e.g., grain ground into flour and then baked into bread).

On the other hand, the *annona* was a government program that provided opportunities for private entrepreneurship. Excavated shipwrecks have produced interesting evidence in this regard. Most cargoes on late ancient vessels were heterogeneous, and appear to have included the government's wheat as well as non-*annona* items such as ceramic plates, glassware, silverware, metals, and building supplies, that is, goods the ship owner "piggybacked" onto the government's trip. The shipper took full advantage of free tolls and duties (which all *annona* ships were granted) as well as direct passage to a port servicing a large city of consumers. The shippers could also profit from the government's underwriting of the risk: if the ship sank, the government paid for its contents and the construction of a new vessel. In other words, the same ship owner burdened by the state's demand for cheap transport could also potentially profit from the system. What is more, he provided private merchants with additional goods that could be sold on the open market to any citizen, regardless of whether she or he was registered to receive the *annona*. In this way, the *annona* indirectly supplied food and other necessities to all inhabitants of the late Empire's largest cities, while at the same time lining merchants' pockets.

The *Annona Civilis* in Action: The Provisioning of Bread to Rome

We know the most about the transport of grain to and provisioning of Rome and Constantinople. Once the state had fixed the amount of grain to be collected from landowners in a given year, it was gathered by local officials, placed in sacks, and transported by carters to the nearest port. To reach Constantinople, for instance, grain traveled up the Nile in barges and then to the city via Alexandria; from Africa, it typically moved directly from Carthage to Rome. The men who orchestrated the transport were the *navicularii*, ship owners who were organized as *corpora*, at least through the fifth century.[24] They were obligated by the government to build, equip, and repair the boats used to transport the Empire's food supply at massively reduced rates (4 percent of the cargo's value, which was about a third of the commercial rate). They also were required to take the shortest distance possible and to make their delivery within two years, lest they face a government inquiry. It is clear that there were never enough *navicularii* to transport all the wheat that was needed in the capitals, so the state relied increasingly on private shippers, who worked either on contract or as what amounted to corvée.

The grain was stored in the holds of ships, sometimes in sacks, but usually just poured directly in. If there were several shipping agents using the same vessel, their cargoes could be separated by planks dividing up the hold. Once the ships reached their destination – Portus near Rome and the harbor of Constantinople – they were unloaded. There, longshoremen removed the grain and emptied it into measuring bins called *modii*.[25] An official then measured the grain and read the figure aloud so that clerks who worked for the office in charge of the *annona* (called the *praefectus annonae*) could record the number. The quantities recorded were compared against those taken when the grain was first loaded. A 4 percent loss was permissible, but anything beyond that required a formal inquiry. From there, the grain was moved into temporary storage facilities at the harbor, and eventually into the city for processing and distribution. In Rome, this meant sending the grain up the Tiber River on special barges, which were pulled by men and, later, oxen walking on towpaths that ran alongside the river.

During this period of heightened activity, there would have been ample opportunity to commit fraud. An inscription from 389 CE documents one such dispute between Rome's official grain measurers at Portus and the Tiber barge drivers. The precise nature of the argument has been lost, but it seems that some grain had gone missing, and each side was pointing fingers at the other. In fact, "inside jobs" were so rampant on this leg of the grain trade that in 417 CE, the emperors in Rome ruled that warehouses at Portus would henceforth have to be guarded by an outside party.

Once the grain arrived, it was distributed to warehouses, where it would sit for months, perhaps for more than a year. Older grain was less desirable, but the state passed laws requiring bakers to finish the old rations before moving to the new ones and to accept mixtures of better- and poorer-quality wheat. Humidity, pests, and theft were the biggest problems, and the Romans tried to combat them by building their granaries on raised floors to allow for air circulation, by coating the insides of the receptacles with *amurca* (olive oil sediment) to drive away rodents and bugs, and by fortifying the warehouses with towers to guard them.

Carting agents transported the grain in animal-pulled wagons from the storehouses to the mills and bakeries. Like the ship owners, the carting agents were organized into *corpora*, and were responsible for hiring the drivers and maintaining the carts and animals (they did not personally drive the carts themselves). As we saw in Chapter 2, many cities like Rome had water-powered mills, where state grain would be processed into flour, after which it was delivered to bakeries that supplied services to the state. Late antique Rome had nearly 250 such public bakeries used for the *annona*, and an unrecorded number of private ones. Less is known about Constantinople's public bakeries. One source claims that the city had only twenty-one state bakeries. If true, these establishments must have been enormous, since they produced enough bread for all registered citizens.

The bread that was distributed as part of the *annona* was called the *panis gradilis*, and it was typically of the fine white type.[26] Until 369 CE, the bread was sold at a heavily reduced price, but thereafter was given away for free at the city's many *annona* distribution points. There were 177 distribution points in Constantinople and an unknown number in Rome. *Panis gradilis*, or "bread from the steps," was called such because it was distributed at one point from tiered platforms. Those who received the *annona* were known as the *incisi*, or "inscribed," a term referring to the practice of inscribing the names of eligible citizens onto tablets that were affixed to the platforms. Presumably the *incisi* also had tickets that identified them as recipients, but no examples have been found. Receiving one's bread ration thus involved standing in line at an appointed station in the city, undoubtedly for a relatively long period of time if we imagine that thousands of citizens received rations. It is important to remember that while we see waiting in line for food handouts as an act associated exclusively with impoverishment, the late Romans viewed it as a mark of citizen status and even privilege.

MOVING GOODS AND PEOPLE: THE *CURSUS PUBLICUS*

A final topic that illustrates the state's role in daily life is the late Roman road system. The Romans are famous for their road networks: thousands of miles of paved and unpaved streets connected cities across the Empire. During Late Antiquity, no new major roadways were built, but the state maintained some preexisting roads and transport systems through the sixth century. Although there is little evidence that the Romans constructed roads for any purpose other than military, the Empire nevertheless was lined by thousands of secondary road networks used for public and private business. Both major and minor networks were integral to the functioning of a large state, whether it was a matter of moving soldiers or olive oil. Everyday people, from merchants and migrant farmers to messengers and missionaries, used these road networks, though they were typically barred from taking advantage of state-funded accommodations.

As we have seen, the state primarily relied on shipping to move grain around the Empire. A preference for shipping was due, in large part, to the higher costs and slower pace of land transport. Land transport was far more expensive than sea transport for the simple reason that late Romans had few technologies that allowed them to haul large and heavy cargoes across terrain. This impediment to commerce did not improve significantly until the invention of steam and internal combustion engines and the establishment of train and trucking networks in the nineteenth and twentieth centuries. Nevertheless, sometimes land transport was the only option. A person with a large cargo and a land route had two choices: pack animal or cart/wagon, which could be pulled by an animal or pushed by a human. Carts were a better and cheaper choice for heavier loads over longer distances on paved roads, but for a light cargo and a short trip, a camel was a much more economical option.

Moreover, carts and wagons required relatively well-maintained paved roads, making them an undesirable option for regional trips on uneven secondary routes. In fact, evidence suggests that during Late Antiquity there was a preferential shift from carts and wagons to pack animals. There are a number of possible reasons for this shift. The territorial contraction of the Roman Empire, and its tax base, meant that fewer resources were funneled into infrastructural maintenance, which led not only to the silting of harbors but also to the deterioration of paved roads. Settlement patterns were also changing, with fewer towns and villages in general, especially in the West. The growing preference for the animal over the wheel was a logical response to changing economic, social, and environmental conditions.

Through the middle of the sixth century, Roman government officials had the option of using a much faster system for land transportation: the public post system. The *cursus publicus* (or *dromos* in Greek) was a system of changing stations (*mutationes*) and lodgings (*mansiones*) that dotted Roman roadways every ten miles or so. These stations and inns were open exclusively to those traveling on official state business who were in possession of the proper documentation. To be clear, the roads themselves could be used by anyone, but only someone with a warrant had access to the changing stations, which provided fresh animals, fodder, water, and veterinary care, and to the inns, which offered travelers food, drink, and lodging. For those with a warrant, in other words, travel was heavily subsidized, with the state paying the bill. Technically, there were two postal systems, a "fast" *cursus* (the *cursus velox* or *oxos dromos*), which provided saddle horses and light two-wheeled carts for luggage, used primarily by officials traveling on administrative business, and a slow wagon post (*cursus clabularis* or *platus dromos*), which mainly served the *annona* transport and the army supply lines. The government used agents to deliver correspondence and documents via the *cursus publicus*, but it was not a publicly accessible mail system. For anyone who wished to send a letter to a distant addressee, the *cursus publicus* was likely out of reach. One would simply wait for a friend or acquaintance to make the trip and deliver the letter on his or her behalf, or, if rich enough, send a slave as courier.

Thanks to two extraordinary sources, we know a great deal about travelling on the late Roman *cursus publicus*, in terms of both the traveler's experience and the routes that were available. For the former, we are fortunate to have the accounts of an early fourth-century Egyptian official named Theophanes, who used the fast *cursus* to travel from his home in central Egypt to Antioch on state business.[27] His personal archive includes letters, receipts, and other records of his trip. We know that the trip took Theophanes about twenty-four days to complete and that it involved some thirty-five different stages. His daily travel distance ranged from sixteen to forty-five (Roman) miles per day, covering an average distance of thirty-two miles per day, which translates to about six hours of traveling, if the speed of travel was five miles per hour. This speed makes sense only if Theophanes rode on horseback and was accompanied by slaves and assistants who rode alongside him in carriages. Interestingly, Theophanes' warrant seems to have been only partial. While he never paid for lodging or the changing stations, he was responsible for purchasing food for his entire entourage. As a lower-level provincial official involved in some kind of litigation on behalf of his hometown, he was only eligible to receive a second-tier warrant. Palace officials, high-level prefects, higher-ranking military officers, and private individuals granted special permission by the emperor would have received a first-tier pass, which included food as well as lodging and animal services. Occasionally, high-status civilians received free rides on the premier post service, such as when Constantine permitted all Christian bishops to use the *cursus* in order to attend the Council of Nicaea in 325 CE.

Our second great source for the late antique *cursus publicus* is a medieval copy of a late ancient document called the Peutinger Map (*Tabula Peutingeriana*). Named for its sixteenth-century owner, Konrad Peutinger, the Peutinger Map is a diagrammatic representation of the Roman road system. It shows not only the major roadways, but also some of the hundreds of changing stations and lodgings along them (in addition to late ancient cities, bath complexes, and fortifications). It was originally created on a single strip of papyrus measuring twenty feet by one foot, and consequently depicts the Empire in a highly distorted frame (all masses are shifted horizontally to fit inside the narrow confines of the strip). For this reason, the Peutinger Map is less a topographical road map of the sort we use today and more of a guide created for someone actually using the post system.[28] A good analogy is the famous diagram of the London tube system, which gives a very clear sense of the train routes and how to use them, but bears little resemblance to the actual topography of London (Figure 4.3).

The *cursus publicus* did not survive the fragmentation of the Roman Empire. As early as the mid-fourth century, emperors began to whittle away at services, typically by simply ending them in specific provinces.

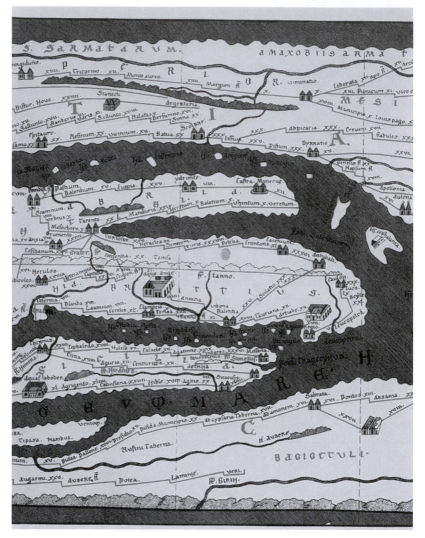

FIGURE 4.3. A section of the *Tabula Peutingeriana*, or Peutinger Map, a late ancient road map depicting route networks on (from top to bottom) the Dalmatian coast, the southern "boot" of Italy, Sicily, and the North African coast. Readers will notice that the map depicts roadways, distances, and pictorial symbols denoting important stopping points for those potentially using the *cursus publicus*, notably baths, changing stations, and hostels. The Peutinger Map was probably first created in the early fourth century, but the image here derives from a thirteenth-century copy.

The West's system eroded first. The post in Sardinia was the first to go, followed by those in Britain, Gaul, Spain, and eventually in the eastern dioceses during the reign of Justinian. The *cursus* was an enormous expense for the state, and the government increasingly relied on compulsory labor provided by local residents to supply and man it. Local farms were typically required to provide food and animals as a form of taxation, making it a burdensome program for many locals. Of course, some profited from the state's oversight of the *cursus*. One sixth-century author notes the dire effects that Justinian's abolition of the *cursus* had on the local economy of interior regions, which had relied on the government's purchases and taxation in grain for their economy. According to the historian Procopius (ca. 500–565 CE), when the government stopped purchasing grain and taking it as a tax to supply the stations, "the unsold crops rotted on the estates ... and the taxpayer was ruined when the tax collectors demanded gold instead of crops, since he could not sell his crops living far from the sea."[29]

***

The late Roman state was hardly a distant entity in the daily lives of its inhabitants. Elites and non-elites benefitted from, and were burdened by, the late antique military, law courts, tax system, and post networks. Whether it was a matter of billeting a soldier, adjudicating a dispute, registering a property for tax assessment, or supplying a changing station with fodder, individual men and women interacted directly and routinely with the government. Of course, there were a number of areas that impacted everyday life where the state had virtually no role. Principal among these were the body, the mind, and health care, topics discussed in the next chapter.

Further Reading

The following primary sources are available in English translation and provide insight into the topics discussed in this chapter:

The Abinnaeus Archive: Papers of a Roman Officer in the Reign of Constantius II, ed. and trans. H. I. Bell et al. (Oxford, 1962).

Eugippius, *Life of Saint Severinus*, trans. L. Bieler (Washington, DC, 1965).

Euphemia and the Goth, with the Acts of Martyrdom of the Confessors of Edessa, ed. and trans. F. Burkitt (London, 1913).

J. Matthews, ed. and intro., *The Journey of Theophanes: Travel, Business, and Daily Life in the Roman East* (New Haven, CT, 2006).

Procopius, *The Wars of Justinian*, trans. by H. Dewing, revised and modernized by A. Kaldellis (Indianapolis, IN, 2014).

Procopius, *The Secret History*, trans. A. Kaldellis (Indianapolis, IN, 2010).

Peutinger Table, see *Die Peutinger Tafel*, ed. K. Miller (Stuttgart, 1962). This is a facsimile of the actual map, with notes and an introduction in German.

Ps-Joshua the Stylite, *Chronicle*, ed. F. Trombly and J. Watts (Liverpool, 2000).

The Theodosian Code, trans. C. Pharr (Princeton, NJ, 1952).

On the late Roman army and everyday life, see especially A. D. Lee, *War in Late Antiquity. A Social History* (London, 2007). There are many excellent general studies on late ancient warfare. Readers should begin with the essays in *War and Warfare in Late Antiquity*. 2 vols., ed. N. Christie and A. Sarantis (Leiden, 2013) and *The Cambridge Ancient History of Greek and Roman Warfare, Vol. 2: Rome from the Late Republic to the Late Empire*, ed. P. Sabin, H. von Wiess, and M. Whitby (Cambridge, 2007). For introductions to the late Roman legal system, see A. H. M. Jones, *The Later Roman Empire* (Baltimore, MD, 1964) and J. Harries, *Law and Empire in Late Antiquity* (Cambridge, 1999). For the *annona* systems, see A. J. B. Sirks, *Food for Rome: The Legal Structure of the Transportation and Processing of Supplies for the Imperial Distributions in Rome and Constantinople* (Amsterdam, 1991). On Roman roadways and the *cursus publicus*, see L. Casson, *Travel in the Ancient World* (Baltimore, MD, 1994), and for a recent reappraisal of the Peutinger Map as imperial propaganda, see R. Talbot, *Rome's World: The Peutinger Map Reconsidered* (Cambridge, 2010).

5

Body and Mind

Sometime in the late third or early fourth century, a Roman wife and mother named Valeria Verecunda died. She was thirty-four years, nine months, and twenty-eight days old when she passed away. Her husband, P. Gellius Vitalio, and daughter, Valeria Vitalis, commemorated her life and death on a marble tombstone, which marked the *loculus*, or humble subterranean tomb, where she was buried.[1] Like many ancient epitaphs, Valeria's tombstone highlighted her most notable achievements: Valeria was a loving mother, a dutiful wife, and, most interestingly, the leading physician of her region in the city of Rome. Female physicians were fairly common in Late Antiquity. Many specialized in treating women and women's diseases, since it was more appropriate for a woman to examine a woman's body. Some, but not all, female doctors were also midwives, experts at delivering babies. We do not know whether Valeria had a specialty like women's health and obstetrics. It is possible that she was a generalist physician, who treated men, women, and children for the myriad common diseases and ailments that regularly affected people of all social classes and backgrounds. She would not have attended a medical school in the modern sense of the institution. In fact, she likely never attended school at all beyond tutoring in her own home. And she had no official license to practice medicine, since there was no regulation of health care at the time. Moreover, Valeria's Rome did not yet have hospitals, which first appeared in the city only at the very end of the fourth century. Instead, Valeria made house calls or met patients at a neighborhood clinic. She probably charged fees for her services, but may have treated some for free.

When Valeria died at thirty-four, she was considered middle-aged. Her immune system would have been relatively strong, having survived the many childhood diseases that killed large numbers of the population in an epoch before vaccines. She had also likely survived multiple pregnancies and childbirths. Although she had only one living daughter, Valeria almost certainly had been pregnant on many more occasions, and probably gave birth to babies who did not live beyond infancy or childhood. As a physician, Valeria was exposed to disease more than most people, but in truth, everyone living in Rome was at high risk for contracting infections. Rome, like many late ancient cities, was a spectacularly dense, dirty, and unhygienic environment. The city's famed sewage system, the *cloaca maxima*, helped move some waste out into the Tiber River, but most residences were not connected to it and had no running water. Human waste was routinely flung into the streets, and public latrines often overflowed. Cholera, typhoid, dysentery, and tuberculosis were commonly contracted diseases, and Valeria could have died from any of them. She may also have been a victim of a seasonal malaria outbreak, which typically erupted in Rome during the late summer months in a pattern tied to the flooding of the Tiber. Or perhaps Valeria died not from disease, but from surgery, since there were no antiseptic operating conditions in Late Antiquity and no antibiotics to prevent infection.

Inscriptions, or what scholars call epigraphic evidence, tell us that Valeria Verecunda was not an anomaly. Similar tombstones from across the Empire demonstrate that women were active members of the medical profession in Late Antiquity, whether working as midwives, physicians, or faith healers. Her death at thirty-four years was fairly average, as was her marital status and single living daughter. If they could survive childhood, most female city-dwellers lived into their forties, and a high incidence of infant mortality made single-child families common. What the inscription does not tell us, but we can piece together from additional evidence, is how Valeria and other late ancient people lived daily in their own bodies and minds: how they physically cared for themselves when ill and when in good health; how much education they received in order to train their minds (in an era before Descartes, the mind was not disassociated from the body); the kinds of sexual activities they engaged in; and what sorts of garments they chose to cover themselves with. To answer these questions, we must turn to a range of late Roman sources, from medical treatises, inscribed amulets, and compilations of herbal remedies to religious dialogues, visual portraits of men and women, and schoolbook exercises. Once again, elite men produced the vast majority of these sources for other elite men, a fact that challenges, but does not undermine, our project of understanding the experience of embodiment for all late Romans.

We will start by looking at how late Romans understood the physical body, that is, how they approached health care, disease, disability, and the culturally central topics of women's health and reproduction. The chapter then shifts to explore what we might call the social body, looking at topics such as sexual behavior, education, and adornment, such as clothing, hairstyles, jewelry, and makeup.

HEALTH CARE AND THE BODY IN LATE ANTIQUITY

Late Ancient Medicine 101: Humoral Theory, Galenic Medicine, and Demons

Before turning to health care workers, hospitals, and disease, we need to establish the basic principles and assumptions that constituted medical science in Late Antiquity, which were substantially different from those that govern medicine today. Valeria Verecunda likely subscribed to an ancient physiological system first established by Greek doctors in the fifth and fourth centuries BCE. Tradition holds that the founder of this system was the Greek physician Hippocrates (ca. 460–370 BCE), the very same Hippocrates credited with the creation of the Hippocratic Oath, a version of which is still recited by American physicians today. Hippocrates and his followers, whom scholars collectively call "the Hippocratic writers" because they wrote using his name, penned treatises on various aspects of medicine, from theoretical studies on human physiology to more practical works on disease. The Hippocratic writers believed that four bodily fluids determined a person's health and well-being. These four fluids, known as the humors, were blood, yellow bile, black bile, and phlegm. The Hippocratic writers associated each humor with an element, certain temperatures, a season, a life stage when it was thought to predominate, and a temperament.

Humor	Temperature	Element	Season	Life Stage	Temperament
Blood	Warmest	Air	Spring	Childhood	Carefree, sanguine
Yellow bile	Warm and dry	Fire	Summer	Youth	Choleric, angry
Black bile	Cold and dry	Earth	Autumn	Adulthood	Serious, depressive
Phlegm	Cold and moist	Water	Winter	Old age	Calm, peaceful, thoughtful

According to the Hippocratic writers, each individual body contains a unique balance of humors, which taken together make up a person's "constitution." A person's constitution, however, was never static. Not only did it change from year to year (i.e., life stage), but it was also influenced by factors such as planetary alignment (astrology), geographic location and climate, gender, social class, diet, exercise, and occupation. According to humoral theory, a healthy body results from a perfect balance of the humors, whatever is needed at a particular moment and place in one's life. Conversely, an unhealthy body results from an imbalance of the humors. Too much or too little of a particular humor upsets the balance and makes a body sick and potentially die. The ancients believed that humoral theory also explained mental health conditions. For instance, they thought that depression, called melancholia, was caused by an excess of black bile, while deep anger and aggression stemmed from too much yellow bile.

If not already obvious, humoral theory is very different from how modern physicians understand the roots of good health and, more significantly, the cause of disease. Without microscopes, no one in antiquity had ever seen a microbe, and thus could not know that many diseases are caused by external pathogens that arise from nonhuman ecologies. Alternatively, according to humoral theory, all sickness was fundamentally caused by an imbalance of the four humors, and was thus exclusively an internal human body problem. This is not to say that the concept of contagion was unknown. A fourth-century CE veterinary manual describes a process of separating healthy from sick animals and culling the sick ones as a means of preventing the spread of disease to the entire flock. Moreover, there was a strong belief that certain diseases, such as malaria spread by "bad air," meaning that people inhaled noxious fumes typically associated with marshes and garbage dumps, which made them sick.[2] Yet ultimately, this explanation of contagion was grounded in the humoral system. Bad air was a feature of a particular geographic location, which directly affected one's balance of humors. In sum, no ancient source ever attributed the cause of any disease to an external organism such as a bacterium, virus, or parasite. Instead, they insisted that diseases were ultimately caused by internal imbalances of the four humors. Hence, all treatment of disease focused on restoring humoral balance rather than eliminating pathogens.

For Valeria and most late ancient physicians, humoral theory was medical common sense, a science built into the background of health care in everyday life. Her reliance on the Hippocratic writers, however, was likely mediated through another Greek medical expert, the great Galen of Pergamum (126–216 CE). Galen read and built on the work of the Hippocratic writers, systematizing their thought while also expanding it. For instance, Galen emphasized the importance of diet more than his Hippocratic forebears, since he believed that the process of digestion initiated the "heating" process within the body, which was necessary to balance the humors properly. Galen was something of a superstar in his day. He became a court physician to the emperor Marcus Aurelius (r. 161–180 CE), and spent his later life in Rome holding public anatomy lessons, where he performed live dissections, mainly on pigs, as it was illegal to dissect human bodies. His writings were bestsellers, and many were translated into Latin and Syriac during Late Antiquity.[3] More important, late ancient medical authorities created streamlined versions of Galen's work, which distilled his often empirical and ambivalent observations about the body into more definitive, declarative passages. In this respect, "Galenic medicine" as a scientific system was born in Late Antiquity.

In Valeria's day, humoral theory was dominant among physicians, but it did not monopolize thinking about health and disease. A parallel system, with deep roots in ancient culture, came to occupy an important place in health care during Late Antiquity. Within this alternative system, people interpreted disease as an effect of demonic possession. The reasons behind demonic possession were multiple: immoral living, the evil eye, cursing the gods, or simply bad luck. One could also have enemies. A binding spell discovered from the Cairo Geniza, a sort of preserved scrap heap of ancient and medieval Jewish texts, called upon *daimones* to bind the victim so that he would "melt and drip and groan and be cast down on a sickbed."[4] As we shall see in the following sections and in the chapter on religion, treatment for disease and health problems in Late Antiquity often involved the use of special healers and magical objects, which were thought to have both apotropaic and medicinal powers. The rise of Christianity, a religion that touted the power of its holy men and women to heal the sick and even raise the dead, played a significant role in making magical medical practices even more mainstream. Typically, the authorities who diagnosed and treated diseases caused by demonic possession were what we might call faith healers, men and women who used their knowledge of the supernatural to drive harmful spirits from sick bodies. This supernatural health care system was not exactly complementary to the humoral system, for some medical authorities flatly rejected "folk cures." In other cases, proponents of faith healing approaches, especially Christians, dismissed humoral medicine as "pagan" health care, and thought it was to be avoided. However, many late Roman medical experts, including the Christian physician Alexander of Tralles (ca. 525–605 CE), increasingly embraced alternative approaches and recommended them in addition to humoral-based treatments.

In sum, health care in Late Antiquity was characterized by two parallel and sometimes competing systems of health and disease: one based on the principles of humoral theory, the other on the role of supernatural forces in illness and infirmity. These two systems coexisted, and people typically moved between them rather than dogmatically positioning themselves in one camp or the other. We shall explore some real-life examples of these dynamics in the following pages.

Late Ancient Health Care Workers: Physicians, Midwives, and Healers

Valeria Verecunda was a female doctor, or *iatromea*, a Latinized version of the Greek word for female physician. To become a physician in Valeria's day, most people trained on the job, learning to diagnose and heal by watching a more experienced doctor, perhaps a family member (medicine tended to run in families), practice. Some physicians specialized in areas such as surgery, obstetrics, or eye problems, the latter of which was the number-one health complaint in the late ancient world. But most were generalists. In Late Antiquity, there were no medical schools in the modern sense, with admissions qualifications, testing, and licensing procedures. Instead, men and women who had the means travelled to one of a handful of cities in the late Roman Empire that was a center of medical learning to hear lectures from established teachers. The most important center was Alexandria, in Egypt, where Galen had first studied, but medical lectures were also traditionally given in Cos, Cnidus, Ephesus, Pergamum, Smyrna, and Rome. Attendance at these lectures was entirely elective, and none led to the acquirement of a special diploma or certificate. Additionally, these schools tended to focus more on medical theory than on practical treatments and diagnostic procedures. Consequently, most doctors learned about practicing medicine from informal apprenticeships. Without any form of certification, a doctor's reputation rested entirely upon public perceptions of his or her knowledge, expertise, and, most important, trustworthiness. A "good" doctor was one you could trust in your home. Nevertheless, there was something of a hierarchy of physicians in Late Antiquity, which ranged from the local barmaid who delivered babies to the cosmopolitan, wealthy author of erudite medical treatises, whose practice was confined to the upper echelons of society. Valeria, we should assume, fell somewhere in the middle of this spectrum.

The background of midwives is harder to assess, because we have no treatises authored by them that would allow us to place them easily in the wider society. Midwives were necessarily women, and typically non-elite in status. Many had day jobs and delivered babies on the side. A humorous anecdote from one fourth-century source recounts how a barmaid who moonlighted as a midwife was pulled away on an emergency delivery one night as she was pouring drinks for custom-ers.[5] As far as we know, midwives received their training entirely on the job. According to a second-century medical authority, the best midwives had good memories and were highly trustworthy, well dis-ciplined, not greedy for money (a point that assumes they expected to be paid), and free from "superstition" that might cause them to refuse a certain treatment.[6]

Physicians and midwives were two categories of late ancient healers. Holy men, magicians, and priests constituted a third. Until at least the late fourth century, sick people could visit temples dedicated to the Greek god Asclepius. Asclepius' temples, known as Asclepeia, were renowned healing centers. Patients would arrive and seek counsel from the temple priests, who would advise them on diet and exercise. The priests might invite them to spend the night in the temple to be treated by the god via dreams, in a ritual healing process called incubation. While the official closing of pagan temples by Theodosius I (r. 379–395 CE) narrowed the possibilities for pagan healing rites, pagan experts continued to use their knowledge to heal. One Neoplatonic philosopher, for example, reputedly used theurgy, a special form of ritual practice, to drive a demon from his wife's body, which he believed prevented her from conceiving.

In addition to priests and philosopher-healers, sick people in Late Antiquity paid visits to the makers and sellers of amulets, curse tablets, and spells, which used magical names and images to direct demons into, out of, or away from the body. They also visited faith healers. Early Christian sources abound with stories of holy men and women healing the sick and infirm, and raising the dead. While all are based on biblical models, there is no reason to dismiss the entire phenom-enon as a literary fiction. Evidence tells us that people regularly visited famous healers, most of whom were ascetics, as well as the tombs of saints and martyrs in the hope that contact with these holy beings might bring respite from their ailments. The Christian bishop and historian Gregory of Tours (538–594 CE) refers repeatedly to people who recovered from ailments by visiting the shrine of St. Martin, a fourth-century holy man, bishop, and saint known to perform healing miracles when alive and dead.[7]

Living with Disease and Disability

Today, everyone gets sick a few times a year, typically with a low-grade viral infection. We often self-diagnose the problem, perhaps using the Internet, and make a trip to the local pharmacy for over-the-counter medicine. If our illness persists, we visit a physician, who may prescribe antibiotics or antiviral medication. Perhaps we need surgery, and so we enter a hospital and undergo a procedure in a sanitized operating room with trained professionals. We feel nothing during the operation, because we have been put under general anesthesia, and when we wake up, we take painkillers and receive antibiotics to prevent infection in our carefully sutured wound. Chances are high in these scenarios that we will recover from our illness and go on to live another year.

In Late Antiquity, sick people had none of these expectations. The absence of vaccines administered in infancy and childhood meant that children died at exceptionally high rates from infectious diseases. Consequently, most children had lost a sibling and/or a friend by the time they reached adulthood, a normalcy that today is hard to fathom. The Roman life expectancy at birth was twenty-five years precisely because of the catastrophically high rates of infant and childhood mortality.

For adults living in urban environments, who had more mature immune systems, the situation was marginally better. Those who resided in the Empire's densest cities, such as Rome, Alexandria, Constantinople, and Antioch, typically lived in filthy environments, in which infectious diseases spread easily. Sewer systems helped, but they did not create hygienic living conditions. Rome's sewers, for instance, emptied directly into the Tiber, and thus human waste regularly contaminated the river that was used for washing, drinking, and fishing. Additionally, whereas some of Rome's sewers were flushed by pipes carrying wastewater, none had traps. This meant that the toilets overflowed whenever the Tiber flooded, which was usually once a year. Moreover, without traps, disease-carrying vermin living in the sewers easily climbed up through the latrines into Rome's streets and buildings. Poor people living in crowded apartments who relied exclusively on public toilets were obviously the worst off, but the rich did not necessarily fare much better. Relatively few houses had their own private toilets. In those that did have toilets, they were often located next to cooking areas. This obviously made dumping kitchen waste more convenient, but it also facilitated the spread of disease from feces to food and encouraged the thick presence of flies. Most used chamber pots and disposed of their waste by hand into receptacles. These were dumped directly onto the street or perhaps stored in ceramic vessels for collection. Urine and human feces were used in industry and agriculture, and people thus collected them to sell. Needless to say, such a recycling system did not promote hygienic conditions.

Alternatively, the countryside was considerably more salubrious. Ironically, a well-fed peasant had less chance of contracting an infectious disease than a rich city-dweller. All matters being equal, rural life was a far healthier environment. However, famine and drought punished the rural poor more than the urban city folk, who lived close to interregional markets. Malnutrition was widespread among the rural poor, as was extreme and continuous physical labor. When a disease hit villages and villa communities, it often wiped out large numbers of people who were simply too weak to withstand infection.

What kind of diseases and disabilities did people suffer from in Late Antiquity? Given the unhygienic conditions and absence of antibiotics, cuts and wounds easily became gangrenous, which in turn could lead to the amputation of limbs and other body parts in unsanitary surgical settings without anesthesia. People regularly contracted a range of infectious diseases, all of which emerged out of dirty and contaminated living conditions. Dysentery, gastroenteritis, infectious hepatitis, typhoid, and tuberculosis were common afflictions, and likely hit urban populations regularly during the warmer summer months. Tapeworms spread easily from fecal matter, and not only to dogs, while leprosy (or Hansen's disease) had been endemic in the Mediterranean since the Hellenistic period. Malaria was arguably the most persistent killer in the southern, low-lying regions of the late Roman Empire, such as the areas around Rome and Athens. Caused by a parasite that infects red blood cells, malaria is contracted through the bite of a particular species of mosquito (the female *Anopheles*) that is a carrier of the parasite. The most obvious symptoms of the disease are regularly occurring fevers, but it also causes fatigue, vomiting, and severe headaches. For women, malaria can result in miscarriages and low-birth-weight infants. There were regular malaria outbreaks in hot, marshy areas of the Roman Empire. Whenever Rome flooded and the city slowly dried out, small pools of water in which malaria-carrying mosquitos nested persisted for months. One recent study links the city's annual spike in deaths during the late summer months to malaria.[8] Malaria was almost certainly the cause of an epidemic during the fifth century in a small Umbrian town near the Tiber, and it appears to have hit children especially hard. Archaeologists uncovered a nearby cemetery in which mostly children and infants were buried within a short period, and DNA testing on one skeleton confirmed that this individual had malaria.

Late Antiquity also witnessed two of the greatest pandemics in human history: the Cyprian and Justinianic plagues. The former (named for its best witness, the Christian bishop Cyprian [d. 258 CE]) struck urban and rural communities throughout the Mediterranean basin between 249 and 270 CE, hitting North Africa especially hard. The second and deadlier of the two, the Justinianic plague (so-called because of the pandemic's initial outbreak during the reign of Justinian [r. 527–565 CE]), initially spread to cities in the southeastern Mediterranean in 541 CE, hitting Egypt first. It quickly moved north to Constantinople, where Justinian caught and recovered from the disease. From there it spread to North Africa, Illyricum, and Italy, likely via shipping, reaching as far north as Germania. This first outbreak ended in 543 or 544 CE, but there were eighteen additional outbreaks of the same plague until 750 CE.

The precise nature of the plague of Cyprian remains uncertain, but some experts believe that it may have been a viral hemorrhagic fever, causing high temperatures, vomiting, diarrhea, bleeding from the eyes, severe debilitation, gangrene, and ultimately death. Scholars concur that the Justinianic-era pandemic was the bubonic plague, a severe bacterial infection caused by the species *Yersinia pestis*. The bacteria first infect fleas and human lice, which pass on the pathogen to human hosts by biting them, although human to human spread is also possible via air droplets in the breath. In the case of the Justinianic plague, the infected fleas were probably carried around the Mediterranean world and northern Europe via black rats, many of which were inadvertently transported on grain ships.[9] Those who contracted the bubonic plague would not have shown symptoms for five to seven days, the typical incubation period. Thereafter, they exhibited a range of horrifying symptoms: mental disturbances, fever, chills, vomiting, diarrhea, severe headaches, black pustules on the skin, and, most characteristically, grossly enlarged lymph glands, or buboes, which form in the upper thigh near the groin and in the armpits. According to one sixth-century witness, some of the buboes opened up and oozed pus.[10] Apparently those whose bodies expelled the infection in this manner were more likely to survive. Nevertheless, the Justinianic plague was a major killer. One recent study estimates that 30–60 percent of the Empire's entire population died in the pandemic during the initial wave in the 540s. Even if this estimate is too high (it is based on epidemiological modeling, not direct ancient evidence), we should assume that the plague profoundly affected daily life for many late Romans.

Later Romans also suffered and died from environmental illnesses, such as lead poisoning. Lead poisoning was a serious problem, though not one that hit all communities equally. It was especially hazardous for those who worked in smelting factories, since silver was produced largely from lead. Similarly, those who made lead pipes and pewter dishware, which contained a large percentage of lead, were also highly susceptible to lead poisoning. People who drew their drinking water from lead pipes and ate off pewter plates were at risk, but much less than those who worked in the smelting and manufacturing factories. In the case of water pipes, the danger might have been mitigated with harder water, because calcium deposits coated the pipes and prevented leaching. However, Romans willingly ingested lead when they ate wine or food that had been "seasoned" with lead-containing ingredients. Lead was regularly mixed with wine in the fermenting process, and late Romans loved a sugary concoction called *sapa* or *defructum*, which was made by simmering fresh grape juice in lead pots. A number of cosmetics, such as kohl and galena, a white powder used on the face, also had high lead contents.

Treating Disease

Treatments for disease were limited in Late Antiquity, but many people found relief through medical regimes and procedures. The dominance of the humoral system meant that the first line of defense against illness was diet: eating the right foods, and abstaining from the wrong ones, was typically the first step in rebalancing out-of-balance humors. Galen recommended barley broth, white meats, especially fish and poultry, and white wine, and warned against consuming red meat and red wine during illness. However, in many cases, patients were told to refrain from eating altogether while the illness persisted. Medical authorities also prescribed exercise, including sexual inter-course, which was thought to be a cure for the disease of melancholia. Bathing was also viewed as a form of medical treatment. Some baths had special times of the day for the sick to visit, but there were no bathing facilities exclusively for sick people.

Medical authorities also recommended medicines. In many cases, these were taken to induce vomiting or defecation as a method of evacuating any excess of humors thought to be causing the illness. All late ancient medicines were "natural" in the sense that they were created from herbs and other organic substances that grew locally and/or could be purchased at an apothecary. A physician likely con-sulted an herbal handbook, like a tiny Coptic-language book from a monastic hospital discovered in Egypt. A physician using this book would learn that marjoram, when mixed with wine and Egyptian incense, relieved thoracic pain, but when mixed with milk and leek seeds was a remedy for headaches.[11] The most famous herbal from Late Antiquity is the Vienna Dioscorides, an early-sixth-century illu-minated manuscript of an herbal handbook called *De materia medica* by the first-century Greek pharmacologist Pedanius Dioscorides. Now housed in a museum in Vienna (hence its name), the Vienna Dioscor-ides originally contained more than four hundred illustrations of plants used to make medicines, as well as detailed descriptions of the plants' various applications. Unlike the Coptic herbal, which was created for a working physician, this large and expensive book was designed for an aristocratic Christian matron in Constantinople named Juliana Anicia, who undoubtedly appreciated the fascinating information about medicines.

If diet, exercise, and medicine failed, late ancient healers typically turned to more invasive treatments. One was bloodletting, or phlebot-omy. It was believed that removing blood from the body reduced the amount of humors and thus rebalanced the patient's constitution. A physician typically used a special cupping vessel, which was placed over a vein that had been cut. The cup created a small vacuum, which drew blood out of the vein. Invasive surgery, we have noted, was generally seen as a procedure of last resort, since it often resulted in death from error or infection. However, archaeologists have found scores of surgical tools, most made of bronze. A typical surgeon's kit included the following instruments: scalpels (typically in sets), forceps, hooks, needles, probes, and cupping vessels. There were also specialized instruments, such as a cataract-couching needle, which was used to remove ocular cataracts.

Not all surgeries failed. Skilled surgeons were often able to relive pain and correct problems, such as cataracts and gallstones. There were also military surgeons trained to remove arrowheads and treat other injuries caused by warfare. The late ancient historian Procopius (ca. 500–565 CE), for instance, describes in great detail the facial injuries sustained by a Roman soldier during the siege of Rome in 534 CE.[12] Apparently, a Gothic archer had struck the soldier through his eye as he approached the city's walls. The Roman survived the initial injury and made his way to a staff surgeon, who successfully removed the arrow without killing the patient. The soldier supposedly went on to live many more years with a single eye. Another extraordinary surgical success story comes from the sixth-century Christian writer John of Ephesus. John tells an astounding tale of an operation performed on a priest named Aaron, who suffered from gangrene of the genitals. The surgeons successfully removed the diseased flesh, applied bandages, and inserted a lead tube into the man's urethra so he could urinate. John claims that Aaron not only survived the surgery, but lived with a lead catheter in his penis for another eighteen years.[13] By late ancient standards of medicine, Aaron's recovery was certainly miraculous.

Nonmedical healers offered an alternative range of treatments, mostly of the spiritual kind. The parallel belief in Late Antiquity that some diseases were caused by demonic possession led many sick men and women to faith healers for remedies that channeled supernatural powers. Amulets of varying types and curse tablets were used to cure physical ailments, as was prayer. Amulets were worn in various ways, as jewelry or even as clothing. A child's hooded tunic from Egypt features two roundels that would have covered the wearer's eyes when the hood was pulled up over his or her head, perhaps protecting the child from infiltration and illness (Figure 5.1). A patient might also purchase a

FIGURE 5.1. This tunic with possible apotropaic designs on the hood was created for a child. The circles on the hood would cover the child's eyes, thus protecting him or her from demons. The tunic was made in Egypt during the sixth or seventh century.
Photo by the Metropolitan Museum of Art (Creative Commons license).

medical armband, sometimes made of silver, with images stamped on it, typically of biblical scenes and verses. Especially popular was Psalm 90: "He that dwells in the help of the Highest," a phrase that likely had both medicinal and apotropaic force. Some included nonbiblical symbols, like the Chnoubis, a mythological half-serpent, half-lion creature with rays emanating from its head, whose image specifically cured stomach problems. The fact that these amulets combined Christian with non-Christian images and verse should not surprise us. As we shall see in the following chapter, religion in everyday life never strictly followed distinctions between "Christian" and "pagan".

The sick also looked to holy men and women, both living and dead, for assistance. Here the healing process was spontaneous and supernatural: a prayer to a god, such as Christ, or a saint acting as Christ's intercessor, was understood as a potential cure for a particular malady. Sick pilgrims, for instance, traveled to the Syrian shrine of St. Symeon Stylites the Younger (ca. 521–597 CE) to purchase stamped

FIGURE 5.2. A ceramic pilgrim's token from the shrine of St. Symeon Stylites in Syria. The token, which dates to the sixth century, depicts St. Symeon atop his famous pillar.
Photo by the Walters Art Museum (Creative Commons license).

clay tokens made from earth that was collected from the peak where Symeon sat on his pillar, known as the "Miraculous Mountain." These tokens, referred to as "blessings" (*eulogia*) in Symeon's biography, supposedly healed a wide variety of illnesses and disabilities (Figure 5.2).

Being Disabled in Late Antiquity

Whereas today many societies endeavor to include and accommodate people with disabilities, Greco-Roman society often viewed the physically impaired as oddities and castoffs. Wealthy families sometimes "collected" disabled slaves (dwarfs were especially popular), who were considered exotic possessions precisely because of their differences. For some, the extremely physically impaired proved ancient myths about the "monstrous races," which ranged from people with anatomical abnormalities to strange human-animal hybrids, like the dog-headed men (the *cynocephali*). Augustine, bishop of Hippo in early fifth-century North Africa, commented on a mosaic depicting "monstrous races" that apparently adorned the walls of a nearby harbor: single-legged men, pygmies, and men without mouths or necks and with eyes on their shoulders were represented as members of an alternative race that was wildly other.[14] Augustine acknowledged that many of these so-called human monsters were imaginary, but his discussion makes clear that real "freak shows" existed in North Africa. What appears to have been a set of conjoined twins, who Augustine described as a single man with two legs, two heads, and four arms, apparently attracted a steady stream of visitors.

In truth, most impaired men and women in Late Antiquity had to overcome more than emotional abuse. Even a relatively minor infirmity, such as poor eyesight, could cause profound difficulties in everyday life. Without corrective lenses, which did not exist, those with severe myopia would have had few opportunities to work and earn a living. Family would have been a nearsighted person's only support network. More severely disabled persons undoubtedly experienced far more serious challenges, from the lack of effective health care to hunger and indigence. While a few might have found their way into Christian hospitals (see "Places for Healing: Homes, Clinics, Hospitals"), most were left at the mercy of their families to care for them, individuals who did not contribute to the household's income. Having an impaired family member put an enormous financial strain on a family, and as a result, most households exposed infants born with anatomical deformities or noticeable disabilities. Babies born with certain congenital conditions, such as a faulty heart valve or cleft palate, would have died within days of birth; today, such conditions are relatively easy to correct with neonatal surgery.

Environmental conditions also meant that children born healthy sometimes became impaired as they matured into adulthood. Chronic malnutrition, especially among children, would have created large groups of disabled people. For example, vitamin D deficiency causes rickets in children, a disease where the bones fail to calcify properly and hence soften, and thus grow improperly into a "bowlegged" posture. Adult bodies, too, might become increasingly distorted over time. Skeletal remains from a fourth-century cemetery in Cirencester (near Gloucester, England) show that nearly 80 percent of the interred suffered from osteoarthritis, a progressive degenerative joint disease that causes debilitating pain and physical deformities in its later stages. Osteoarthritis is a common disease that still affects (typically elderly) men and women today, but the high percentage of those who suffered from it in fourth-century Cirencester suggests that this particular community may have had a disproportionately large number of people with deformed bodies in pain.[15] Moreover, relatively minor injuries could result in lifelong deformities if they did not heal properly: a fractured thigh bone that was set incorrectly, for example, might result in legs of different lengths.

Women's Bodies and Reproductive Health

Women's bodies were the focus of extensive attention from medical authorities, largely because of their reproductive capacity. Most ancient medical writers believed that the female body was distinct from the male in terms of its humoral constitution: it was colder, wetter, spongier, less active, and hence less likely to fully absorb the body's blood. Consequently, they reasoned, women expelled blood monthly through menstruation. As women aged and approached menopause, it was thought that their bodies became warmer and drier (more like the male body), and thus no longer needed to expel blood. Anatomically, fewer differences were noted. In fact, Galen famously argued that the female reproductive system was essentially a smaller, less perfect, internalized version of the male system. Instead of testes, women had ovaries; instead of a penis, they had a clitoris. Moreover, both Galen and his contemporary Soranus, a second-century medical authority whose writings on gynecology were read in Late Antiquity, asserted that although women contributed "seed" to conception, the female seed was inferior to the male seed, and the male seed drove fetal development. The fact that ancient medical authorities believed that the female body was inferior to the male body, even in reproduction, is hardly surprising given the deeply patriarchal nature of Roman society.

On a daily basis, women obviously dealt with unique bodily functions. Menstruation was considered not just normal, but necessary for maintaining a woman's humoral balance, but precisely how real women handled their monthly periods is difficult to know. Menarche likely began around the age of twelve, the legal minimum age for marriage in the Roman Empire. We have very little literary evidence and no material evidence for "sanitary protection" in Late Antiquity. Women presumably used napkins made of cotton, linen, or wool, the latter of which can be highly absorbent. However, we have no sense of how they secured the napkins, since women did not typically wear underwear except during exercise. They may have used some kind of sanitary belt, such as women in the modern West wore before the invention of adhesive strips and tampons. The napkins were likely made at home, and disposed of there, although, as with urine and feces, there was resale value in used sanitary pads. In Alexandria, groups of poor women collected *phulakia* ("protection") from houses, ostensibly to clean and resell.

Most women in Late Antiquity were pregnant several times in their lives, having on average five or six live births during their fertile years. Then as now, conceiving a child was not always easy and infertility was a problem, though undoubtedly less so, given that most women had children when they were still quite young. The late Romans had no effective means of dealing with infertility. They erroneously believed that ovulation occurred after, rather than before, menstruation, rendering futile any attempt at timing sex for conception. Some resorted to fertility enhancing medicines and amulets. Prayer and magical rites were also used. A Neoplatonist, we recall, attempted to cure his wife's infertility by driving a demon from her body. Once a woman conceived, she had essentially no prenatal care. Miscarriages were common, especially given the high rate of infectious diseases and lead exposure. And delivering a stillborn could be very dangerous without effective drugs to induce labor. According to a Christian source, a young woman was unable to deliver a seven-month stillborn baby, and to make matters worse, her jaw had broken from excessive vomiting during the pregnancy.[16] As the girl was nearing death herself, her mother brought in physicians and midwives, but the only help came from the relics of St. Stephen, which, according to the narrative, enabled the girl to give birth to the dead child and healed her jaw.

When a pregnancy advanced normally and labor began, the family called in a midwife, who came to the house to deliver the baby. Virtually all infants were born in private homes during Late Antiquity, although there was at least one lying-in hospital in early seventh-century Alexandria. Birthing chairs were commonly used, as was a special seat for the midwife, which allowed her to be positioned beneath the woman's vagina so that she could massage the vaginal opening with olive oil, just as some midwives and doctors do today. However knowledgeable the midwife was, and many undoubtedly had considerable experience dealing with difficult labor and birth, her skills were limited in the case of a true emergency. Physicians were sometimes called in to assist in these situations, but late ancient medical doctors had few effective solutions to offer. Contrary to popular belief, Julius Caesar was not delivered via C-section, and there is little evidence that late Roman surgeons resorted to opening up the uterus to remove babies who could not be delivered vaginally. In cases where babies became stuck in the birth canal, forceps were used, and if that was not successful, the baby eventually died. Moreover, hemorrhaging was difficult to stop without effective surgical treatment and clotting drugs, and hence posed an additional danger to women during childbirth. After birth, mothers were highly susceptible to puerperal fever, an infection women contract from bacteria in the reproductive system following a birth or miscarriage.[17] In sum, pregnancy and childbirth were potentially deadly experiences for women and babies, and late ancient medicine was not well equipped to deal with most of the relatively routine problems that arose in the course of bearing a child.

Not all women, of course, wanted to become pregnant and have a child. Prostitutes, poor mothers who already had too many mouths to feed, and rich society ladies who had committed adultery all had reasons to avoid pregnancy or to terminate one. With regard to contraception, there were few, if any, effective methods available. Medical treatises often prescribed remedies such as pessaries (pieces of wool smeared in ointment, in this case inserted into the vagina), vaginal plugs, and creams applied to the penis. Soranus, our second-century expert on women's health, suggested that a woman squat down immediately after sex and wipe her vagina and uterus with olive oil. Although some used the rhythm method, the fact that late Romans believed that women ovulated after menstruation made the technique utterly ineffective. Breastfeeding gave some women several months of birth control, but it was neither permanent nor certain.

Abortion was probably a more viable option for women than contraception. Medical texts recommended exercises such as jumping, carrying around heavy loads, and constricting the body, as well as loud and violent sneezing. They also suggested pessaries and certain medicines known to stimulate labor. According to the famous herbal handbook by Dioscorides, there were two varieties of a plant called Aristolochia that promoted menstruation and the expulsion of a fetus. Surgical abortion was also known, but like all surgical procedures, it was seen as a last resort. To be clear, performing abortions and prescribing abortifacients were illegal in Late Antiquity, though only because they potentially denied the father an heir (poisons were also deemed illegal in general). The fetus's life or death was not a concern to the Roman state. Some Christian authorities characterized abortion as murder, although many drew a distinction between formed and unformed fetuses, and allotted harsher spiritual punishments for those who aborted the former.[18] Some physicians probably sidestepped criminal charges by claiming that they prescribed a drug for an ailment and the resulting miscarriage was unrelated. Aristolochia, for instance, was also used to treat asthma, hiccups, and convulsions. In truth, abortion was never the most common means of dealing with an unwanted pregnancy in Late Antiquity. The majority of women carried their babies to term, gave birth, and then abandoned them. Infant exposure, we noted earlier and in Chapter 3, was practiced in Late Antiquity, though typically only under the most extreme circumstances.

Places for Healing: Homes, Clinics, and Hospitals

Valeria Verecunda likely practiced medicine in private clinics, making house calls as needed. There was nothing like preventive care in Late Antiquity, and people did not have annual checkups with their physicians. Illness, either chronic or acute, was the reason to call a doctor. Depending on the wealth of the household, a private home might be the best place to undergo a procedure and convalesce. The rich had many slaves, who could keep the room and bedding relatively clean, bring water as needed, pick up medicines, and attend to the patient's needs. A poor family living in a single room would have had a very different experience of illness. Even if they were able to afford a doctor's fees, the patient could suffer in a dirty space without running water, in a bed infested with insects (if the family had a bed; the poor mostly slept on mats), and would have had minimal access to medicines or the appropriate foods because of cost. Although disease hit rich and poor indiscriminately in Late Antiquity, especially in dense urban settings, the poor fared far worse when it came to receiving health care and recovering from any serious illness.

Outside the home, physicians' clinics provided medical care to local communities. Some offered specialty services. In late fourth-century Antioch, for instance, there were separate clinics for surgery and eye ailments. Wounded soldiers would also receive medical care, but probably not in military infirmaries. Although the infirmary was a regular feature of the early imperial military camp, it is unclear whether late Roman armies continued to build and staff them. Lack of evidence for military infirmaries suggests that soldiers stationed along the Empire's frontiers relied on local medical services rather than on permanent military facilities. However, physicians routinely accompanied field armies on campaign, as we saw in the case of the Roman soldier who underwent successful surgery to remove an arrow that had entered his head through an eye.

Outside the army, the Roman government historically provided little to the people in terms of medical services. Generally speaking, sick men and women paid for health care out of their own pockets. In some cases, members of specific religious communities, notably Christians and Jews, provided assistance for health care. Charity was a key component of both ancient Judaism and Christianity, and religious authorities encouraged members to give alms as a way of offering material support to those in need, typically food, clothing, and shelter – all necessarily elements for an effective physical recovery. It is also likely that some provided funds for medical care for their most needy members.

The Christian commitment to charity inspired fourth-century clerics and monks to establish Late Antiquity's greatest innovation in health care: the hospital. Christians founded the first hospitals in the eastern Mediterranean during the second half of the fourth century. These were not hospitals in the modern sense, in that their primary function was not to provide inpatient medical services by professional physicians and nurses. Rather, the late antique hospital was a charitable institution that offered housing, food, and, in some cases, medical assistance to individuals in need. In fact, those who entered late ancient hospitals were not necessarily sick, but they were necessarily poor. In some cases, those who were ill might receive free medical attention from doctors and other healers and nursing assistance from staff who were not nurses in the modern sense, since the profession did not yet exist. The words late ancient writers used to refer to these hospitals underscores their charitable function. Most were called *xenodocheia*, or "guest houses," that is, places for the homeless (whether transient or local). It is believed that the bishop Basil of Caesarea (330–379 CE) established the first hospital on his property near the episcopal see of Caesarea (central Turkey). He called the entire complex a "poor house" (in Greek, *ptochoptopheion*), and it included buildings for the very sick as well as lepers and orphans. A few decades later, another Christian cleric, John Chrysostom (349–407 CE), used church funds to found a sick house in Constantinople, where he was bishop. Similar institutions gradually appeared throughout the eastern and western Mediterranean, most established with ecclesiastical funding and directed by church authorities. By the sixth century, Constantinople had a network of hospitals, including St. Sampson's, the archaeological remains of which have been recently excavated. Unfortunately, scholars are unable to determine from the site how many beds the hospital provided or whether it had separate wards for surgery, convalescing, etc. In late sixth-century Spain, the bishop of Mérida founded a hospital in the city to which he assigned physicians and attendants. The hospital served both travelers and the sick, Christians and Jews, providing beds, food, and medical care. The bishop earmarked half of the church's annual revenues for the hospital, suggesting that it was the focus of his administration and served a large population of needy people.

SEXUALITY, EDUCATION, AND ADORNMENT

Having Sex in Late Antiquity

Soon after her marriage to P. Gellius Vitalio, Valeria Verecunda probably had sex for the first time. She was almost certainly a virgin before she married Gellius, because this was expected for all girls from respectable families, regardless of wealth or social status. Yet, losing her virginity to a husband in a legal marriage was precisely what

Valeria's family and society wanted. A married woman was supposed to have sex with her husband and to produce many children. On the other hand, it is unlikely that Gellius was a virgin when he first slept with Valeria. For one thing, he was probably older than Valeria. He might have been previously married to another woman, who died or whom he divorced (or who divorced him). But even if this was his first marriage, Gellius was a man. It was perfectly acceptable for him to "experiment" sexually with slaves, prostitutes, and concubines outside of marriage. Even after he and Valeria wed, he could have continued to force his slaves to have sex with him or paid a prostitute for it. He might even have preferred to sleep with men outside his marriage. So long as Gellius remained the "active" participant in the sexual relationship, meaning that he penetrated his partner and was not penetrated by him, Gellius did not violate any Roman cultural norms. Where Gellius could run afoul of the law and society was in coupling either with a married woman (adultery) or with an unmarried woman or boy of status whose family had intended her or him to wed in the proper fashion. The latter situation was a criminal offense known as *stuprum*. *Stuprum* was the closest the Romans came to acknowledging rape, and it only applied to sex with freeborn women and men of otherwise marriageable status. Single women, too, could be charged with *stuprum* if they behaved in what was perceived as a promiscuous manner with other men.

Had Valeria sought extramarital partners, she would have faced severe social disapproval and possible criminal charges. Adultery, defined narrowly in Roman law as sex with a married woman, was a criminal offense in the late Empire. As a respectable married woman, Valeria had one acceptable "normal" sexual choice: to be the passive – that is, the penetrated – sexual partner with her husband.

In Late Antiquity, there was no such thing as a sexual identity. People did not self-identify as "gay" or "straight," nor did they distinguish biological sex (male/female) from gender (the various cultural constructions of masculinity and femininity). Instead, they understood sexual experiences and appetites to be both natural and defined primarily by power and status. A freeborn, active male lover in a same-sex relationship was a respectable citizen, but a freeborn man who preferred to be the passive partner was considered deviant and labeled effeminate. What we call lesbianism was harder for the

Romans to grasp, especially if neither female partner appeared to play the active sexual role. However, female same-sex relationships clearly existed. For example, a woman named Sophia purchased a Greek binding spell to attract a female love interest named Gorgonia.[19] A woman who actively sought another woman and pursued her "like a man" was seen as masculine (and called a *tribadis* or *virago*), and hence also violated the norm, which associated femininity with sexual passivity. Whether Sophia's peers branded her a *tribadis* for her active pursuit of Gorgonia is impossible to know.

It is also clear that pederasty, that is, sexual relations between an older man and a teenage boy undertaken for the boy's social education, existed in late Roman culture, especially in the East (even if it was less common than in earlier periods). In fact, what mattered most to the vast majority of late Romans was less the gender or age of a person's sexual partner than that the person's sex life reflected social status and an appropriate level of self-mastery. The Romans perceived moderation of sexual desire as a gendered moral virtue. For women, the goal was to refrain from all sexual activity outside marriage and to limit one's sex life to passive experiences with a husband. For men, the rules were different, since they could have sex outside marriage. However, this double standard did not entirely exclude them from potential moral censure. Having too much sex, or engaging in it either with the wrong type of person (e.g., an unmarried freeborn girl or boy) or in a passive manner, could lead to social stigma and perhaps legal penalties, such as *stuprum*.

To a certain extent and for some people, the emergence of Christianity as a major religion modified the sexual mores of the late Roman Empire. Christian authorities, especially bishops, typically took a black-and-white position on the matter of extramarital sex: all of it was sinful, regardless of who performed it and their role in the sex act. For the first time, husbands who committed adultery were condemned to the same extent as their wives, while all same-sex relations were branded "fornication." These important ideological developments laid the foundation for harsher imperial legislation proscribing prostitution, male adultery, and ultimately, if the sixth-century historian Procopius can be believed, pederasty. In his salacious narrative about the emperor Justinian and his wife, Theodora, known as *The Secret History*, Procopius claimed that Justinian passed laws not merely condemning pederasty, but punishing the participants with castration.[20] Additionally, some Christian authorities privileged virginity and celibacy in a way and to an extent that was unknown in classical Greco-Roman culture. As we shall see in greater detail in the next chapter, asceticism – the renunciation of sex, money, and other material pleasures for spiritual reasons – was gaining adherents throughout the period, and an increasing number of men and women were eschewing sex at various points in their lives. From a Roman cultural perspective, this extreme form of self-mastery was an odd departure from the norm. But for many late Romans, achieving moderate sexual self-control was closely related to the proper education of the mind.

Educating the Elite Mind

In an earlier chapter on the household, we learned that children received their early and perhaps only education within the home. Whether they were tutored by a parent or a special slave, homeschooling was the norm for young girls and boys across the social spectrum. But beyond this early stage, education was dramatically different for non-elites and elites. Both Valeria and her husband, Gellius, for instance, almost certainly received their entire education in an informal domestic context. They also may have taught their daughter some basic Latin literacy and numeracy skills, but none of them would have been capable of reading complex texts in any language. Moreover, Valeria's medical training was entirely practical and acquired through an apprenticeship, perhaps with a family member. For non-elites, schooling was essentially vocational. Simply put, academic education was a luxury that the vast majority of families could not afford, since it came not only with tuition and boarding costs, but also (and more significantly) with the loss of a potential worker for years at a time. When we consider education at this high level, therefore, we necessarily examine a small fraction of late Roman society.

Elite education was both a privilege and an obligation. All respectable young men were expected to be not simply literate, but trained in the proper manner of speaking, writing, and maintaining composure. Elite women were supposed to be able to read as well, and it was common for highborn girls to achieve a relatively advanced level of literary knowledge. Elite schooling began when children were four and five, with basic literacy and numeracy in their primary language, but many learned second languages. Wealthy Latin-speaking families often owned Greek-speaking slaves, whose role in the household was to teach the children the Empire's other main language. Fewer elite Greek-speaking families would have taught their children Latin, unless they intended their sons to have a career in government, in which Latin was the official language until the sixth century. The ability to read longer works of literature, whether from the classical or the newer biblical canon (increasingly popular among Christian families), was also expected of both boys and girls, and thus was part of schooling in the early stages.

For aristocratic boys and, more rarely, girls, schooling went beyond literary fluency, and might involve traveling to classes taught by expert teachers outside the home. To be clear, the schools these elite children attended were not like the institutions that we have now, a set of physical facilities with an administrative and instructional staff. Rather, late ancient schools were relatively informal organizations centered on a single teacher, who perhaps had a few assistants. In a sense, the late Roman educational system was more accessible than a modern Ivy League university. Admission was "open" and informal, meaning that interested students did not apply to these schools and entrance was not contingent on any particular metric, such as grade point average or extracurricular activities. If a teacher had space, and the expenses could be met, then a boy could attend.

Teachers and assistants in late Roman schools were almost always men. One exception is Hypatia (d. 415 CE), a pagan female teacher of philosophy in Alexandria who tutored a number of famous men (and was subsequently murdered by an angry Christian mob). Students who studied abroad were expected to live independently, as schools provided neither lodging nor adult supervision. Instead, slaves would have accompanied children studying away from home, acting as babysitters. But slaves had only so much control over their young masters. Hazing was common in many late ancient schools, as were street fights between students of rival teachers. Due to these experiences, not to mention the high cost of tuition and living expenses, attrition rates were high. Even a world-famous teacher, such as the great orator Libanius (314–394 CE), could not always persuade his students to stay on: in one entering class of fifty-seven students, thirty-five dropped out in the second year.

What exactly did elite kids study? Children typically followed three sequential courses: the study of grammar, followed by the study of rhetoric, and finally the study of philosophy or law. In ancient education, grammar was more than simply learning the formal mechanics of Greek and Latin. Rather, the study of grammar was more like a course in the language and interpretation of "great" literature and its moral and historical significance. The first stage of grammatical training entailed the reading of what late Romans deemed "classical" texts, such as Virgil's *Aeneid* and Cicero's orations or Homer's epic poems and Demosthenes' speeches. Teachers taught students how to identify important references in the texts and recognize their moral or historical significance. Students who mastered this basic level of grammatical training would advance to the next, in which they engaged in compositional exercises. Through these, students learned how to shape their own texts, wherein they elaborated upon stories or themes using the linguistic and interpretive skills acquired in the first level of grammatical training. After mastering grammar, students moved on to the second stage, where they learned rhetorical techniques, that is, skills in the art of public speaking and written persuasion. Here students worked closely with a teacher, first listening to him give speeches, and then practicing with him to make speeches of their own, in which they adhered closely to specific rules of argumentation, diction, and style.

A few especially gifted students might further their education through the formal study of philosophy or law, the third stage. By philosophy, we primarily mean the writings of Greek thinkers such as Plato and Aristotle, as well as disciples of the Roman Stoics and the Epicureans. Students at this level were expected to identify the specific thinkers behind a particular idea, and to explain how a particular philosophical issue or problem related to their living a morally outstanding life. Here the choice of a teacher was especially significant, since each would specialize in the writings and ideas of a particular philosophical school. The study of law entailed further rhetorical training, especially in forensic argumentation. Unlike today, it did not involve studying current legal codes; rather, late ancient law students focused on the conceptual dimensions of the legal system.

Of course, not all families wanted their children to study pagan philosophy or secular law. Leading Christian households preferred to send their boys to schools where they would study biblical writings and the works of venerated church authorities. Jewish households in the East might have elected to send their sons to a rabbinic school, where they would study not only scripture, but also the emerging body of Talmudic literature, the Jewish legalistic writings that were collected and codified during Late Antiquity. In fact, over time, finding a school for pagan philosophy became increasingly difficult, especially after Justinian shut the main schools in Athens in 529 CE. Instead, the brightest boys would attend religious-affiliated schools, where the classics might be read, but only as a gateway to the more important religious literature. By the end of the sixth century, Christian monasteries and rabbinic schools became the leading centers of learning in the Empire.

Dressing the Body: Clothing, Cosmetics, Jewelry, and Hair

Valeria Verecunda and her husband, P. Gellius Vitalio, were neither rich nor aristocratic, but they likely dressed with care, choosing clothing that was gender appropriate, but that also emphasized their respectable status and Roman heritage. Valeria wore one or more linen tunics most days, and when it was cooler, she donned a woolen *palla*, a sort of draped cloak that was popular among women in Late Antiquity. Her great-grandmother probably wore a *stola*, a signature clothing item for Roman matrons, but by the third century it had gone out of style. When she was working, Valeria likely belted her tunic just beneath her breasts, which would have made it easier for her to move around when seeing patients. Her sense of personal style would have come through in her choice of color and pattern for her tunic. If she could afford it, she wore a few items of handmade jewelry, such as glass beads. Valeria probably did not cover her long hair in public, only perhaps when she participated in sacrifice, or, if she was Christian or Jewish, when she attended church or synagogue.

While her husband was almost certainly a Roman citizen, Gellius probably did not wear a toga, the traditional "uniform" of the male Roman citizenry. By the third century, the toga was worn by relatively few men, and instead was becoming more ceremonial garb for high-status civil magistrates. More likely, Gellius sported a tunic like his wife's, but he would have worn it with a military-style cloak, which was becoming fashionable for men, even for those who were not (or had never been) soldiers. Gellius was probably clean-shaven, with short hair, and might have worn a few rings.

Clothing in Late Antiquity, like clothing today, was both a necessity and a social code. The vast majority of late Romans owned only a few items, and clothing was considered so valuable that people itemized individual garments in wills and handed them down to their heirs, just like pieces of land. Generally speaking, clothing was relatively simple and standardized in Late Antiquity, at least by later measures. For all late Romans, male and female, free and enslaved, rich and poor, the tunic was the basic dress item, worn at home and in public. Increasingly, the fashion was to layer two tunics. The under-tunic often had long sleeves to the wrist and was more tight-fitting, while the outer-tunic was typically looser, wider, and shorter. Men and children usually wore their tunics to just below their knees, women to their calves or ankles (Figures 5.3 and 5.4). Slaves dressed similarly to their

FIGURE 5.3. A typical linen tunic from Egypt, dated to the fifth century, with designs featuring images of the god Dionysius. The tunic was the most common article of clothing worn in Late Antiquity by men, women, and children. Photo by the Metropolitan Museum of Art (Creative Commons license).

FIGURE 5.4. An early fifth-century ivory diptych depicting a Roman official with his wife and child, most likely the high-ranking general Stilicho (d. 408 CE), his wife, Serena, and their son, Eucherius. All three wear styles of clothing common to the rich and aristocratic: Serena dons two high-belted layered tunics, the bottom tunic featuring long, tight sleeves, a *palla* around her shoulders, heavy jewelry, and what appears to be a snood in her hair. Stilicho is dressed in military-style garb, as was common for all late Roman officials regardless of whether their service was military or civilian: a short, belted tunic covered by a *chlamys*, the soldier's cape, fastened at his shoulder with a fibula. Note the circular designs, or *segmenta*, decorating the fabrics of Stilicho's clothing. Eucherius dresses similarly to his parents, with layered, unbelted tunics and a pinned *chlamys*.
Photo by akg-images.

masters and mistresses in terms of the tunic. A mosaic from a house in Piazza Armerina in Sicily, one of Late Antiquity's best preserved elite villas, depicts slaves accompanying their mistress to the baths. Everyone in the image is dressed in tunics, although the slaves'

FIGURE 5.5. An early fourth-century mosaic image of a mistress with her slaves walking to the baths. All of the female figures wear similar tunics, but the slaves' are belted. From the Villa Romana del Casale in Piazza Armerina, Sicily.
Photo by Jorge Tutor, Alamy stock photo.

garments are belted, since this was more practical for working. What seems to differentiate the mistress from her slaves is largely the length of her tunic. It is longer, more impractical for labor, and probably understood to be made of a costlier fabric (Figure 5.5).

Indeed, what differentiated clothing along status lines was quality and quantity. There were numerous grades of linen on the market, and several types of wool. Silk, the costliest textile in Late Antiquity, was also available, especially from the sixth century, when workshops in Constantinople started breeding silkworms. Previously, all silk was imported from the Far East. Linen, woolen, and silk fabrics could be dyed when finished. Skilled weavers added intricate patterns. Lateral stripes called *clavi* were popular for both sexes, and were typically woven in white or purple. Also favored were patch-like or roundel markings called *segmenta*. Some *segmenta* were illustrated with images of popular pagan gods or biblical scenes. Contrary to modern presuppositions, the Dark Ages were not actually dark, at least when it came to clothing. Ancient fabrics became increasingly colorful

FIGURE 5.6. A bronze crossbow-shaped fibula dating to the fourth century. Such pins were regularly used to fasten clothes.
Photo by the Metropolitan Museum of Art (Creative Commons license).

and ornate over time. Fifth- and sixth-century clothing can appear simply garish when compared to third- and even fourth-century styles (see Figure 5.3).

In the hot summer months around the Mediterranean Basin, one or two linen tunics would have sufficed for comfort. But in northern climates and in the winter months, late Romans typically wore a woolen cloak or cape over their tunics. Buttons, zippers, and snaps had not yet been invented, so people fastened their cloaks using a brooch or pin known as a *fibula* (Figure 5.6). Men and women also wore similar types of shoes: sandals were popular in warm climates, especially the "thong" style, while boots and closed-toe shoes were favored during cooler periods and in colder regions. All shoes were completely flat with no heels, and in most cases the leather soles were sewn or nailed into leather uppers (Figure 5.7).

Although men and women dressed more similarly to one another in Late Antiquity than they do today, not all clothing was unisex. Military-style clothing, we noted above, was especially popular among male civilians and civilian administrators. In the case of the latter, the uniform of the late Roman civil magistrate closely resembled that of an army officer. He wore a short tunic made from an elaborately

FIGURE 5.7. A pair of leather sandals, likely made for a child, from fourth-century Egypt. The thong style, shown here, was popular in the late Roman world.
Photo by the Metropolitan Museum of Art (Creative Commons license).

decorated fabric, a *chlamys* or similar-styled cloak, and a large belt (*cingulum*) (see Figure 5.4). The inspiration for this new hybrid style was the emperor, himself both a military and civilian leader. For men who did not want to look like soldiers or officials, a *pallium* was another option. Originally a Greek-style cloak worn by philosophers and physicians, the *pallium* symbolized another form of ancient masculinity, one oriented around wisdom and expertise. Because of these associations, Christian bishops gravitated toward the *pallium*, and most artistic representations of Christian saints depict them wearing one. Late Roman men also wore colored leggings and sometimes even trousers, a clothing item borrowed from northern barbarian neighbors that became popular among Romans (Figure 5.8).

Women typically wore more and heavier jewelry than men, and styled their hair more elaborately. For special occasions, a very wealthy woman likely wore big pieces of jewelry, preferably made of gold. She would have been especially fond of collar necklaces and banded bracelets adorned with gems like amethysts and garnets or pearls. These were the prominent jewels of the period, made popular by the ladies of the imperial court and their goldsmiths in Constantinople and Ravenna. Although the Romans knew about diamonds, they were unable to cut them, and hence relied on softer stones for jewelry making. The less well-off lady, by contrast, might opt for jewelry made of glass beads, which were ubiquitous in the late Empire. Elite women had long hair, which they elaborately coiffed on top of their heads, often using hairpieces and even wooden strips to prop up vertiginous beehive-like piles. The snood, a fitted hairnet, was increasingly popular beginning in the later fourth century, although it is uncertain whether women outside the imperial court followed this trend. As we observed in the case of Valeria, women did not necessarily cover

FIGURE 5.8. In this mosaic from the Villa Romana del Casale in Piazza Armerina, Sicily, men wear short decorated tunics with colored leggings. Photo by Ivan Vdovin, Alamy stock photo.

their hair and head at home or when traveling in public, though hoods were both typical and fashionable.

Many women wore makeup in Late Antiquity, and not only actors. Decorative facial creams and materials were relatively cheap, and women from a wide range of backgrounds wore makeup some of the time. Women liked to use either galena, a white lead-based power, or a compacted white clay on the face to create the illusion of smooth white skin, which was the physical ideal. They also applied rouge to the cheeks and kohl (which also contained lead) to decorate the eyelids and brows.

Facial hair for men was also a fashion statement. The beard came in and out of fashion throughout Roman history, but it was traditionally associated with the figure of the Greek philosopher. The fourth-century emperor Julian grew a beard precisely because of its Greek connotations, much to the chagrin of his courtiers, who ridiculed him for departing from his predecessors' "Roman" clean-shaven look.[21] Thereafter, beards became more common. Another trend in Late Antiquity was the mustache, originally associated with non-Roman men, perhaps especially with northern barbarian males. Although the mustache was not a novelty in Late Antiquity (earlier images of Roman soldiers sporting mustaches predate the period), it nevertheless become a signature style for several western barbarian kings, such as the Ostrogoth rulers Theodoric and Theodahad, as well as at least one fifth-century Roman emperor. Just as a beard connoted the philosopher, so the mustache symbolized martial virility and invincibility, two qualities that the Romans both admired and closely associated with barbarian peoples.

The question of whether Late Antiquity witnessed the emergence of a "Christian" style of clothing has long intrigued scholars, with some suggesting that men and women took heed of the church's critique of sexuality and began to dress more modestly in their daily lives. However, this trend appears to have been little more than wishful thinking by bishops, at least for the average Christian. Images from late ancient mosaics and other objects show that women wore increasingly form-fitting clothing that was anything but solemn in terms of decorative color and style. Men dressed in silks and multicolored tunics that were excessively patterned. The heavy bejeweled accessories worn by the late Empire's elite emphasized wealth, not ascetic values. Moreover, Christian women were not obligated to veil themselves outside of the home, though some may have done so. Of course, some ascetic Christians deliberately dressed differently from their non-ascetic counterparts, choosing simpler fabrics and more somber colors, and eschewing jewelry and makeup. Pinianus, the ascetic husband of Melania the Younger (383–439 CE), reportedly downgraded the quality of his linen tunics in an effort to appear humble. A few Christian women ostentatiously veiled themselves in public, even when it was socially inappropriate. According to her biographer, Melania the Younger insisted on covering her entire head when meeting with Serena, the emperor's sister and wife of Stilicho, the West's leading general at the time (Figure 5.4).[22] Serena apparently ordered Melania to unveil herself, but Melania refused to go without a covering, breaching court decorum. Jewish women in the eastern regions of the Mediterranean, and especially from the conservative rabbinic communities of Palestine, may have worn veils more often when outside of the home, but the evidence is hardly conclusive.

Finally, the most pressing question about late ancient clothing: did people wear underwear? Believe it or not, scholars still cannot definitively answer this question. Most historians of clothing believe that men usually did not wear underwear, except perhaps when sporting very short tunics. They did wear underwear-like garments during exercise, however. More like a leather loincloth or pair of shorts than underwear, the garment, sometimes called a *subligaculum*, covered the man's private parts and was worn exclusively during physical activities and competitions. Images of men exercising and of gladiators offer us our best insight into what these garments looked like, and their function as light, unencumbering clothing for athletic pursuits (see Figure 2.10).

Women, we noted in an earlier section, did not regularly wear panties. Like men, however, some wore special garments when exercising. Mosaics from Piazza Armerina in Sicily depict late Roman women exercising, wearing what we would describe as bikinis: briefs to cover their lower parts and a bandeau strip around their breasts to secure them. In fact, this bandeau strip may have been a fairly common clothing item worn outside of athletic events. While the modern bra is a nineteenth-century invention, late ancient women relied on strips of linen to hold their breasts in place. Called a *strophium*, the female breast band had both utilitarian and aesthetic functions, since it could be tied in a manner to increase or decrease bust size. The ideal late Roman woman apparently had a small to medium-sized chest (Figure 5.9).

***

The experience of embodiment varied for men and women, rich and poor in Late Antiquity, especially when it came to education. Sexuality, too, was deeply gendered and status-oriented. Double standards governed expectations about sex outside of marriage: men were given considerable latitude and women none, while internalized ethical notions of self-control caused many to feel shame for wanting too much sex or sex in the wrong manner. Of course, slaves and prostitutes (as "infamous persons"; see Chapter 2) did not count in this high-stakes game of reputation building or destruction. Their bodies were simply there to use. Disease, we have seen, was far less

FIGURE 5.9. The "bikini girls" mosaic from the Villa Romana del Casale in Piazza Armerina, Sicily. Though they may look to us like girls in bathing suits, these female athletes wear the typical exercise gear of the time: a breast band with short briefs, perhaps made of leather.
Photo by Richard Hodges.

discriminatory, hitting all genders and social statuses relatively equally, with the largest differences determined more by where one lived (rural or urban setting) than how one lived. Recovering from or avoiding illness was a preoccupation of many late Romans, for obvious reasons, and people explored a variety of paths to better health. Religion, we have seen, provided one such path, a central topic of late Roman life that we will now explore.

Further Reading

Augustine, *The City of God*, trans. H. Bettenson (London, 2004, reprint).
J. Gager, *Curse Tablets and Binding Spells from the Ancient World* (Oxford, 1992).
Gerontius, *Life of Melania the Younger*, trans. E. Clark (New York, 1984).
Gregory of Tours, *Miracles of Saint Martin of Tours*, trans. R. Van Dam, in *Saints and Their Miracles in Late Antique Gaul* (Princeton, NJ, 1993), 199–303.

Jerome, *Letter* 121, trans. P. Schaff, in *The Nicene Fathers and Post-Nicene Fathers*, vol. 6; most easily accessed at www.tertullian.org/fathers2/NPNF2-06/Npnf2-06-03.htm#P4384_1197838.

John of Ephesus, *Lives of the Eastern Saints*, trans. E. W. Brooks (Leiden, 2003, reprint).

Procopius, *The Wars of Justinian*, trans. H. Dewing, revised by A. Kaldellis (Indianapolis, IN, 2014).

Procopius, *The Secret History and Related Texts*, trans. A. Kaldellis (Indianapolis, IN, 2010).

Soranus, *On Gynecology*, trans. O. Temkin (Baltimore, MD, 1991).

Readers interested in the general history of ancient medicine, including that of Late Antiquity, should consult H. King, *Greek and Roman Medicine* (London, 2001), and V. Nutton, *Ancient Medicine* (London, 2004) and "From Galen to Alexander: Aspects of Medicine and Medical Practice in Late Antiquity," *Dumbarton Oaks Papers* 38 (1984): 1–14. On the history of health care in Late Antiquity, the earliest hospitals in the Roman Empire, and their link to early Christianity, see A. Crislip, *From Monastery to Hospital: Christian Monasticism and the Transformation of Healthcare in Late Antiquity* (Ann Arbor, MI, 2005). Those interested specifically in disease should read Ralph Jackson, *Doctors and Diseases in the Roman Empire* (London, 1988), especially for its images of surgical instruments, R. Sallares, *Malaria and Rome: A History of Malaria in Ancient Italy* (Oxford, 2002), and B. Shaw, "Seasons of Death: Aspects of Mortality in Ancient Rome," *Journal of Roman Studies* 86 (1996): 100–138. Contraception and abortion are discussed in E. Eyeben, "Family Planning in Greco-Roman Antiquity," *Ancient Society* 11/12 (1980–1981): 5–82. For the Justinianic plague, see the essays in *Plague and the End of Antiquity: The Pandemic of 541–750*, ed. L. Little (Cambridge, 2006).

For ancient education, see E. Watts, *City and School in Late Antique Athens and Alexandria* (Berkeley, CA, 2006), R. Kaster, *Guardians of Language: The Grammarian and Society in Late Antiquity* (Berkeley, CA, 1988), and H. I. Marrou, *A History of Education in Antiquity* (New York, 1956). For a general introduction to ancient sexuality, see M. Skinner, *Sexuality in Greek and Roman Culture* (London, 2005). And for the impact of Christianity on sex and the body, start with P. Brown, *The Body and Society: Men, Women, and Sexual Renunciation in Early Christianity* (New York, 1988). On clothing, see A. T. Croom, *Roman Clothing and Fashion* (Stroud, UK, 2002), M. Harlow, "Female Dress, Third-Sixth Century: The Messages in the Media," *Antiquité Tardive* 12 (2004): 203–215, and K. Olson, *Dress and the Roman Woman: Self-Presentation and Society* (Milton Park, UK, 2008). On apotropaic clothing, see J. Ball, "Charms: Protection and Auspicious Motifs," in *Designing Identity: The Power of Textiles in Late Antiquity* (Princeton, 2016), pp. 54–65. J. Arnold, "Theoderic's Invincible Mustache," *Journal of Late Antiquity* 6.1 (2013): 152–183 tackles the always pertinent matter of male facial hair.

6

Religion in Daily Life

INTRODUCTION: AN AMULET AND AN EVERYDAY
RELIGIOUS ACT

Sometime in the sixth century, a person living in a small town near the
modern city of Split (Croatia) visited a religious practitioner. This particular practitioner was an expert in prophylactic amulets, objects that
men, women, and children wore or displayed to ward off malignant
divine beings. The practitioner listened closely to the client's woes, and
carefully crafted a special lead amulet, with holes poked through on
one side so that it could be worn as a necklace. The amulet's power
was contained in the tiny words that the practitioner carefully etched
onto the tablet. Using a mix of Greek and Latin letters, the magician
covered both sides of the amulet with the following protective spell:

(Side A) In the name of the Lord, Jesus Christ, I denounce you, most foul
spirit of Tartarus, whom the angel Gabriel bound with burning letters, you
who hold ten thousand barbarians, came to Galilee after the resurrection.
There (Christ) commanded that you be kept in the hilly, mountainous wild
places, and only from that hour on to be invoked without difficulty. Therefore
see, most foul spirit of Tartarus, that whenever you hear the name of the Lord
or recognize the scripture you are not able

(Side B) to harm when you wish. In vain you hold the Jordan River which you
have not been able to cross. When asked how you are not able to cross you
said, because it runs there to the fire (which comes) from fiery hell, and for
you everywhere and always, may it run to the fire from fiery hell. I denounce
you through my Lord. Beware![1]

For the man or woman who purchased and wore this amulet, the power of Christ had manifold uses. Presuming that the client was a Christian – by the sixth century, it was the dominant religious system in the late Roman Empire – she or he likely learned from a cleric in church that wearing magical objects and invoking Christ in this manner was sinful. Generations of Christian authorities had drawn sharp lines separating the practice of "pure" and "true" Christianity from versions "adulterated" by traditions like amulet wearing. Yet, this amulet is hardly a unique piece of evidence. In fact, we possess hundreds of similar spells and objects from all over the Late Roman world, which were used by real Christians, Jews, and pagans. They reflect the messier reality of religious practice in daily life, what scholars call lived religion.

Late Antiquity is characterized by an astounding diversity of religious practice and thought. Not only were there four major religious systems – Christianity, Judaism, paganism, and Manichaeism[2] – there was also extraordinary diversity *within* each of these systems, making it very hard to identify what any particular Christian, Jew, pagan, or Manichean regularly did and thought on any particular day. Indeed, the very concept of lived religion rests on the understanding that people and communities make their own choices about how they interact with the divine, and that these choices are typically driven more by a desire for efficacy, or upholding family traditions, than by orthodoxy. We should never doubt, therefore, that the wearer of this amulet saw him- or herself as anything less than a true Christian.

This chapter is based on the assumption that religion mattered to men and women on a daily basis. But the assumption itself needs to be qualified. First, there were some late Romans who both rejected available forms of organized religion and questioned the prevailing system of divinity. It is hard to identify these men and women, since they left few traces on an historical record that is dominated by deeply religious writers and authorities. Yet, a range of attitudes, from atheism to skepticism about divine intervention in human affairs, existed in the ancient world.[3] Second, even among the majority who accepted the power of the divine in human activity, we might still ask: how frequently and in what ways did people's thoughts and actions turn to religion? Honest answers to these questions will necessarily vary, not only from religious community to religious community, but also from individual to individual. Members of the Manichean elect, Palestinian rabbis, and Christian monks saw their entire day organized around a sequence of religious rituals and/or periods of intensive study, whereas less observant Manicheans, Jews, and Christians may have engaged formally with their religion a few times a year, if that. Additionally, their experiences may have been marked by informal interactions with the divine, driven by self-interest or limited by social pressure, and mediated by a range of practitioners, such as the person who crafted the amulet with the protective spell. In short, it is very difficult to distinguish between norms for prayer and ritual prescribed by religious authorities, on the one hand, and what people were actually doing, on the other. What follows, therefore, is necessarily speculative, but likely hits close to the mark as to what lived religion meant for some people, some of the time.

LIVED RELIGION

Religion permeated all aspects of daily life in Late Antiquity. No late Roman would have recognized separate and exclusive "secular" and "religious" spaces, as we do today. In fact, there was no word in Late Antiquity for "religion" in the modern sense.[4] Instead, there were varieties of practices, symbols, and beliefs, some systematized, some not, which oriented how people interpreted the relationship between human and divine. Men, women, and children in all social statuses performed rites, studied sacred scriptures, and recited votive prayers in both public buildings open to the larger community and privately owned spots accessible only to an exclusive group. Some of these spaces were carefully controlled by religious authorities, but others, such as the household, were less directly governed, and hence offered individuals more opportunity to practice their religion according to local, familial, and personal preferences.

Household Spaces, Rites, and Traditions

The household was arguably the most common place of quotidian religious practice. It is surely one of the oldest. Long before the third century CE, pagans linked the prosperity of a household and its master to the good favor of domestic deities, who were worshiped regularly by family members and their slaves. In some cases, householders constructed small shrines in their homes known as *lararia*, where they performed bloodless sacrifices, typically of incense or cakes, and recited prayers. In return for these offerings, ancient Romans expected the household gods to protect the home from evil spirits, which might bring bad weather or illness, and to shower the family with prosperity and fertility.

Late Romans continued to view the household as a space of divine presence and ritual practice, albeit in new ways. Protecting the home and body from evil spirits remained a priority. Material evidence of amulets and other apotropaic symbols have been recovered in households from across the late Empire. In Sardis, several apartments over the shops along Marble Road show signs of prophylactic practices in the form of crosses etched on walls and doorways. Similarly, some late Roman Jews affixed small wooden cases with pieces of parchment stuffed inside at the tops of their doorways. The parchment contained verses from the Torah, which they believed warded off demonic spirits. Mezuzahs, as they are called in Hebrew, are still used in many Jewish households today.

In addition to invoking divine protection through apotropaic objects, late ancient households performed a wide variety of rituals. Jews, for instance, recited several groups of prayers in their homes daily, including the *Shema*, an affirmation of their commitment to Judaism, every morning and night. They also said a lengthier prayer called the *Amidah* once a day, usually in the morning. Some Jews, most likely those directly influenced by rabbinic authorities in the East, habitually offered blessings before eating, especially when they consumed privileged items such as bread. Blessings also might end a meal. Some regularly followed food laws, prescribed in part by the Torah and in part by the rabbis. These laws both prohibited certain types of foods (e.g., pork and shellfish) and created categories of foods that could not combine (e.g., meat and dairy). While not all late ancient Jews followed dietary laws carefully, or at all – pig bones have been recovered from Jewish areas in Palestine – those who did experienced the very act of eating as an at-home ritual.

Observant Jews also followed a weekly worship schedule that centered on the household. For centuries, they marked their Sabbath, called *Shabbat*, from sundown on Friday to sundown on Saturday, with abstention from all forms of work, and with a ritual meal on Friday evening. Once *Shabbat* started with the lighting of candles, all work was supposed to cease. Some Jews clearly took this prohibition very seriously and refrained from doing even necessary household duties. They might even use technology to help them meet their Sabbath requirements. Archaeologists, for instance, have discovered clay oil lamps with reserves, which did not need constant refilling. The fact that some of these lamps are decorated with Jewish motifs suggests that Jews used them during the Sabbath. Not all were so observant, of course. The remains of Aramaic-language *ostraka* (pottery shards reused as cheap writing tablets) from first-century Palestine show that some Jews worked during the Sabbath delivering bread and other food, thereby directly defying the law; we may infer that late Roman Jews broke Sabbath laws too. But one at-home activity that the rabbis actively encouraged Jews to engage in was procreation. Marital sex was strongly advised during the Sabbath.

As temples shut or were abandoned, late Roman pagans increasingly lived their religion exclusively within the domestic sphere. State laws prohibiting sacrifices only gradually included non-blood offerings, such as incense and cakes, which were traditionally the sort used in domestic settings. Behind closed doors, people continued to worship in the old way. Archaeology reveals one fourth-century pagan home in Rome that contained a small shrine for the worship of Mithras, a Persian-Roman deity, while other contemporary evidence suggests that a network of elite households in the city maintained the cult through the end of the fourth century. Similarly, the main centers of Neoplatonism in Athens and Alexandria were often located inside wealthy people's homes, which functioned as both residences and schools for philosophers in training. And from its origins, Manichaeism was a religion without temples and altars, and could be described as a highly institutionalized domestic cult. The elect lived and studied exclusively within private houses, where they performed all the rites, including a central daily ritual meal, described in "The Extraordinary Daily Lives of Religious Elites."

As historians have often noted, the history of Christianity began in the home. In general, Christians did not worship in publicly accessible, purpose-built churches until the early fourth century. Before then, they assembled in privately owned spaces, such as storefronts, warehouses, and, most frequently, homes. These "house churches" were places to gather, teach, learn, read, share meals, and engage in developing ritual activities. The end of the persecution along with an influx of wealthy Christian patrons led to a building boom of public churches, which we shall examine shortly.

The rise of the monumental public church, however, did not lead to the fall of Christian domestic worship. Late Roman Christian authorities still encouraged people to spend part of their day in prayer, and in some cases required them to worship at specific times. A third- or fourth-century text known as the *Apostolic Tradition* calls for at-home prayer during the third, sixth, and ninth hours of the day, with a suggested fourth session at midnight.[5] Other authorities pre-scribed the reading of specific biblical passages (e.g., the psalms in the Hebrew Bible) on certain days of the week as an antidote to illness. The most devoted Christian might orient his or her daily schedule around Bible study and prayer. Jerome, a Christian writer and spirit-ual advisor, who died in 430 CE, counseled aristocratic Roman women to forgo dinner parties and social visits for time alone in their bedrooms reading the Bible.[6] Although Jerome's advice to these ladies was extreme, his understanding of the household as an active religious place reflects a general cultural consensus.

Late ancient Christian householders also physically adapted their domestic spaces to incorporate worship. Wealthier householders might construct shrines or chapels inside their homes for family worship. In Rome, for instance, a fourth-century mansion on the Caelian Hill contained a small shrine on a stair landing. The shrine, which can still be seen today, included a niche, perhaps once containing a box of relics or a container of bread from a Eucharist celebration in a public church that was brought home for consumption.[7] The niche is sur-rounded by wall paintings of men and women, some making offerings, others perhaps enacting scenes from a martyr narrative (Figure 6.1). In rural settings, Christian householders constructed self-standing chapels on their estates, which served not only their close family, but also their slaves, clients, and tenants.[8] Some estate chapels even had baptisteries, that is, small pools for performing the Christian initiation rite. Owners of estate chapels often employed local clergy to carry out the same rites performed in public churches, including Eucharistic celebrations and baptisms. Less well-off Christians might simply paint crosses in a room, like the owners of a small house in the suburbs of

FIGURE 6.1. A small niche, perhaps a place for relics or reserved Eucharistic bread, in a decorated prayer space built in a home during the fourth century. The space was undoubtedly used by the family for private worship, and features several images, including what appears to be a depiction of martyrdom. The house is still extant beneath the medieval church of SS. Giovanni e Paolo in Rome.
Photo by Kimberly Bowes.

Alexandria (House D in Kom el-Dikka). In these more modest homes, rites were performed that did not require a priest or bishop, such as ritual lamp-lighting to mark the evening prayer hours.

Evidence also tells us that Christians lived their household religion in more complex ways. For many, the home was a space to display not only signs of Christian devotion, but also allegiance to a shared classical past. The same fourth-century Christian family in Lullingstone, Britain (in the modern county of Kent), who constructed a chapel in their country villa for private worship decorated their dining room with images drawn from pagan myth. A scene on the mosaic floor

FIGURE 6.2. This mosaic floor in the dining room of a late Roman villa in Britain features a number of distinctly pagan motifs, including the mythic figure Bellerophon riding his winged horse, Pegasus (top), and Jupiter's rape of Europa (bottom). Elsewhere in the home, the same family built a small Christian chapel, suggesting that these Christians also enjoyed pagan images. Photo by Ian G. Dagnall, Alamy stock photo.

depicts the god Jupiter in the form of a bull abducting the goddess Europa, while beneath, the mythic hero Bellerophon slays the Chimaera while riding the winged horse Pegasus (Figure 6.2). Silver collections belonging to some of the richest late Roman Christians reveal a similar comfort with polytheist symbolism. A hoard dating to the late fourth century from Britain includes a large silver dish featuring images of dancing Greek gods as well as three silver spoons with explicitly Christian signs (Figure 6.3a,b). Presuming that the owner was a Christian (of course, she or he could have been a pagan who appreciated the power of the Christian god), we might ask how she or he and the Lullingstone residents accepted such images in the home. In truth, the owners would not have seen any great contradiction in possessing such silver and living in a home decorated with both Christian and pagan images. For many Christians, pictures of the gods no longer conveyed the sacrificial notions of pagan ritual, but the concept of *paideia*, that is, a sense of erudition and what we would call "class."

(a)   (b)

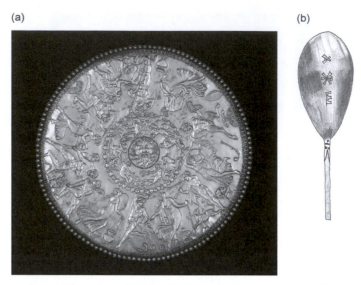

FIGURE 6.3. (a) A silver platter with Greco-Roman mythological designs is among the many objects of the Mildenhall Treasure, a silver hoard from Britain dating to the fifth century. Photo © The Trustees of the British Museum. (b) A silver spoon with Christian symbols, specifically the Greek letters alpha and omega, along with a Chi-Rho sign, from the Mildenhall Treasure. Drawing by Chris Otter.

Public Religious Life and the Everyday

While the home was a central site of ritual life, the public sphere was also a critical venue for lived religion. In fact, Late Antiquity witnessed a number of profound changes in the use of public space for all of the major late Roman religious systems. For Christians and Jews, the period was nothing short of revolutionary, since it heralded the beginning of both religions' history of grand, monumentalized community buildings, known more colloquially as churches and synagogues. As we saw in Chapter 2, churches and synagogues were among the few types of new buildings that were regularly constructed in cities across the late Empire. With the construction of these buildings came new habits of daily life.

The Christian church in the modern sense of the term, that is, a building constructed exclusively for religious worship, containing an altar and space for the community to stand, including perhaps a baptistery, became a center of worship for the first time in Late

Antiquity. The earliest known Christian church that largely fits this description dates to the mid-third century, and was created by renovating a former home located in the eastern frontier town of Dura Europos. Purpose-built churches, however, first appeared only in the early fourth century, after the legalization of Christianity and its adoption by the imperial family and aristocratic patrons. Whereas earlier Christians both shunned the idea of distinct buildings for worship (they felt they were too much like pagan temples) and were prohibited by law at times from having public meeting places, late Roman Christians were free from these constraints. They used their private fortunes to construct large, grand churches in cities across the Empire, from Rome to Constantinople, Brixia to Ephesus. The largest churches were built and adorned by the imperial family, but their efforts were soon mimicked by elites in large metropolises and small towns (albeit on a far smaller scale). In Brixia, we recall, local Christians Theodorus and Marta paid for a small section of mosaic floor decoration and were commemorated for their efforts by an inscription still visible in the remains of the late Roman church. In this way, church building and decoration became a new outlet for civic patronage.

What was it like to worship in one of these new churches? Like everything, it depended on a range of factors. Churches differed in size and grandeur, with those constructed by imperial families typically dwarfing the humbler buildings erected by clergy and local lay elites. There were, of course, some common architectural features. Most late Roman churches had one or more apses, that is, semicircular recessed areas with a domed or vaulted ceiling. Apses were borrowed from a classical public building type called the basilica, which was typically used by magistrates hearing legal cases (hence why we call churches "basilicas").[9] The altar and nave of the church were usually situated within the largest apse, centered at the front of the church. There, the priest or bishop would have led the service and performed the Eucharistic celebration. The apses and other parts of the interior of a Christian church could be lavishly decorated with colorful mosaics, marble inlay, and frescoes. Biblical scenes were typically the subject matter, but in some cases the history of the church's foundation was represented in the art. Alternatively, the exterior of most late ancient churches was nondescript. Most had

(a)

(b)

FIGURE 6.4. (a) The church of St. Sabina was built in the early fifth century on the crest of the Aventine Hill in Rome. Its simple brick exterior, with a row of clerestory windows, is typical of late Roman churches. Photo by Hackenberg-Photo-Cologne, Alamy stock photo. (b) Elaborate polychrome wall paintings dating to the fifth and sixth centuries adorn all three apses of the Church of the Red Monastery in Sohag, Egypt. Pictured here is the southern apse, with images of an enthroned Christ (top) and Coptic Christian patriarchs (bottom). Skilled craftsmen produced these paintings using both tempera, a paint made of pigment combined with egg, and encaustic, a mixture of beeswax and pigment. Photo by Caroline T. Schroeder.

plain walls and doorways, with the tradition of exterior sculpture not emerging until the Middle Ages (Figure 6.4a,b).

However grandiose many of these churches might have felt to the common visitor, most were physically small by modern standards. Assuming that people stood during church services and needed about a square meter of space, the majority of early Christian churches could accommodate no more than one hundred worshipers. A handful, such as the Church of the Anastasis in Jerusalem, could hold approximately eight hundred, but most were considerably smaller. Consequently, the largest cities had many churches in order to accommodate the entire community. Rome, for instance, had about forty churches by 400 CE, which could collectively hold around twenty-two thousand people. We should add, however, that even at the city's lowest population level (perhaps around sixty thousand in the mid-sixth century), Rome's churches still could not accommodate all its Christian citizens. Some, of course, were prevented by work or enslavement from attending. But we should assume that a number of them chose to spend their Sundays worshipping at home or doing something else altogether.

Technically, early Christians were expected to attend church services once a week, on Sunday. Sunday became an official "holiday" during the reign of Constantine, who forbade engagement in certain forms of work on that day. Of course, these expectations were not always met, and there is ample evidence from Christian sources that regular church attendance was a problem. In fact, church services often had to compete with other forms of entertainment, such as the games or theater. This is one reason why the cleric John Chrysostom railed against the theater, as we saw in Chapter 2: it was drawing away his parishioners. Similarly, the Roman Pope Leo (441–461 CE) rebuked his community for choosing to attend a chariot race rather than divine services.[10] In some cases, bishops insisted that congregants go to church in the early morning hours before the start of work (and the games), a request that perhaps helps to explain why attendance was sometimes low.

Those who lived in cities likely had at least two or three churches to choose from, and probably made their selection depending on location and, more likely, social connections. When services began, the entire congregation arrived, including those men and women who were not yet baptized. They were called catechumens. The baptized stood toward the center of the building, the catechumens in the aisles. In some assemblies, men and women worshipped separately, but there were no universal rules about gender division. Most stood for the entire service, which could last several hours, although there was some seating for lay elites and clergy. Together the congregants listened to the cleric deliver a sermon, offer interpretive readings of biblical texts (known as homilies), and lead the whole group in prayer. This was a crucial part of the service, since it was during these sermons and prayers that everyday Christians pondered some of their religion's most complex ideas: How, precisely, ought we to understand Jesus

Christ's relationship to God? Was Jesus himself both human and divine or just divine? What might we face in the afterlife? The cleric's role was to offer answers to these deep questions and to present them in a manner that was accessible to a wide audience, comprising elites and non-elites, baptized and nonbaptized Christians.

Toward the end of the service, the catechumens were required to exit the building (this is why many churches had doorkeepers), so that the Eucharist celebration could ensue. The Eucharist was the central rite for Christians, and only the fully initiated could participate in it. It began when the bishop or presbyter (the two grades of cleric theoretically capable of performing the rite) recited a special prayer and made the sign of the cross over an offering of bread and wine on the altar.[11] At this moment, Christians believed that the bread and wine were transformed mystically into Christ's body and blood, recreating on the altar Jesus' great sacrifice. After the community said "amen" and recited the Lord's Prayer, the bread and wine were distributed, with each person receiving a tiny portion of Christ's body and blood. The Eucharist typically marked the end of the service.

For late antique Jews, the synagogue was the primary public space for fellowship and prayer. Jews would have attended a local synagogue on their Sabbath, Saturday, where they sang liturgical hymns (called *piyyutim*) and listened to lectures by a teacher or rabbi on the Scriptures and Jewish law. In Late Antiquity (as today), synagogues were not temples or churches, for they were not spaces of sacrifice or sacred rites. Rather, they were assembly halls, where late Roman Jews gathered to study the Torah and other aspects of Jewish law with an educated leader. By 500 CE, all but the smallest Jewish communities had a synagogue, with more than one hundred and twenty excavated in Palestine alone. In many cases, these were purpose-built constructions with rich decorative programs (Figure 6.5). Some drew on the same basilican form as Christian churches, with an apse serving as the site not of an altar, but the Torah shrine, wherein a chest held the biblical scrolls. While some Jews were avowedly aniconic, many visited synagogues that were decorated with Jewish symbols like the menorah, figures from the Bible, and, in some cases, pagan images.

Consider, for example, the great synagogue of Hammat Tiberias in modern Israel, which underwent major renovations in the fourth century (Figure 6.6). The renovations included the construction of

FIGURE 6.5. The archaeological remains of the monumental synagogue in Sardis (Turkey) was built by the city's Jewish community as its meeting place in the late third century.
Photo by Carole Raddato (Creative Commons license).

FIGURE 6.6. The zodiac panel from the central floor mosaic of the synagogue at Hammat Tiberias in Israel dates to the fourth century. The twelve zodiac signs, with each month identified in Hebrew, surround a central image of the pagan god Helios or Sol Invictus, a popular late Roman image that connoted belief in a central, all-powerful deity.
Photo by Bukvoed (Creative Commons license).

a new nave with aisles and an elaborate three-panel mosaic. The top panel around the Torah shrine presents standard Jewish motifs, such as a menorah and a shofar (a ceremonial horn blown on certain holidays), while the bottom panel contains eight dedicatory inscriptions, each preserving (in Greek) the name of one of the synagogue's major donors for the renovations. The middle panel is the most surprising: an entire zodiac calendar centered on an image of a pagan sun deity, either Helios or Sol Invictus ("the Inconquerable Sun"). The inclusion of blatantly non-Jewish images has long perplexed scholars, and they have offered a range of explanations. However, the most likely reason for the inclusion of a zodiac and a sun god in a fourth-century synagogue is probably the most prosaic: this is what the community wanted, and found most meaningful for their experience of religion. If we keep in mind that hard divisions between religions did not define the reality of lived religion, then we are less bothered by Jewish interest in alternative divine systems, especially those connected to astrology, which profoundly oriented daily life for many late Romans.[12]

While Jews and Christians enjoyed an expansion of public monumental space and ritual during Late Antiquity, pagans and Manichaeans experienced a gradual contraction of options. Except for a short burst of sacrificial activity and temple renovation during the brief reign of the emperor Julian (r. 361–363 CE), polytheists witnessed a succession of imperial laws that illegalized not only the performance of most sacrifices, but also attendance at them. They watched as imperial officials redirected funds away from the maintenance of their once grand urban temples, a move that contributed to the buildings' abandonment and ruination. In Brixia and Ephesus, we recall, the cities' two most magnificent temples slowly suffered the indignation of spoliation and decline, as their most valuable materials were stripped, reused in other buildings, or sent to other cities for display.

Consequently, the public performance of pagan sacrifice in temples ceased during Late Antiquity. However, polytheistic rites had long spilled into the streets and fields, and a few of the larger public festivals endured in one form or another. In Rome, Christian elites continued to attend the Lupercalia, an annual festival focused originally on the Roman god Lupercal, another name for Faunus. The late ancient Lupercalia appears to have involved a group of young men wearing goat skins, who ran a course through the city while singing bawdy songs about local public figures and slapping women on their rears with a leather thong. Most scholars believe that the late ancient version of the Lupercalia bears little resemblance to its earlier form, which was directed by a dedicated priesthood and focused on a sacred cave associated with Rome's mythic founding by Romulus and Remus. Nevertheless, we know from Pope Gelasius (492–496 CE) that the Lupercalia was still held in the 490s, when some of the participants apparently sang about a local cleric caught up in an adultery scandal. In fact, Gelasius' discussion of the Lupercalia makes clear that its sponsors were none other than local Christian elites, for whom the festival was a perfectly legitimate expression of their dedication to civic tradition. Unsurprisingly, Gelasius condemned the festival and its aristocratic Christian patrons in no uncertain terms, yet there is no clear evidence that his rebuke formally ended the practice.

The Cemetery: Death and Religion

A final space to consider as a site of religious activity is the cemetery. Cemeteries were traditionally viewed as intensely spiritual places. Among other things, they were where the shades of the dead roamed, particularly those who had died an untimely or violent death. Generally, dead bodies were seen as sources of pollution, and hence could not rest near the living. Consequently, urban ancients traditionally buried their dead in cemeteries located outside city walls. Until the second century, most Greeks and Romans preferred to cremate their dead, but from this time inhumation gradually became the norm across the Empire. Many ancient cemeteries were located along main roads, and aboveground tombs and mausolea were visible to those passing by. Tombstones were often elaborately constructed, and their inscriptions presented résumés of the dead, highlighting their achievements and the sadness felt by loved ones still alive. A rich Roman might have selected an elaborately carved sarcophagus, typically covered with images and inscriptions.

During Late Antiquity, some of these traditions endured, but new burial customs also emerged. Subterranean cemeteries, for instance, were largely a phenomenon of the third and fourth centuries. In places where the ground was soft enough to dig into, such as around

FIGURE 6.7. The catacombs of St. Gennaro in Naples (Italy) were primarily used during the third and fourth centuries.
Photo by Dominik Matus (Creative Commons license).

the cities of Rome and Naples, people created cemeteries in deep underground tunnels, which we collectively call catacombs.[13] One scholar estimates that the third-century sections of Rome's largest catacombs featured some forty-one thousand burial spaces, a figure that is likely a gross underestimation (Figure 6.7). We tend to think of the catacombs as exclusively Christian burial spaces, but Jews and pagans were buried in them too. Significantly, the catacombs, like all ancient cemeteries, were rarely segregated by religious faith. Consequently, pagans, Jews, Christians, and Manicheans were buried side-by-side. It is often difficult to distinguish between them through the evidence of tombstones, especially if the interred was represented only by a symbol and a name. This is because late ancient people liked to borrow symbols from different systems, creating tombstones, mausolea, and sarcophagi that combined images in unique ways.

In fact, while scholars used to believe that the Christian church in Rome controlled all the catacombs, they now think that the clergy had authority over a relatively small number of burials, and that family preferences, rather than an ecclesiastical monopoly, drove burial practices in late antique Rome at least until the fifth century. Families interested in interring a loved one in one of Rome's underground cemeteries would have to independently purchase the space and pay a gravedigger to dig the tomb. In some cases, poor families may have relied on organizations such as the church to help with these costs. Those living in Constantinople were provided with free burials, but this was a unique provision. Outside of cities, rural communities typically buried their dead along roads, in ditches that marked property boundaries, and even under the floors of buildings that were still in use. Without city walls around their villages, traditional strictures governing intramural burials would not have applied. After the fifth century, the Christian church played a more direct role in burying the dead, though the control was limited to burial spaces located in close proximity to saints' tombs or to intramural churchyard cemeteries, a very new phenomenon.

As we noted in Chapter 2, late Romans in many cities (especially in the West) gravitated away from extramural burial over the course of the fifth and sixth centuries. During this time, the dead were increasingly interred in tombs dug just under the ground (as in modern American cemeteries), and increasingly *inside* city walls. In cases where burials were dug around or inside churches, we can assume that the clergy played a much larger role in regulating burial space, and we know that payments were made directly to churches in some cases. Precisely why this shift to intramural burials took place remains an open question, but it was likely a combination of cultural and material factors and has much to do with the shifting contours of urban space discussed in Chapter 2. Additionally, inscribed tombstones became increasingly rare after the fourth century, a development that further challenges archaeologists in search of the late ancient dead.[14]

Despite the presence of the dead, people were not fearful about visiting cemeteries in Late Antiquity. Pagans traditionally staged feasts at the tombs of their dead relatives on certain days (such as on the ninth day after death) to remember them. Some sarcophagi even had tubes drilled through them so that visitors could pour wine directly into them. Christians, too, visited the dead in cemeteries. There they ritually commemorated both their own ancestors and a new group of very special dead: those venerated as martyrs and saints.

The martyrs were Christian men and women believed to have clung steadfastly to their religious principles in the face of extreme pressure to renounce them, especially during the persecutions of the third and very early fourth centuries. They refused, for example, to sacrifice or pray to a pagan god when Roman authorities demanded it.

By choosing execution or imprisonment over apostasy, the martyrs were branded "saints" by later Christians, who believed that their suffering and death brought them uniquely close to Christ in heaven.[15] Christians thought that the martyrs possessed special intercessory powers, which enabled them to work on behalf of the living before God. The martyrs were later joined by another set of "special dead," Christians who had achieved memorable feats of ascetic practice during their lifetimes (discussed further in "The Extraordinary Daily Lives of Religious Elites"). Figures such as Symeon Stylites (ca. 390–459 CE), who sat on a pillar in the Syrian desert for twenty years, and the Gallic ascetic bishop Martin of Tours (316–397 CE) were widely perceived as powerful intercessors long after they had died.

Consequently, the saints' bodies and tombs took on immense importance in Late Antiquity. Christians traveled to their burial sites, where they prayed and offered food, hoping that their special attention to the saint might bring them God's attention and assistance. In many cases, church authorities constructed more permanent shrines over these tombs, so as to mark the sites' importance and provide ample space for visitors and, in some cases, elite burials. The basilica of St. Peter's in Rome, today the headquarters of the Roman Catholic Church and the city's largest cathedral, began as a small memorial erected in the third century over what the city's Christians then believed was the tomb of the apostle Peter in a cemetery just outside the city walls. Miracles were widely associated with the saints' tombs, body parts, and contact materials (e.g., oil or dirt from the tomb, rags that had touched the bones, chains that had once imprisoned the body), which in the form of relics became a new, transportable medium of healing and power. For this reason, relics were sometimes broken apart, distributed, and exchanged all over the Empire (Figure 6.8; see also Figure 5.2).

Special Rites: Feasts, Festivals, and Magical Interventions

In addition to these more regular religious activities, late ancient men and women participated in a range of special rites, performed on certain days of the year or as special needs dictated. Whether to commemorate the death of a founding prophet (like the Manichaean holiday of Bema) or to seek divine intervention for an acute health

FIGURE 6.8. A sixth- or seventh-century metal tourist flask, likely from the shrine of St. Sergios in Sergiopolis, Syria, the supposed site of his martyrdom in the third century. Sergios is depicted on horseback, and the Greek inscription circling him reads: "Blessing of the Lord Saint Sergios."
Photo by the Walters Art Museum (Creative Commons license).

problem, late Romans engaged in occasional rituals. The Jewish calendar was (and still is) full of annual festivals, such as Shavuot, which commemorates Moses' receiving the Ten Commandments; Passover, celebrated in the early spring to remember the Jews' exodus as slaves from Egypt; and, most important, Yom Kippur in the fall, when Jews pray, fast, and repent for their sins. And although no one in Late Antiquity used the Hebrew word *seder* to describe it, Jews began Passover with a ritual meal.[16] Hanukkah was also celebrated as a day of remembrance of the Maccabean revolt (167–160 BCE), though its significance was less than it is now.

The Christian festival calendar expanded considerably during Late Antiquity. Christmas, or Christ's birth, has been celebrated on December 25 since at least the middle of the fourth century (though it was a relatively minor feast day that accrued additional traditions, such as gift-giving, from association with the Roman winter festival of Saturnalia); Pentecost was marked in the late spring to remember the descent of the Holy Spirit as described in the Acts of the Apostles (2:1–31);

and the Easter cycle took shape as the most important part of the Christian liturgical year. Many late ancient Christians fasted during Lent, the forty days leading up to Easter. Typically, Lenten fasting involved abstention from meat, milk, or wine. And although baptism could be performed at any time of the year, many catechumens preferred to wait until the evening of Easter Saturday, so that they could experience their first Eucharistic celebration on Easter Sunday. At this time, the calendar began to include additional holidays, such as the "birthday" of a martyr or saint. Actually, this would be the date of the saint's death. Early Christians commemorated it as a moment of "rebirth," since the saint was understood to have been reborn in heaven through his or her death. Every month, several saints were feted, whether in a church through a special sermon delivered by a cleric, or at the saint's tomb, where the faithful gathered to remember the saint and perhaps ask for intercession. In some cases, these celebrations took the form of funeral meals that closely paralleled the pagan tradition of feasting at the tombs of ancestors. The North African bishop Augustine's mother, Monica, reputedly liked to picnic with the saints in the cemeteries, despite having another bishop censure her for the behavior. In Monica's mind, of course, her rites were properly Christian.

Indeed, religious calendars were often personal, fluid enterprises. People might first celebrate a decidedly "Christian" holiday and then a decidedly "pagan" one. For example, one might honor Christmas on December 25, and then attend a Kalends festival in early January, which marked the new year. Alternatively, one might combine celebrations to create what might seem to us a confused religious schedule, but made great sense to the participants. The earliest known calendar of Christian festival dates is a case in point. Called the Codex-Calendar or Chronography of 354, this richly illustrated document was produced in Rome during the fourth century (sometime after 354 CE, the latest recorded date in the calendar, and hence its name) for a wealthy patron named Valentinus.[17] Among other items, the Codex-Calendar of 354 contains a list of the names and birthdates of the emperors; many pages of astrological material, including a fully illustrated zodiac; two chronicles, one for biblical history, the other for the history of the city of Rome; a list of Rome's urban prefects from 254 to 354 CE, followed by a list of its Christian bishops from

255 to 352 CE, and a list of names, burial sites, and death dates of local martyrs; dates for Easter; histories of both biblical figures and the city of Rome; and a consular list. In other words, the Codex-Calendar of 354 combines Christian and pagan material, religious and secular, into a single document. It shows that when it came to marking time, an absolute division between "pagan" and "Christian" simply did not exist for some people.

Neoplatonists, who were pagan, also practiced occasional rites, all of which were performed as a means of lifting their souls to the higher, immaterial world of the divine. In many cases, the rites in question were largely intellectual and abstract, for they involved periods of intensive philosophical contemplation. Contact with the divine might also be achieved through concrete rituals collectively known as theurgy, most of which are vaguely understood, precisely because Neoplatonic rites were secret and deemed unknowable to uninitiated outsiders. Until the end of the fourth century, sacrifice had been a key element of Neoplatonic theurgy, but imperial legislation combined with Christian antipagan sentiment made it difficult, and even dangerous, for Neoplatonists to perform them. Instead, they performed ceremonies aimed at purifying the body, understood as the vehicle for the soul. Precisely what form these ceremonies took is difficult to determine, but Neoplatonic authors describe practices such as the use of magical signs to mark out a ritual space to evoke a specific deity; the wearing of special clothing by the practitioners; and the use of plants, herbs, stones, and incense to draw the divine closer to the soul.

In fact, the Neoplatonic belief in magic and esoteric rites as paths to divine knowledge and assistance is broadly characteristic of all lived religion in Late Antiquity. Evidence overwhelmingly shows that the period's three major monotheistic communities – Jews, Christians, and Manichaeans – engaged in forms of magical practice. By "magic," we do not mean the opposite of religion. In fact, during Late Antiquity, performing magic was as religious an enterprise as participating in the Eucharist service or attending a *sabbah meal*. Late ancient magic is best understood as a set of concrete practices through which individuals engaged with, and attempted to direct, various spiritual beings. In some cases, magical activities unlocked malignant forces, which brought ruin and pain upon enemies and competitors; in other cases, magic unleashed wholly benign spirits, who brought relief from suffering and protected one from evil demons. Another form of magical practice, called divination, involved methods for reading the future. Christians were especially attracted to a form of divination that involved randomly selecting passages from the Bible and treating them as oracular responses to specific questions, in what was known as the *sortes*, or "lots." Others used dice and an oracular book of corresponding "answers" provided by an expert.[18] One such book from southern Gaul dating to ca. 600 CE presents answers to questions on topics ranging from "slaves" and "romantic problems" to "struggling with a child who hates school."[19]

Astrology, the study of astral and planetary alignments in relation to a particular place, time, and date, such as an individual's birthday and birthplace, was also widely popular among late Romans as a means of predicting future experiences and/or helping make decisions. Zodiacs, we recall, were integrated into the flooring of several Palestinian synagogues, while Christian and Manichaean literary sources abound in references to what was considered astrological science. At least one Christian emperor, Zeno (r. 474–491 CE), had his own horoscope drawn up when rival leaders threatened to depose him. Late ancient men and women also believed that the stars and planets were linked to rhythms of earthly weather, climate, and fertility. Late ancient agronomy manuals, we recall, explicitly directed farmers to use astrology as a guide for agricultural decisions.

Generally speaking, the Roman government had long been highly intolerant of malignant forms of magic and modes of divination used to discern the emperor's fate. To know how or when an emperor would die could potentially be used as leverage in an attempted palace coup. Christianity did not change the government's position on magic in any radical way, although some Christian bishops attempted to prohibit all forms of magic, regardless of whether it was used for good or for ill. Material artifacts, such as the lead amulet discussed in the beginning of this chapter, along with the fact that authorities repeatedly reissued rulings against magic and astrology, demonstrate that proscriptions were ineffective at curbing these religious practices.

For example, a sixth-century chariot-racing fan from Apamea, Syria, purchased a lead tablet in preparation for a major race between his team, the Greens, and their rivals, the Blues, which he buried in the starting gate of the track.[20] The curse calls upon "the most Holy Lord," identified further with "Topos" and "Zablos," divine names for angels known from contemporary Jewish texts, and "the spirits [of those] who have died violently" to "tie up, bind the feet, the hands, the sinews, the eyes, the knees ... the victory and the crowning of Porphuras and Hapiscrates, who are the middle left, as well as his co-drivers of the Blue colors in the stable of Eugenius."[21] The identities of Porphuras and Hapiscrates are uncertain (they may have been horses or jockeys), but the goal of the tablet is clear: prevent the Blues from crowding out the Greens on the racecourse and ensure a victory for the Greens.

Late Romans used curses and magical spells as forms of self-help for a range of problems: financial or legal troubles, physical illness, and especially romantic crises. Many of these are rather innocent pleas for a clearly uninterested woman to be drawn to a lovesick man, but some suggest a darker and more violent understanding of magical power. The Louvre figurine (so-called because it is owned by the Louvre Museum in Paris) is a small clay figure of a woman, kneeling with her hands tied behind her back; thirteen bronze needles pierce her eyes, breasts, anus, vagina, and elsewhere (Figure 6.9). This visually disturbing object was found in Egypt in a ceramic vessel with a lead curse tablet, which invokes a spirit called Antinoos (the name of a man who died violently or prematurely) to "bind" a woman named Ptolemais, the love interest of a man named Sarapammon. Little is known about Sarapammon and Ptolemais other than that they lived in Egypt sometime in the third or fourth century. "Drag her by the hair and her heart until she no longer stands aloof from me," the curse exclaims, and goes on to order the spirit to prevent Ptolemais from being "had in a promiscuous way, let her not be had anally, nor let her do anything for pleasure with another man, just with me alone, Sarapammon."[22] On the one hand, the highly misogynistic nature of the curse attests to the powerful gender hierarchy that ordered relationships between men and women in the ancient world, and allows us a glimpse at a late ancient notion of "romantic pursuit" that looks a great deal like violent sexual coercion. On the other hand, it demonstrates how one man resorted to the power of supernatural forces in order to effect potential solutions for two of the most ordinary problems of everyday life: unrequited love and sexual competition.

FIGURE 6.9. A clay figurine of a kneeling woman with thirteen bronze needles piercing her body. Now preserved at the Louvre Museum in Paris, the figurine was originally discovered in Egypt along with a rolled-up lead tablet containing an accompanying love spell, wherein a man named Sarapammon calls upon spiritual forces to "bind" his love interest, Ptolemais. Both objects were buried in a small clay vessel. The entire ensemble likely dates to the third or fourth century.
Photo by Marie-Lan Nguyen (Creative Commons license).

The Extraordinary Daily Lives of Religious Elites

For most late Romans, belief in supernatural powers and participation in rituals did not translate into a lifestyle governed by strict religious rules. For a small minority, however, rules and strictures derived from religious ideas and texts guided how they lived. This final section briefly examines the lives of Christian clergy and monks, Jewish rabbis, Neoplatonist sages, and Manichean elect. These were not, by definition, ordinary people. By choice or obligation, religious elites followed rules that marked them as distinct from, and perhaps in their minds better than, their more typical counterparts. Of course, many failed to live up to these ideals, which were often at odds with contemporary Roman social norms and traditions.

For Christian religious elites, an ascetic regime might orient their daily lives. Asceticism, from the Greek *askesis*, meaning "exercise," was a set of practices through which one trained the body and mind to be purer and hence closer to God. This lofty goal was approached through various forms of self-denial and renunciation. Ascetics abstained from certain foods (especially meat and wine) and fasted assiduously on a regular basis; forwent sex, marriage, and family life; and rejected wealth and, in some cases, all forms of private property. Christians did not invent asceticism as a transformative spiritual discipline; they have Greco-Roman philosophers and Jewish radical communities to thank for that. However, Christians made asceticism a distinct mode of living during Late Antiquity, when ascetic practices were adopted by clerics and nonclerics. For the clergy, asceticism most directly affected their marriages, which had to be especially pure. For those who aspired to a higher office, such as the priesthood, this meant that they could be married, but only once and to a woman who was a virgin at the time of marriage. Once ordained to the office, they were expected to cease from all sexual relations permanently and could not remarry or, if unmarried, marry for the first time. Clerical celibacy was never consistently or universally embraced in Late Antiquity, but it was widely seen as a desirable goal.

Nonclerical ascetics often followed even more extreme ascetic regimes, and established a new form of social community based upon them: the monastery.[23] The monastery, which derives from the Greek word *monachos*, meaning "solitary," was a community oriented around the renunciation of worldly things: traditional family ties (including marriage), good food and wine, property ownership, and sexual contact of all kinds. Instead of laboring for their families, monks were supposed to work for God, praying throughout the day at set times, studying Scripture, and performing physical tasks to maintain the livelihood of the monastic community, whether it was weaving mats or farming. The earliest Christian monasteries were established for men in Egypt during the fourth century, but the concept caught on quickly and monasteries were founded for men and women all over the late Empire (Figure 6.10). In some cases, late ancient monasteries were guided by elaborate regulations or "rules," which dictated where and when to sleep, pray, study, and work, what clothing to wear, and when to leave the monastery, if at all, and required the communal

FIGURE 6.10. The earliest purpose-built monasteries appeared in Egypt. Here is the White Monastery in Sohag (Egypt), which dates from the fifth century. Photo by Caroline T. Schroeder.

possession of all property. Of course, the existence of a rule did not mean that people always followed it. The *Benedictine Rule*, attributed to the sixth-century monk Benedict of Nursia (Italy), delineates a series of punishments for monks who defy the rules, suggesting that this was expected. Moreover, most late ancient monks probably did not observe any particular set of written rules, which were just beginning to develop. Not all late Roman monks lived in monastic communities, in fact. Jerome's friend Marcella (d. 410 CE), for instance, lived as a nun in her own home outside of Rome, where she followed a rigid ascetic regime as a widow.[24]

These particular monastic and ascetic regimes distinguished Christianity from other religious communities in Late Antiquity. However, the notion that religious leaders ought to behave differently from common men and women was pervasive. The Manichaean elect adopted strict codes of sexual renunciation and eschewed marriage. But their motivations were rather different from those of Christian clergy and monks, who renounced sex in order to become more like God. The Manichean elect abstained from sex because they viewed procreation as the generation of matter, which only further imprisoned the light particles. Alternatively, rabbis and Neoplatonist sages were never expected to be permanently celibate and could marry at any time, though they did abstain from sex during key periods. Neoplatonists believed that sex immediately before a theurgistic ritual polluted the rites, and hence they adopted temporary celibacy for the purpose of ritual purity. For rabbis, the concern was that sex might interfere with a teacher's focus and attention during periods of intense Talmudic study; hence they, too, did not sleep with their wives during these times. Of course, not all late ancient synagogue leaders were devoted Talmudic scholars.

Among all late ancient religious elites, the daily lives of the Manichean elect were arguably the most extraordinary. Because they were prohibited from killing any living thing, including plants, the elect were theoretically unable to grow, purchase, or even cook their own food. Consequently, a ritual system emerged wherein the hearers, the non-elite religious members of the community, provided all the food for the elect on a daily basis. Each day, hearers were expected to collect alms in the form of food, which they delivered to the tables of the elect at the beginning of a daily ritual meal. This was the elect's only meal of the day; it began with the presentation of the alms, and concluded after several hours of prayer and eating. In fact, for the elect, eating was itself a sacred act, since the Manicheans believed that the digestive process refined the food and released the "light" from the dark matter.

***

For many inhabitants of the late Roman Empire, engaging in some form of regular religious ritual was a part of everyday life. Whether it was collecting food alms to present to your local Manichean elect, purchasing a love spell from a specialist practitioner, celebrating a Sabbath meal, or attending church services, the spiritual world was experienced in daily, highly material ways. In many respects, the embedded nature of religion in everyday life is among the continuities that link Late Antiquity with earlier periods in ancient Mediterranean history. Still, by all accounts, religion – and especially Christianity – came to play an even greater role in the daily lives of Roman men, women, and children over the course of Late Antiquity.

Further Reading

The following primary sources were cited in this chapter:

Apostolic Tradition: A Commentary, by Bradshaw, Johnson, and Phillips (Minneapolis, MN, 2002), with full English translation.
J. Gager, *Curse Tablets and Binding Spells from the Ancient World* (Oxford, 1992).
Leo, *Sermons*, trans. J. Freeman (Washington, DC, 1996) and online at www.newadvent.org/fathers/3603.htm.
Jerome, *Letters* 22 and 127, most easily accessed online at www.newadvent.org/fathers/3001.htm.

As yet, there is no general history of the religions of Late Antiquity. Consequently, readers must consult introductory studies dedicated to individual religions. For early Christianity, see H. Chadwick, *The Early Church* (London, 1993) and P. Brown, *The World of Late Antiquity* and *The Rise of Western Christendom* (both cited in the Introduction). For late Roman Jews, see the multiple volumes of *Judaism in Late Antiquity*, ed. J. Neusner (Leiden, 1995–2001). For late Roman paganism, see the first volume of *Religions of Rome*, eds. M. Beard, N. North, and S. Price, 2 vols. (Cambridge, 1998) and R. L. Fox, *Pagans and Christians* (New York, 1986). For Manichaeism, see *The Light and the Darkness: Studies in Manicheism and Its World*, eds. P. Mirecki and J. Beduhn (Leiden, 2001). On various aspects of daily life and Christianity, see the collected essays in *Late Ancient Christianity* (*People's History of Christianity*), ed. V. Burrus (Minneapolis, MN, 2010) and *Byzantine Christianity* (*People's History of Christianity*), ed. D. Krueger (Minneapolis, MN, 2010), along with R. MacMullen, *The Second Church: Popular Christianity, AD 200–400* (Leiden, 2009) and K. Bowes, *Private Worship, Public Values, and Religious Change in Late Antiquity* (Cambridge, 2008). For Judaism, see *The Oxford Handbook of Jewish Daily Life in Roman Palestine*, ed. C. Hezser (New York, 2010). For burial habits, see E. Rebillard, *The Care of the Dead in Late Antiquity*, trans. E. Rawlings and J. Routier-Pucci (Ithaca, NY, 2009). Finally, readers interested in the surprising fluidity of late antique lived religion should explore D. Frankfurter, *Christianizing Egypt: Syncretism and Local Worlds in Late Antiquity* (Princeton, 2017).

Appendix: Late Roman Time and Money

DATING AND TIMEKEEPING

For the most part, late ancient Romans used the same calendrical system that was in place since the time of Julius Caesar, the so-called Julian calendar. This solar calendar of 365 days and 12 months included leap years. Months were divided into seven-day weeks. However, to designate particular dates, Romans used day markers rather than ordinal numbers. These markers were the *Kalends* (first of the month), the *Nones* (eight days before the *Ides*), and the *Ides* (the fifteenth of the month in March, May, July, and October; the thirteenth of all other months). Individual dates were given in relation to these day markers, always counting backwards: for example, February 8 would have been written and understood as "six days before the Ides of February" (the Romans counted inclusively). Readers should note, however, that regional calendars remained in use throughout Late Antiquity. Dating conventions as well as the names of the months and days of the week were different in Egypt, for example.

To designate a particular year, late Romans used several different conventions. Some used the regnal years of a particular emperor or "consular years," referring to the names of the two consuls (in Rome or Constantinople, depending on location) in office during that year (consuls served one-year terms). Of course, this convention required readers to know which year(s) these particular consuls or emperor served in order to determine the date. Another common dating convention was the "indiction year." This was the year in which empire-wide tax assessments were made, once every fifteen years (after 312 CE). Many state documents thus read "on the fourth year of the indiction of Emperor X." An indiction year dating system obviously required knowing the exact year in which any particular indiction cycle began, as well as the regnal dates of the emperor.

Several different religious dating conventions existed during Late Antiquity. These included biblical dating schemes, some oriented around creation, others an impending apocalypse, such as was associated with the year 500 CE. In the early sixth century, a Christian monk named Dionysius Exiguus invented the construct of Christ's birth year as a date marker, which he designated *in anno domini*, or "in the year of our Lord." Our modern convention of BC/AD (or BCE/CE) dating was thus born in Late Antiquity, though *in anno domini* did not become standard usage until the Middle Ages.

The Roman day was divided into twenty-four hours, with twelve hours of daylight and twelve of darkness. Because daylight hours varied according to the season, the Romans modified the length of an hour seasonally in order to maintain the twelve/twelve division. They began to count the hour following sunrise, which was the first hour of the day, continuing through sunset, when the count resumed from one. Generally, the first hour began at six o'clock AM, with the sixth hour at noon and the ninth hour at three o'clock PM. However, modern equivalencies are hard to determine with any precision because of the variable nature of the Roman hour, and the fact that the Empire itself encompassed different latitudes with more or fewer hours of daylight. To measure time, Romans relied on sundials (which measured on the hour, not on the minute) as well as more sophisticated devices, such as water clocks.

COINS

Late Antiquity witnessed the emergence of new types of currency. Gradually, the primary silver-based Roman coins, such as the *denarius* and *sesterce*, fell out of use and were replaced with gold and bronze coins. Diocletian created the gold *solidus* to replace a preexisting gold coin (the *aureus*), and it became the main high-value currency throughout the period. Smaller issues included the bronze *nummus* (valued at anywhere between one twelve-thousandth and one six-thousandth of a *solidus*) and the larger *follis* (the equivalent of forty *nummi*). Lightweight *solidi* called *siliquae* were also minted from the sixth century, and were valued at around one-twenty-fourth of a *solidus*. While state transactions (e.g., taxes, salaries) were typically assessed and paid in *solidi*, most daily transactions involved the smaller issues.

Notes

Introduction

1 Roger Bagnall and Rafaella Cribiore (eds.), *Women's Letters from Ancient Egypt, 300 BC–800 AD* (Ann Arbor, MI, 2006).

2 There are notable exceptions to this generalization, such as during the brief reign of the usurper Magnus Maximus, who was one of two recognized western Roman emperors from 383 to 388 CE.

3 The most significant exception is the Gothic language, which was codified in the fourth century so that the Bible and other Christian texts could be disseminated among the newly converted Gothic people.

4 In fact, Julius Nepos, who was deposed in 474 CE by Romulus Augustulus' father and driven into exile, was the last surviving western Roman emperor. His death in 480 CE arguably marks the true end of the Roman Empire in the West as a political entity.

5 Late ancient women might have designations such as *femina illustra* ("illustrious lady"), even though they could not hold public office. The honor was achieved through marriage or birth, and connoted the highest social status for women.

6 The phrase is based on the Latin legal term for such men: *curialis* (s.), *curiales* (pl.).

7 Classical paganism made a brief return to prominence during the reign of Emperor Julian ("the apostate," so called because he was born a Christian and converted to paganism), from 361 to 363 CE.

8 Mani was also influenced by a Persian religion called Zoroastrianism, which provided the foundational idea of a universe divided by forces of good/light and evil/darkness/matter. Zoroastrianism was the principal religious system of the late ancient Persian or Sasanian Empire.

9 Nicene Christianity is centered on the theological supposition that God the Father, Jesus Christ the Son, and the Holy Spirit are of the same substance

and co-equal, and hence three expressions of a single godhead. Scholars call it "Nicene" Christianity because this is the theological definition first articulated at the Council of Nicaea in 325 CE.

1.   Rural Life

1 The archive of Aurelius Sakaon is available in English translation (see *The Archive of Aurelius Sakaon* "Further Readings"). Unfortunately, there is no English translation of the Apion archive, but interested readers can learn more about its contents from Sarris 2006 and Hickey 2012, both cited in "Further Readings."

2 See, for example, S. Rippon, C. Smart, and B. Pears, *The Fields of Britannia: Continuity and Change in the Late Roman and Early Medieval Landscape* (Oxford, 2015). An ongoing archaeological investigation undertaken by scholars at the University of Pennsylvania, called the Roman Peasant Project (www .sas.upenn.edu/romanpeasants/project.html), endeavors to map out the movements and living conditions of late Roman peasants in Italy.

3 From the archives of Dioscorus of Aphrodito, cited in Jones 1964, p. 847 (see Introduction, "Further Reading").

4 For a more detailed discussion of late ancient housing, see Chapter 3, pp. 108–119.

5 Ps-Joshua the Stylite, *Chronicle* 37–38.

6 Palladius, *Opus agriculturae* ("Treatise on Agriculture") and the anonymous Byzantine *Geopontika*, an admittedly later text, demonstrate the enduring significance of astrology in agriculture.

7 For the arrangement, see *P. Sakaon* 36 in *The Archive of Aurelius Sakaon*.

8 For the lawsuit in question, see Chapter 4, pp. 141–43.

9 *P. Sakaon* 59 in *The Archive of Aurelius Sakaon*.

10 Symmachus, *Letters* 1.5, 2.3, 3.23, 5.78, and 7.2.

11 For the late antique tax system and its development, see Chapter 4, pp. 144–150.

12 Beer made from barley or wheat was consumed mainly in the northwest regions of the late Empire (e.g., northern Gaul). While enjoyed in Late Antiquity, it was far less popular than wine.

13 All of these wheat crops are sometimes called "corn" in modern scholarship. Actual corn, however, is a New World crop and was unknown to the Romans.

14 Some non-wheat grains, such as barley and oats, were also consumed whole in porridge. Generally speaking, however, late Romans preferred to eat wheat rather than other grains.

15 In earlier periods, Romans preferred pork over sheep and goat meat; during Late Antiquity, there appears to have been a preferential shift toward sheep and goat meat, although pork remained popular.

16 Readers can learn more about the site and view pictures of the excavations (including a reconstruction of the entire villa complex) at www.basilicata turistica.it/turismi/area-archeologica-di-san-giovanni-di-ruoti-le-ville-di-eta-romana-e-tardo-antica/?lang=en.

17 For directions on how to make Lucanian sausage with modern ingredients, see www.coquinaria.nl/english/recipes/12.4histrecipe.html.

2. Urban Life

1 This early Christian church, known today as Santa Maria Maggiore de Dom, underwent centuries of repair and renovation before it fell into ruin during the eleventh century. Only sections of the mosaic pavement, such as this inscription, are extant.

2 *Agora* is the Greek word for "marketplace." The Latin equivalent is *forum*.

3 The dating of the palace of the governor in Ephesus is unclear. It could have been built as early as the reign of Diocletian (r. 284–305 CE) or as late as the sixth century.

4 In fact, the Greek word *embolos* literally means a large colonnaded street.

5 For late ancient churches, see Chapter 6, pp. 206–210.

6 On late Roman burial habits, including the new tradition of intramural burials, see Chapter 6, pp. 213–216.

7 On health and the body, see Chapter 5, pp. 161–181.

8 A more detailed discussion of the late Roman legal system appears in Chapter 4, pp. 139–145.

9 Readers can learn more about the Byzantine shops at Sardis, including pictures of the remains, at www.sardisexpedition.org/en/essays/about-byzshops.

10 The document is a papyrus, *P. Cairo* 67126, cited in Jones 1964, p. 863 (see Introduction, "Further Reading").

11 Julian of Ascalon, *Treatise of Construction and Design Rules*.

12 The late Roman *corpora* are different from the early imperial organizations known as *collegia*. While sometimes organized around the members' shared profession, the *collegia* were more like social clubs, where members paid dues and collectively contributed to their individual burial costs, for example.

13 An English translation of the Greek inscription is in Foss 1976: 110–113.

14 For the law, see the Justinianic Code 3.12.2(3).

15 Translation from Harper 2013: 49.

16 Valentinian, Theodosius, and Arcadius, *Collatio Legum Mosaicarum et Romanarum* ("A Collation of Mosaic and Roman Laws") 5.3 (a. 390).

17 For more on this experiment, see Yegül 2010: 85.

18 *Circus* is the Latin equivalent of the Greek *hippodromos*. Both words mean "racetrack" in English.

19 For these graffiti, see Roueché 1989, n. 186, pp. 227–228.

20 Some forms of classical South Asian dance perhaps offer a closer approximation.

21 Cassiodorus, *Variae* 4.51.

22 A brief history of the sewer in Late Antiquity can be found at: https://visualisinglateantiquity.wordpress.com/2015/09/07/going-down-the-drain-in-late-antiquity/.

23 Ps-Joshua the Stylite, *Chronicle* 50–53.

24 A more extensive discussion of urban sieges and the late Roman army appears in Chapter 4, pp. 127–139.

25 Ps-Joshua the Stylite, *Chronicle* 280.

26 Ammianus Marcellinus, 27.3.12–13.

3. The Household

1   Readers familiar with this evidence will note that I follow A. Cameron's dating and identification. See A. Cameron, "The Date and Owners of the Esquiline Treasure," *American Journal of Archaeology* 89.1 (1985): 135–145.

2   Chapter 1, pp. 32–33.

3   Sidonius Apollinaris, *Letter* 5.19, dated to 459 or 460 CE.

4   *Codex Theodosianus* (the Theodosian Code), 5.18.1.2.

5   The Romans did not practice primogeniture, and male and female children could inherit equally.

6   Roman law prohibited marriage within four degrees of consanguinity.

7   Introduction.

8   Alternatively, a fatherless married woman over the age of twenty-five still depended on her husband as her de facto guardian for legal transactions.

9   This is the *Lex Julia de adulteriis coercendis*, from 17 BCE.

10 We return to the subject of sexuality in Chapter 5, pp. 181–184.

11 *Inscriptiones Christianae Urbis Romae*, NS II. 4187, trans. from Lançon 2000: 128 (cited in Introduction, p. 18).

12 Imperial laws were more likely to protect the rights of people who recovered foundlings, many of whom were slave dealers, than to punish the parents who abandoned them.

13 Gregory, *Letter* 11.56a to Augustine of Canterbury (601 CE).

14 See Chapter 5, pp. 184–187 which examines elite education more fully.

15 Gregory of Tours, *Ten Books of History* 4.46.

16 Roman law did prohibit owners from killing a slave without legal cause, or from prostituting him or her.

17 Chrysostom, *Homily on Ephesians* 15.3–4, trans. Harper 2011: 207.

18 Cassiodorus, *Variae* 8.33.4

19 Augustine, *Letter* 10*.

20 *Codex Theodosianus* (the Theodosian Code), 9.40.2.

21 Readers can scroll through the images on two interactive websites dedicated to the late Roman villa: Villa Loupian, a late Roman villa in modern France (www.villa.culture.fr/index.php?lang=en#/en/annexe/intro/t=Introduction); and the Villa Romana La Olmeda in Spain (www.villaromanalaolmeda.com/contenido?id=70385ee5-1a03-11de-84a2-fb9baaa14523&lang=en).

22 The Crypta Balbi museum in Rome offers visitors an opportunity to see these precise changes to housing and daily life in the archaeological record. See http://archeoroma.beniculturali.it/en/museums/national-roman-museum-crypta-balbi.

23 *De re coquinaria* ("On Cooking"), trans. Grocock and Grainger (Totnes, UK, 2006). There is also a fun website dedicated to food history: www.coquinaria.nl/english/index.htm.

24 Sidonius Apollinaris, *Letter* 1.2.

4. The State in Everyday Life

1 A critical edition and English translation of the entire Abinnaeus papyrus archive is available. See the "Further Reading" section at the chapter's end.

2 By comparison, only 0.5 percent of America's current population serves in the armed forces.

3 *P. Rylands* 609, trans. Roberts, in Lee 2007, p. 79.

4 *P. Abinn.* 35 in *The Abinnaeus Archive.*

5 Ibid., 19.

6 Ibid., 18.

7 Wounded soldiers might also have been honorably discharged, but they did not receive the same privileges and bonuses as those who served to retirement.

8 In 364 CE, the emperor Valentinian amended the law and gave veterans only the land grant.

9 Procopius, *Wars* 7.11.15.

10 Cyril of Scythopolis, *The Lives of the Monks of Palestine.*

11 Ps-Joshua the Stylite, *Chronicle* 86.

12 *P. Abinn.* 9 in *The Abinnaeus Archive.* Natron is a naturally occurring form of soda ash that was used as a cleaner and preservative; its acidic, drying properties made it a key ingredient in mummification.

13 Eugippius, *Life of St. Severinus* 20.

14 *P. Sakaon* 34 in *The Archive of Aurelius Sakaon* (cited in Chapter 1).

15 *Codex Theodosianus* (the Theodosian Code) 1.13.7 (331 CE).

16 See *P. Sakaon* 31 and 36 in *The Archive of Aurelius Sakaon.* We met Artemis and her deceased husband, Kaët, in Chapter 1, p. 29.

17 A fourth potential option was the use of a military tribunal. Theoretically, only cases involving soldiers could be tried before a military court, but as Abinnaeus' archive shows, this rule was often broken.

18 By Late Antiquity, a single judge rendered all decisions, including sentencing. Trial by jury had long ceased to be a feature of the Roman judicial system.

19 For the Romans, a *census* was a registration process and type of document solely linked to tax collection. The Romans never held a census for demographic purposes, that is, to estimate population; this is a modern use of the term.

20 The fifteen-year indiction cycle was also used as a dating convention.

21 For the conversion chart, see Decker 2009, p. 118, cited in Chapter 1, "Further Reading".

22 *P. Abinn.* 15 in *The Abinnaeus Archive.*

23 The word *annona* derives from the name of the Roman goddess Annona, who was the personification of the grain supply for the city of Rome.

24 On the *corpora*, see Chapter 2, p. 60.

25 A *modius* was also a dry measure, equal to approximately two US gallons.

26 The three grades of Roman bread are discussed in Chapter 1, p. 36.

27 For Theophanes and the records of his trip, see J. Matthews 2006, cited in the "Further Reading" section.

28 Alternatively, one recent study argues that the Peutinger Map was not actually made for traveling on the *cursus publicus*, but rather was a form of early fourth-century imperial propaganda created to celebrate the successes of the emperor Diocletian's reforms. See R. Talbot 2010.

29 Procopius, *Secret History* 30.5–6.11.

5. Body and Mind

1 For the inscription, see *Corpus Inscriptionum Latinarum* VI.9477. A discussion of late ancient burial habits appears in Chapter 6, pp. 213–216.

2 This is also known as miasma theory. In fact, the word malaria comes from the Italian *mal'aria*, meaning "bad air."

3 Medieval Islamic medical researchers read Galen's work largely through Syriac translations, which they rendered into Arabic. As with many other Greek texts, the medieval Latin West only came to know Galen's work through Latin translations of Arabic translations of Syriac translations of the Greek originals.

4 For this spell, see Gager 1992, no. 113 (Egypt), pp. 210–211.

5 Eunapius, *Lives of the Sophists* 463.

6 Soranus, *On Gynecology* 1.3–4.

7 Gregory, *The Miracles of Saint Martin* 2.1 and 4.36.

8 On late ancient Rome's annual death rates, see Shaw 1996.

9 In fact, the rats were the primary victims of the *Yersinia pestis* microbe. It was only when the bacteria killed off a rat population that the fleas – and hence the pathogen – jumped to human hosts.

10 See Procopius of Caesarea's account of the plague in *Wars* 2.22–23.

11 For an English translation of sections of this handbook, see Crislip 2005: 32–33.

12 Procopius, *Wars* 6.2.25–29.

13 John of Ephesus, *Lives of the Eastern Saints* 38.

14 Augustine, *City of God* 16.8.

15 Of course, the fact that so many people in this town lived long enough to develop arthritis is a sign of generally good health overall.

16 See Clark 1993, p. 82 (cited in Chapter 3) for the tale.

17 Puerperal fever or sepsis remains a major killer; according to the World Health Organization, it is the sixth leading cause of death of women in the world.

18 See, for instance, Jerome, *Letter* 121.4.

19 Cited in B. Brooten, *Love Between Women: Early Christian Responses to Female Homoeroticism* (Chicago, 1996), 82.

20 Procopius, *Secret History* 11.

21 Julian wrote a satirical treatise on this alleged abuse entitled "The Beard-Hater," in which he poked fun at his own admiration for Greek philosophers and their beards from the perspective of his clean-shaven contemporaries.

22 Gerontius, *Life of Melania the Younger* 11–12.

6. Religion in Daily Life

1 For the amulet and this text, see Gager 1992, no. 119, pp. 224–225.
2 A brief introduction to these four systems appears in the Introduction, pp.14–17.
3 See the new study by T. Whitmarsh, *Battling the Gods: Atheism in the Ancient World* (New York, 2015).
4 The Latin root of our word religion, *religio*, meant something like a regard for sacred things, moral obligation to the gods, or piety. It did not refer to any particular system of ideas and practices, pagan or otherwise.
5 *Apostolic Tradition* 35 and 41.
6 See, for example, Jerome, *Letter* 22 to the aristocratic girl, Eustochium.
7 This is known as the reserved Eucharist, and it seems to have been a fairly common practice.
8 See www.villa.culture.fr/accessible/en/uc/02_05_10 for a reconstruction of the early Christian chapel built in the fourth century on the grounds of the Villa Loupian in Gaul.
9 Apses were also found in late Roman elite housing, in what was yet another borrowing of the form from the public sphere.
10 Leo, *Sermon* 84, dated to 442 CE.
11 In reality, lower clergy, such as deacons, sometimes performed the Eucharistic celebration, especially in areas with a shortage of clerics. We know this because late ancient church documents frequently complain about lower clergy "forgetting their place" and irregularly performing the Eucharist and baptismal rites.
12 The Jews of Hammat Tiberias were not alone. In the nearby synagogue of Bet Alpha, built in the sixth century, there is a similar astrological mosaic.
13 The word "catacomb" derives from a place name of a subterranean cemetery outside Rome on the Via Appia called *Ad catacumbas*, meaning "near the hollows."
14 The decline in the number of inscribed tombstones mirrors a general decline in inscription production (or what scholars call "the epigraphic habit") that began in the early third century.
15 The epithet "saint" (from the Latin *sanctus*; Greek *hagios*) was popularly attributed to a wide range of early Christian heroes, from martyrs to bishops and monks, who were seen as especially holy. In Late Antiquity, there was no official canonization process for sainthood. A community simply decided that a particular holy person deserved to be a saint.
16 The term *seder* (meaning "order") does not appear in our sources until the Middle Ages.
17 An online version of the Calendar of 354, with extant illustrations and a partial English translation, is available at www.tertullian.org/fathers/chronography_of_354_00_eintro.htm.
18 This form of divination is known as kleromancy. The client rolls a die or dice, and the expert practitioner looks up the corresponding answer in the oracular "answer" book.

19 This document, available only in Latin, is discussed at length in W. Klingshirn, "Defining the *Sortes Sanctorum,*" *Journal of Early Christian Studies* 10 (2002): 77–130.

20 On chariot racing and the Blue and Green circus factions, see Chapter 2, p. 73.

21 For a full English translation of the tablet inscription (from the Greek) and a potential connection with an actual chariot race in sixth-century Apamea, see Gager 1992, no. 6, pp. 56–58.

22 English translation of the full text is in Gager 1992, no. 28, pp. 97–100.

23 Clergy could and did join monasteries in Late Antiquity, and monks could be ordained. For the sake of clarity, however, we shall discuss their elite lives separately.

24 For a description of Marcella's at-home monastic life, see Jerome, *Letter* 127.

Index

Note: Page numbers followed by n and a number refer to endnotes.
Page numbers in italics indicate illustrative material.